Imagining the Modern City

WITHDRAWN

Imagining the Modern City

JAMES DONALD

THE ATHLONE PRESS
LONDON

First published in 1999 by
THE ATHLONE PRESS
1 Park Drive, London NW11 7SG

British Library Cataloguing in Publication Data
*A catalogue record for this book is available
from the British Library*

ISBN 0 485 00401 1 HB
0 485 00601 4 PB

Typeset by RefineCatch Limited, Bungay, Suffolk
Printed and bound in Great Britain by
Bookcraft (Bath) Ltd

Contents

	Acknowledgements	vii
	Preface	ix
1	Fog Everywhere	1
2	Metaphor and Metropolis	27
3	Light in Dark Spaces: Cinema and city	63
4	The Citizen and the Man about Town	95
5	Fat Lady in the Cab: Imagining urban space	121
6	Noisy Neighbours: On urban ethics	147
	Afterword: Postcards	173
	Notes	188
	Bibliography	202
	Index	211

Acknowledgements

Although versions of most of the chapters have appeared before, all have been revised or expanded to a greater or lesser extent – mostly greater. I have in all cases retained copyright. Nevertheless, I happy to acknowledge that this work reproduces material that has appeared in the following:

'Metropolis: the City as Text', in Robert Bocock and Kenneth Thompson (eds.), *Social and Cultural Aspects of Modernity*, Cambridge: Polity, 1992
'The City, the Cinema: Modern Spaces', in Chris Jenks (ed.), *Visual Culture*, London: Routledge, 1995
'The Citizen and the Man about Town', in Paul du Gay and Stuart Hall (eds.), *Questions of Cultural Identity*, London: Sage, 1996
'This, Here, Now: Imagining the Modern City', in Sallie Westwood and John Williams (eds.), *Imagining Cities*, London: Routledge 1996.

ILLUSTRATIONS

We have gone to considerable lengths to trace and contact copyright holders of all images used in this text. In a very few cases, this has proved impossible, for which the publisher apologises in advance. We are grateful to those copyright owners who have granted permission to reproduce their works.

Art Institute of Chicago, Julien Levy Collection, Gift of Julien and Jean Levy: p. 83 (Eugène Atget)
Bauhaus-Archiv, Berlin: p. 131 (Erich Comeriner)
Berlinische Galerie, Photographische Sammlung: p. 120 (Marianne Breslauer)
Bibliothèque Historique de la Ville de Paris: pp. 26, 40 (Charles Marville)
British Film Institute, Stills Collection: pp. 78, 80, 85, 88, 90, 91
Victor Burgin: p. 9
Cahiers du Cinema: p. 115
Centre Georges Pompidou/Mnam-Cci, Paris: p. 56 (Germaine Krull); p. 129 (Raoul Hausmann)
Collection of the J. Paul Getty Museum, Malibu, California: p. 67 (August Sander); p. 113 (Germaine Krull)

Collection Viollet, Paris: p. 48

Condé Nast: p. 15 (Ira Martin)

Ted Croner/The Howard Greenberg Gallery, New York: p. 94

James Donald: p. 126

Graphische Sammlung Albertine, Vienna: p. 108 (Adolf Loos)

Historisches Museum der Stadt Wien: p. 53

Magnum Photos: pp. 62, 153 (Henri Cartier-Bresson); p. 158 (Bruno Barbey); p. 163 (Gilles Peress); p. 172 (Richard Kalvar)

Museum of the City of New York: p. 34 (Jacob Riis)

Museum of Modern Art, New York: p. 43 (Eugène Atget)

Rheinisches Bildarchiv. Köln: p. 110 (August Sander)

Royal Photographic Society, Bath: p. xiv (Alvin Coburn); p. 23 (John Thomson); p. 134 (Captain Alfred Buckham)

Sotheby's, London: cover

Studio Chevojon, Paris: p. 50

Bernard Tschumi: p. 141

University of Leeds, Brotherton Library: p. 38

Viscopy: p. 12 (Georg Grosz); p. 58 (Le Corbusier); p. 75 (Paul Citroën/University of Leiden)

David Vestal: p. 16

Walker Evans Archive, Metropolitan Museum of Art, Collection of Jack Reynolds and Suzanne Hellmuth: p. 111 (Walker Evans)

Preface

As my work on this book finally neared completion, a screen memory kept returning to my mind. A Japanese detective looks at a street guide and tries to figure out where he is in the city. He scratches his head, and looks around with a bemused expression. Is he lost? Is he looking at the wrong map? Doesn't he know how to read the map? Or is it just that he doesn't know where he is going?

The image, I soon remembered, refers to a film I saw at the London Film Festival thirty odd years ago. It was called *The Man Without a Map*. In an act of almost self-conscious disavowal – I *know* finding out more about the image won't explain why it is presenting itself now – I started asking around about the film, and even posted a request for information onto the Internet. My investigations turned up some results. Also known as *The Burned Map*, the film was directed in 1968 by Hiroshi Teshigahara, whose best known work was *Woman in the Dunes*. It was apparently based on a novel by the Nobel Prize-winning author Kenzaburo Oe, which doesn't seem to be in print in English at present. Nor is any video or print of the film easily available for me to look at to check whether I have remembered it right, or how I have transformed it. Some people thought Teshigahara had given up film making for pottery and/or gardening in the early nineteen seventies, but subsequent information revealed a limited number of later films – as well as the existence of a gardening school. One generous informant even passed on, in confidence, a contact number for someone working in the office of his production company.

But if I had followed up that tip, what could I have asked? And what would be the point, given that the impulse behind the fantasy is clear enough? Even my ineffective attempt to exorcise the image by getting hold of the 'real' version in a video or a book was another repetition of what the image was telling me. As I recall, what I particularly liked about the film was not just that it was about a detective failing to solve a case, nor its use of the imagery of being adrift in the city as a metaphor for that failure (or vice versa). The twist to the film was that, even in the end, the detective still has not the slightest inkling what the case was about.

This book represents my attempt to find my way around the city, with all the anxiety of following my nose rather than the reliable directions of a map. Contrary to all the good advice I give my students, I set off without knowing exactly where I was heading, or what question I was supposed to explain once I got there.

I know that there are maps that I could have followed, but their projections never quite fitted my hunches and intuitions. If I look at an atlas of world cities, that simply reminds me that I am not here attempting to provide a synoptic analysis of their contemporary reconfiguration, nor their global or geopolitical significance. That task is far more expertly done by writers like Manuel Castells, Anthony King, or Saskia Sassen.[1] Equally, though, my book does not offer a reading of any actual city or cities, in the sense Christopher Prendergast writes so elegantly about *Paris in the Nineteenth Century*, or Victor Burgin teases out through word and image the secret meanings of *Some Cities*, or Mike Davis offers his *noir* analysis of Los Angeles in *City of Quartz*, or Sharon Zukin discerns *Landscapes of Power* from New York to Disneyland, or Ackbar Abbas conjures up the 'disappearing' cultural space of Hong Kong.[2] Rather, this book consists of a series of improvisations on the possibility that the concept or category of the city may illuminate some topics entailed by the contentious notion of modernity.

Some of the more obvious guide books to the idea of the modern city are not followed here. That perhaps requires explanation, if not justification. Marshall Berman's magisterial *All That is Solid Melts into Air*, for example, seems to cover much of the same territory.[3] Both he and I are concerned with the way that people have tried to create some sense of self and some form of communal living in what he calls the 'maelstrom' of the city of modernity. To be honest, though, with the unscholarly indiscretion allowed by the informality of a preface, I have to admit to a temperamental incompatibility with his book. I respect its achievement. I can see why people love it and are changed by it. Personally, though, I have always found it unbearably garrulous and sentimental. The fault and loss are, without doubt, mine. But they mean that I have had to find my own path, rather than follow his.

Similarly, I tend to steer clear of the excursions mapped out along the boundaries between cultural geography and social theory (and usually around the Bonaventura Hotel in downtown Los Angeles) by guides like David Harvey, Fredric Jameson, and Edward Soja.[4] Each of them, in his own way, and often in dialogue with the others, has addressed the spatialisation of contemporary social relations, and in doing so they have done much to redefine the field of contemporary social theory. My anxiety may simply be the tourist's familiar neurosis about seeing the sights without being seen to stick unadventurously to the rubber-necker's package tour. But I do know that I did not want to spend most of my time explaining where and why I disagree with these guides – and also, of course, what I have learned from them. Putting up my hand to a degree of anxiety about influence, let's just say too that mine is a different city from theirs. It is not just that my city is somewhere else. It is the experiential, imaginative, and political differences that are significant.

My city is at the same time abstractly conceptual and intensely personal. It is *the* city, not *a* city. It is an imaginary space created and animated as much by the urban representations to be found in novels, films, and images as by any actual urban places. But to leave the impression that my city is wholly abstract, that it has no implicit referent, would be disingenuous. 'Every time I describe a city, I say something about Venice,' admits Marco Polo to the Khan in Calvino's *Invisible Cities*.[5] In the same way, for me to write about the city is inevitably to invoke London.

Or, increasingly, a bit like Polo if he ever did make it even part of the way to China, it is to invoke memories and projections of London from afar. I began work on what was to become this book just as I moved out of London, after living there all my life. Admittedly, to begin with, I only got as far as Brighton, the capital's playground by the sea. Drafts of most of the chapters were first written during that period, while I was working at the University of Sussex. I have finished the book in the months since making a more radical displacement, to Fremantle, just south of Perth in Western Australia. Roger Silverstone, my erstwhile colleague at Sussex, would no doubt cite this curious provenance as evidence for his claim that suburbia rather than the city is the typical backdrop to everyday life in the twentieth century. He points out that 'for millions, and mostly by choice, the city was too much to bear. It was a place to leave.'[6] Demographically true, no doubt, even if he has moved in the opposite direction, from the Liverpool suburb of Birkenhead eventually to live and work in the heart of central London. As for me, to adapt an old blues line, this book testifies that, even though I have taken myself out of London, it has not been so easy to get the city out of me.

My new perspective from the most geographically remote metropolis in the world enables me to see just to what extent this is a European book. I defend my use of the problematic term modernity later, but I acknowledge fully that it is a Eurocentric term. Juxtaposing the category of the city with the concept of modernity is to ask about an experience, a repertoire of ways of acting and feeling, that is culturally and historically bounded. It is an attempt to explore the limits to the ways I see and think, and so to test those limits. I am absolutely *not* saying that this is the only way, or even the best way, to tell the story of the modern city. To do that would, I guess, require a conversation between millions of citizens likewise enacting the limits of their citizenship and their modernity not only in Europe and North America, but perhaps especially in Hong Kong, Algiers, Buenos Aires, New Delhi, Cape Town and Perth. My ambitions here are, as I say, more modest in scale.

Finally, though, this is also a book about the city and politics: not about city politics, but about the city as an idea with which to think politics. In *Hegemony and Socialist Strategy*, Ernesto Laclau and Chantal Mouffe warn against two extremes that would undermine the attempt to construct a radical democratic politics. One is 'the totalitarian myth of the Ideal City'. The other is 'the positivist pragmatism of reformists without a project.'[7] What might lie between these two?[8] To reject the utopianism of the Ideal City is to reject a fantasy of pure space, not the need to imagine how we might live differently. To reject positivist pragmatism should not entail a disdainful withdrawal from an engagement with those activities and rationalities that lead to changes in the fabric of the city: urban policy, planning, architecture, and so forth.

That is why, especially in the later chapters of the book, I focus on the city as an attempt to imagine not only the way we live, but above all the way we live together. That is only in part a sociological question. The city has always stood not only for the vanities, the squalor and the injustice of human society, but also for the aspiration to civilized sociation. The question then is how we *do* live today in the city. In a short paper on architecture, the Italian philosopher Gianni Vattimo considers how this existential space may be changing. He quotes Heidegger quoting Hölderlin:

> *Voll Verdienst, doch dichterisch, wohnet*
> *Der Mensch auf dieser Erde.*
>
> Full of merit, yet poetically, man
> Dwells on this earth.

For Vattimo, these lines define a shift away from the life of modernity, a life 'full of merit' – 'which is to say, full of activity.' This post-Enlightenment European modernity was 'characterised by an existence defined essentially in terms of projective activity and a drive towards the rationalisation of reality by means of structure founded on thought and action.' Hölderlin's 'yet' signals a turn, a transition to what Vattimo calls the postmodern. This is 'the time when "poetic" characteristics are rediscovered'.[9]

Vattimo identifies *indefiniteness* as one of the defining features of the 'poetic'. 'To dwell poetically does not mean to dwell in such a way that one needs poetry, but to dwell with a sensitivity to the poetic, characterised by the impossibility, in a sense, of defining clear-cut boundaries between reality and imagination.' He then relates this to the way that the media have worn away the boundaries of the real. His comments on the media are quite conventional. More important for me is his insistence on *the impossibility of defining clear-cut boundaries between reality and imagination.*

One of the things I try to show is that this impossibility is not (or is not just) a feature of postmodernity. The disconcerting poetics of dwelling is a definitive fact of modern urban existence. I know that this premise will make the book way too poetic for many of my pragmatic reformist friends. In my view, it is a necessary starting point for a realistic politics. It is a simple acknowledgement of the complexity of the problems to be addressed by urban policies, plans for reform, or achitectural designs. It is this stubborn poetic complexity, common to the modern city and the modern media, that I seek to explore in the chapters that follow.

Chapter one traces the urban imaginary to which it gives rise in literature, sociology and contemporary theory. In chapter two, I offer a short history of how certain metaphors and images helped to shape modern European cities roughly in the century from the eighteen thirties until the Second World War. Chapter three introduces in a more sustained way the idea that cinema both shares with the city a certain structure of visibility, and also institutes a number of related ways of imagining the city. Chapter four sees a shift of emphasis from the city to its citizens. After considering what citizenship might be, I explore how agency and performance are enacted in the theatre of city. In chapter five, I return to the question of how we imagine urban space, linking the city of novel and film to some recent discussions in the field of architecture. In chapter six, I address directly one theme that emerges with increasing insistence from the preceding chapters: that is, not just how we live in the city, but how we can live together. Then some parting thoughts on the past and the possible futures of imaginable cities.

I have accumulated many debts in the course of writing this book. Mark Gibson, Jeremy Gilbert, Maria-Christina Lutter and Wendy Parkins read and commented on a full draft. Mark has helped with some of the intricate and time-consuming work on notes, bibliography and picture research, as well as beginning to instruct me in the importance of Hume. I am grateful to Curtin University of Technology for a research grant that has enabled me to have him as my research assistant in 1998.

For invitations to write, for comments on drafts and versions, for difficult but focusing questions, for apposite references, or for teaching me new ways of seeing things, my thanks to Stephen Barber, Tony Bennett, Stevie Bezencenet, Iain Borden, Rachel Bowlby, Victor Burgin, Iain Chambers, Daryl Cohen, Terry Diffey, Paul du Gay, David Frisby, John Frow, Stuart Hall, Chris Jenks, Laura Marcus, Doreen Massey, Chantal Mouffe, Graham Murdock, Brian Nelson, William Outhwaite, Kevin Robins, John Tagg, Nigel Thrift, Caroline Welsh, Sophie Watson and Sallie Westwood. I have learned a good deal from my research students, among them Redmond Bridgeman, Rangan Chakravarty, Ken Fox, and Ana Reynaud.

Sections of the book, or earlier versions of them have been presented at a number of conferences, seminars, and university departments. Among them have been the Architectural Association, London; Birkbeck College, London; the British Sociological Conference *Contested Cities* (1995); the Cultural Studies Association of Australia conference, *In Search of the Public* (1997); the symposium *The Contemporary Study of Culture* (1997) organised by Internationales Forschungszentrum Kulturwissenschaften and the Federal Ministry of Science & Transport, Vienna; the University of Kent; the Institute of Romance Studies, University of London; the Philosophy Department, University of Malta; the University of Middlesex; the Centre for European Studies, University of New South Wales; the University of Queensland; the Signs of the Times *Cityscapes* conference (1996); the University of Southampton; the *Citizenship* conference, University of Staffordshire; the John Logie Baird Centre, University of Strathclyde; the *Theory, Culture and Society* conference *Culture and Identity*, Berlin (1995); the American Center in Warsaw; the Department of Architecture and Art History at the University of Western Australia. Among those not already named, let me thank for invitations and hospitality Lou Bondi and Catherine Roe, Glenn Bowman and Elizabeth Cowie, Mark Cousins, Geoff Craig, Selim Eyuboglu, Simon Frith, John Milfull, Lutz Musner, David Pinder, and Richard Read.

Above all, the years of writing this book have been bound up with my developing relationship with three people. My daughter Morag was born during the writing of the first draft of what is now chapter three. My second daughter, Ellen, arrived between chapters four and five. Without them, the thing might have been finished more quickly, but it wouldn't have been half so much fun. My deepest gratitude is to Stephanie Donald for sharing the adventure of this book with me. Having grown up on Dartmoor, a passion for space often makes her impatient with the sacrifice of cities to motor traffic. Nevertheless, she retains an affection for the convivial urban life of Stoke Newington and Brixton. I hope I have been able to explain to her why, despite the cars, I still believe in the principle of the city.

Alvin Langdon
Coburn, Thames
Embankment,
London, ca. 1905–
1910 (The Royal
Photographic Society
Collection, Bath,
England)

chapter 1

Fog Everywhere

We start in the midst of things, in the city of benighted day, at the opening of Charles Dickens's novel *Bleak House*, published in 1853.

London. Michaelmas term lately over, and the Lord Chancellor sitting in Lincoln's Inn hall. Implacable November weather. As much mud in the streets, as if the waters had but newly retired from the face of the earth, and it would not be wonderful to meet a Megalosaurus, forty feet long or so, waddling like an elephantine lizard up Holborn Hill. Smoke lowering down from chimney-pots, making soft black drizzle with flakes of soot in it as big as full-grown snowflakes – gone into mourning, one might imagine, for the death of the sun. Dogs, indistinguishable in mire. Horses, scarcely better; splashed to their very blinkers. Foot passengers, jostling one another's umbrellas, in a general infection of ill temper, and losing their foot-hold at street-corners, where tens of thousands of other foot passengers have been slipping and sliding since the day broke (if this day ever broke), adding new deposits to the crust upon crust of mud, sticking at those points tenaciously to the pavement, and accumulating at compound interest.

Fog everywhere. Fog up the river, where it flows among green aits and meadows; fog down the river, where it rolls defiled among the tiers of shipping, and the waterside pollutions of a great (and dirty) city. Fog on the Essex Marshes, fog on the Kentish heights. Fog creeping into the cabooses of collier-brigs; fog lying out on the yards, and hovering in the rigging of great ships; fog drooping on the gunwales of barges and small boats. Fog in the eyes and throats of ancient Greenwich pensioners, wheezing by the firesides of their wards; fog in the stem and bowl of the afternoon pipe of the wrathful skipper, down in his close cabin; fog cruelly pinching the toes and fingers of his shivering little 'prentice boy on deck. Chance people on the bridges peeping over the parapets into a nether sky of fog, with fog all around them, as if they were balloon, and hanging in the misty clouds.

Gas looming through the fog in divers places in the streets, much as the sun may, from the spongey fields, be seen to loom by husbandman and plough-boy. Most of the shops lighted two hours before their time – as the gas seems to know, for it has a haggard and unwilling look.

Although this passage represents a there (London) and a then (the middle of the nineteenth century) rather than a here and now, the city conjured up by Dickens is not a place we have left behind. His London remains familiar territory. As the architect Kevin Lynch once observed, 'Dickens helped to create the London we experience as surely as its actual builders did.'[1] The city presented by *Bleak House* remains part of the present in which we live, part of our common sense. It does so less through its vivid representation of that city then, however, than through its pedagogy. The novel teaches us how to see the city, and how to make sense of it. It defines the co-ordinates for our imaginative mapping of urban space.

What is this London mapped by Dickens? The opening of *Bleak House* teaches a relationship between city and nature. The city is, by nature, unnatural. Its landscape and weather are shaped by human dirt: the mud, the November fog, the soot. As the gas-lamps struggle to penetrate the murk, so the city's fragile veneer of civilisation barely holds nature in check. Or, rather, its suppression produces a nature that always threatens to return as monstrous: the spectre of the Megalosaurus.

The passage defines a *here*, the space of the city, as it maps but also names London. It locates the reader. We are on Holborn Hill, by Lincoln's Inn. London as a whole is defined in relation to the (unnamed) Thames, from its source to its mouth in the east. It is the eastern boundaries that are named: Essex, Kent, Greenwich. This space is already too vast and sprawling to be captured in a panorama: hence the montage of apparently random figures and events – pensioners by the fire, the skipper with his pipe, the shivering apprentice, the pedestrians gawping from the bridges – which constitute London as a place.

Dickens locates the reader in time as well as in space. This is the city *now*. That is only in part the sense of London on *this* late afternoon in *this* November. More broadly, Dickens begins to render a way of experiencing the urban space of London which we shall learn to call modern. The contemporaneity, the now-ness, of his city suggests a style of living in the present. This style entails an historically specific psychological response. Dickens captures the modern citizen's reaction to this unnatural new landscape and to the oppressive presence of crowds of strangers, always on the move, jostling the observer, their anonymity emphasised by their umbrellas. Equally, he describes an anxiety externalised and figured in the cityscape and the crowd. Here Dickens's pedagogy teaches his readers not only how to articulate that anxiety, but also how to manage it. However opaque its ever-changing surface and however labyrinthine its social structures, for Dickens the metropolis *was* still legible. He always looks beyond the apparent randomness of the bustle and the business. The modernity of this overture to *Bleak House* lies in its brief prefiguring of institutions and social interactions that bind the city together. These, it will emerge later, are the law, money (here linked to the capital accumulation of mud), and trade (embodied not only in London's shops but also in international shipping).

Dickens's London is a city of networks. In part, these are social, economic or administrative networks: the railways of *Dombey and Son*, the dust heaps of *Our Mutual Friend*, the prisons in *Little Dorrit*.[2] But they are also narrative networks. London becomes a space constituted by the possibility of the narration of its social relations. In *Bleak House*, the narrative moves beyond or behind the empirical reality of fog and bustle to unravel a hidden reality, the link between an aristocratic landowner and an impoverished crossing sweeper. Through the interminable and pettifogging delays of the Court of Chancery, the law colludes in obscuring this connection. The narrative device for discovering it is to turn the lawsuit into a mystery through the murder of the lawyer who knows the city's secrets. This prepares the stage for the entrance of that other figure of the law, the police detective who can then solve the mystery and so resolve the case.

The policeman is thus a figure of the modern city, the personification of the power to decipher its networks. This power the policeman shares with the modern poet. The anthropologist Marc Augé cites the presentation of the city in the first poem in Baudelaire's *Tableaux parisiens* as a spectacle of modernity.

> *Les deux mains au menton, du haut de ma mansarde,*
> *Je verrai l'atelier qui chante et qui bavarde;*
> *Les tuyaux, les clochers, ces mâts de la cité,*
> *Et les grands ciels qui font rêver d'éternité.*

> Chin on my two hands, from my mansarded eyrie,
> I shall see the workshop with its song and chatter,
> Chimneys, spires, those masts of the city,
> And the great skies making us dream of eternity.

What makes this modern, for Augé, is first of all a sense of decipherable and cohering networks of meaning that Baudelaire shares with Dickens. Here, the ancient church spires are still integrated into the industrialised landscape of Paris, and so mark both the passage and the continuity of time in the space of the city. Second, though, and this is different from Dickens, the poet looking at the city has himself become part of the spectacle, a constitutive part of the landscape. His gaze is observed by a second self sensitive to the eternal that transcends the contingency – the this, here, now – of the temporal city.

By the time of high literary modernism after the Great War, this second way of seeing had intensified to the extent that it had absorbed the city into its own mental landscape. By 1922, in T.S. Eliot's *The Wasteland*, London's fog and river and anonymous crowds are still there as they had been in the opening of *Bleak House* seventy years earlier. But now the city has become *unreal*.

> Unreal City,
> Under the brown fog of a winter dawn,
> A crowd flowed over London Bridge, so many,
> I had not thought death had undone so many.
> Sighs, short and infrequent, were exhaled,
> And each man fixed his eyes before his feet.
> Flowed up the hill and down King William Street,
> To where Saint Mary Woolnoth kept the hours
> With a dead sound on the final stroke of nine.[3]

In modernist aesthetics, despite their national and political variability, the city for the most part was used to define this type of experience, this way of seeing, rather than to portray a place. Or rather, place comes to be understood as this way of experiencing urban space in human consciousness. 'The forces of the action have become internal,' Raymond Williams observes of James Joyce's *Ulysses*, also published in 1922; 'in a way there is no longer a city, there is only a man walking through it.'[4] Williams quotes this passage from the novel to illustrate both Joyce's new way of seeing Dublin – 'fragmentary, miscellaneous, isolated' – and also the way that it is 'actualised on the senses in a new structure of language.'[5]

> He walked along the curbstone. Stream of life. . . .
>   . . . Cityful passing away, other cityful coming, passing away too: other coming on, passing on. Houses, lines of housing, streets, miles of streets. Miles of pavements, piledup bricks, stones. Changing hands. This owner, that. Landlord never dies, they say. Other steps into his shoes when he gets his notice to quit. They buy the place up with gold and still they have all the gold. Swindle in it somewhere. Piled up in cities, worn away age after age. Pyramids in sand. Built on bread and onions. Slaves. Chinese wall. Babylon. Big stones left. Round towers. Rest rubble, sprawling suburbs, jerrybuilt, Kerwan's mushroom houses, built of breeze. Shelter for the night.
>   No one is anything.

In a slightly earlier novel, the first volume in Dorothy Richardson's massive thirteen-volume *Pilgrimage*, the city has been rendered not to a man walking through it, but to a woman cycling back into London.

> This was the true harvest of the summer's day; the transfiguration of these northern streets. They were not London proper; but to-night the spirit of London came to meet her on the verge. Nothing in life could be sweeter than this welcoming – a cup held brimming to her lips, and inexhaustible. What lover did she want? No one in the world would oust this mighty lover, always receiving her back without words, engulfing and leaving her untouched, liberated and expanding to the whole range of her being. In the mile or so ahead, there was endless time. She would travel further than the longest journey, swifter than the most rapid flight, down and down into an oblivion deeper than sleep; and drop off at the centre, on to the deserted grey pavements, with the high quiet houses standing all about her in air sweetened by the evening breath of the trees, stealing down the street from either end; the sound of her footsteps awakening her again to the single fact of her incredible presence within the vast surrounding presence. Then, for another unforgettable night of return, she would break into the shuttered house and gain her room and lie, till she suddenly slept, tingling to the spread of London all about her, herself one with it, feeling her life flow outwards, north, south, east, and west, to all its margins.[6]

Although Richardson's London is as thoroughly internalised as Joyce's Dublin, the flux and force of the city are not here centred into the consciousness of the observer walking through it. Rather, the woman's very being is dissolved into the enveloping, liquefying spread of the city. This might be read as a contrast between centripetal, taxonomising maleness and centrifugal, feeling femaleness. But remember then the same nocturnal sense of the self dissolving across space and time to be found at the end of 'The Dead' in Joyce's *Dubliners*.

> A few light taps upon the pane made him turn to the window. It had begun to snow again. He watched sleepily the flakes, silver and dark, falling obliquely against the lamplight. The time had come for him to set out on his journey

westward. Yes, the newspapers were right: snow was general all over Ireland. It was falling on every part of the dark central plain, on the treeless hills, falling softly upon the Bog of Allen and, farther westward, softly falling into the dark mutinous Shannon waves. It was falling, too, upon every part of the lonely churchyard on the hill where Michael Furey lay buried. It lay thickly drifted on the crooked crosses and headstones, on the spears of the little gate, on the barren thorns. His soul swooned slowly as he heard the snow falling faintly through the universe and faintly falling, like the descent of their last end, upon all the living and all the dead.

This may be more conventional than *Ulysses*. Nevertheless, it conveys something of the modern city-dweller's imagination, the ability to live both here and elsewhere – a way of being encouraged in more mundane ways by new and largely urban technologies of communication: here the newspaper, but also advertising, cinema and, later, broadcasting.

The snow in 'The Dead' performs similar functions to the fog in *Bleak House*. That continuity may be of passing interest to literary historians. It makes me wonder whether such tropes tell us anything about a broader repertoire of cultural responses to the city. Consider another imagined city at another time, in a different place, and inscribed in a less rarefied genre: the middle of the twentieth century, an unnamed city in America's mid-West which is clearly Chicago, and a narrative located squarely in the traditions of popular fiction.

A dark, blustery night had settled down like a cowl over the huge, sprawling Midwestern city by the river. A mistlike rain blew between the tall buildings at intervals, wetting the streets and pavements and turning them into black, fun-house mirrors that reflected in grotesque distortions the street lights and neon signs.

The big downtown bridges arched off across the wide, black river into the void, the far shore blotted out by the misty rain; and gusts of wind, carrying stray newspapers, blew up the almost deserted boulevards, whistling faintly along the building fronts and moaning at the intersections. Empty surface cars, and buses with misted windows, trundled slowly through the downtown section. Except for taxis and prowl cars, there was no traffic.

River Boulevard, wide as a plaza and with its parkways and arched, orange street lights stretching off into the misty horizon in diminishing perspective, was as deserted as if a plague had swept the streets clean. The traffic lights changed with automatic precision, but there were no cars to heed or disobey them. Far down the boulevard, in the supper-club section of the city, elaborately glittering neon signs flashed off and on to emptiness. The night city, like a wound-up toy, went about its business with mechanical efficiency, regardless of man.

Finally the wind died down and the rain began to fall steadily all over the huge city: on the stacks of the steel plants in Polishtown; on the millionaires' mansions in Riverdale; on the hilly regions of Tecumseh Slope, with its little Italian groceries and restaurants; on the massed tenement apartments along the upper river, where all the windows had been dark for hours and men would start awake cursing as the alarm clocks blasted at five a.m.; on the fanned-out suburban areas to the north and east, where all the little houses

and the little lawns looked alike; and finally on the dark and unsavoury
reaches of Camden Square and its environs, the immense downtown slum
beyond the river, where there was at least one bar at every intersection, prowl
cars by the dozens, and harness bulls working in pairs.

A taxi pulled up at a dark store front near Camden Square, and the driver
turned to speak to his fare.

'You sure you know where you're going, buddy?'[7]

This is from W.R. Burnett's gangster thriller *The Asphalt Jungle*, published in 1949
and turned into a successful film the following year. Strangely, this imagined
Chicago is still in many ways Dickens's London, and in some sense also Joyce's
Dublin. The implacable weather still indiscriminately buffets different districts.
The city still seems somehow alien, and civilisation, however mechanically sophisticated it has become, remains fragile. The narrative is again woven around the technologies and forces that constitute the life of a city – transport, lighting, police, and
so forth. Obviously, there is going to be a crime. So what is new in this urban here
and now of Burnett's?

First, Burnett offers a double take on the city which intensifies and makes explicit
images that were emergent in Dickens. On the one hand, the urban networks traced
by Dickens are here transformed into the city as *machine*: 'The night city, like a
wound-up toy, went about its business with mechanical efficiency, regardless of
man.' On the other hand, the uncanny edge to this machine-like city is made manifest. Gone are the haggard gas lamps. The wet pavements have become 'fun-house
mirrors that reflected in grotesque distortions the street lights and neon signs.'

Second, then, this unnamed city may refer to Chicago, but it is also recognisably
the modernist city. It is as de-centred and de-centring as Richardson's city,
suspended between life and death like Joyce's, and as unreal as Eliot's.

Third, however, this city is modernist in another sense. Burnett takes it for
granted that readers of a popular novel in the middle of the twentieth century will be
at ease with the idea of mapping class and ethnic differences onto the geography of
the city. That assumption invokes another tradition for talking about the city: not
the nineteenth century novel, nor literary modernism, but modern sociology. There
is at least an affinity between Burnett's urban ecology and the microscopic mapping
of their home city by the Chicago School of sociologists in the inter-war decades.

Compare Burnett's description of rain-soaked enclaves with Louis Wirth's observation in his 1938 essay on 'Urbanism as a Way of Life':

> Cities generally, and American cities in particular, comprise a motley of
> peoples and cultures, of highly differentiated modes of life between which
> there often is only the faintest communication, the greatest indifference and
> the broadest tolerance, occasionally bitter strife, but always the sharpest
> contrast.[8]

Compare too the tone and perspective of *The Asphalt Jungle*, or American hard-
boiled crime fiction generally, with the advice given to his students by Robert Park,
the leader of the Chicago School.

> Go and sit in the lounges of the luxury hotels and on the doorsteps of the
> flophouses; sit on the Gold Coast settees and on the slum shakedowns; sit in

the Orchestra Hall and the Star and Garter Burlesque. In short, gentlemen, go get the seat of your pants dirty in real research.[9]

I have no idea whether Burnett knew the work of the Chicago sociologists (any more than I know whether he had read Dickens or Joyce). He probably did, but influence is not the important issue.

I take two broader lessons from this Chicago contribution to my montage of quotations. First, *The Asphalt Jungle* reveals a perspective on the city – a certain way of seeing and narrating the city – which transcends literary modernism, gangster novels and the sociological imagination. Historically, what linked popular fiction and sociology seems to have been a journalistic eye for the drama of the city and a nose for social investigation. Like Dickens before him, Park worked as a journalist and editor in New York and Chicago in the eighteen nineties before going to Berlin to study with Georg Simmel. Burnett's day job was also as a Chicago journalist. The attitude which unites novelist and journalist in their fascination with the city – an attitude raised to heroic status in the mythical figures of gangster and detective – is captured by Park in his 1915 essay on 'The City':

> . . . a great city tends to spread out and lay bare to the public view in a massive manner all the characters and traits which are ordinarily obscured and suppressed in smaller communities. The city, in short, shows the good and evil in human nature in excess. It is this fact, more than any other which justifies the view that would make of the city a laboratory or clinic in which human nature and social processes may be most conveniently and profitably studied.[10]

The second lesson from Burnett's Chicago follows from this. If sociologists, journalists and novelists carry out their research in the *laboratory* of the city, then their moral tales about social differences and about human nature in turn help to construct the city as *archive*.

This archive, this city of modernist texts, is to some extent my object of study. But, more than that, it is where I live. I am less interested in literary archaeology than in understanding the imaginary city which, snail-like, I carry around with me. Part carapace and part burden, this shell has been moulded, of course, by experience. But both that experience, and the imagined city it has produced, are shot through by the contents of the archive city. It has been learned as much from novels, pictures and half-remembered films as from diligent walks round the capital cities of Europe. It embodies perspectives, images, and narratives that migrate across popular fiction, modernist aesthetics, the sociology of urban culture, and techniques for acting on the city.

This starting point produces a distinctive paradox in the way I see the city. *The city* suggests an immediacy of experience: the *this, here, now,* so beloved of empiricist philosophers, that is conjured up in Dickens's rendering of London on a foggy November afternoon and (as we shall see in a later chapter) made explicit in Virginia Woolf's London on a June morning in *Mrs Dalloway*. Yet, as those references already show, this experience of immediacy is mediated through and through by the pedagogics and aesthetics of the city. It involves not immediacy but contingency. The city teaches us the arts, the techniques, and the tactics of living in the present.

A STATE OF MIND

'The city is a state of mind,' wrote Robert Park in 1915. If that is true, does it mean that there is no such thing as the city? It is tempting to say yes, but that answer might set up a false opposition. Of course, cities are not only mental constructs. Of course, there are real cities. Each city has its own location and climate, its own history and architecture, its own spatial and social dispositions, its own cacophony of languages, its own soundtrack of traffic, trade and music, its own smells and characteristic tastes, its own problems and pleasures. But why reduce the reality of cities to their thingi-ness, or their thinginess to a question of bricks and mortar? States of mind have material consequences. They make things happen.

Starting from there, what particularly interests me is the power of *the city* as a category of thought. *The city* is an abstraction, which claims to identify what, if anything, is common to all cities. The category designates a space produced by the interaction of historically and geographically specific institutions, social relations of production and reproduction, practices of government, forms and media of com-munication, and so forth. By calling this diversity *the* city, we ascribe to it a coherence or integrity. One way of thinking that coherence would be to treat the category of *the city* as a representation. But the concept of representation, although in the end it is indispensable, may raise more problems than it solves when we try to think about both the thinginess of the city and the city as state of mind. It is true that what we experience is never the real city, 'the thing itself'. It is also true that the everyday reality of the city is always a space already constituted and structured by symbolic mechanisms.[11] But representation does not quite get the measure of the relationship between those two realities, for it implies that one reality must be a model for the other, or a copy of it. More to the point, maybe, is Ihab Hassan's invocation of the *immaterial city* which, he suggests, has 'in-formed history from the start, moulding human space and time ever since time and space moulded themselves to the wag-ging tongue.'[12] The City of God, the republican *polis*, the Ville Radieuse, the city as public sphere: none of these is just or quite a representation, nor has any of them ever existed as a real (in the sense of physical) place. Rather, these immaterial cities are ideas or ideals that have played a powerfully important role in shaping the spatial organisation and architectural design of cities. What such images point to is a social and even spiritual element invested in space, a material and so inevitably unsuccess-ful embodiment of the will to create relations between people that transcend the animal or the tribal; the will to community.

If it is not quite a representation, maybe (taking the imagined community of the nation as an analogy[13]) it would be more accurate to think of the city as an *imagined environment*. This environment embraces not just the cities created by the 'wagging tongues' of architects, planners and builders, sociologists and novelists, poets and politicians, but also the translation of the places they have made into the imaginary reality of our mental life. In that sense, I live in the same city as Victor Burgin; or, at least, I live the city in the same way.

> The city in our actual experience is *at the same time* an actually existing phys-ical environment, *and* a city in a novel, a film, a photograph, a city seen on television, a city in a comic strip, a city in a pie chart, and so on.[14]

The important point, which Burgin himself explores and illuminates in both his

Work and love meld in the romance of consumption staged on the Kings Road in London in the 1980s. 'The Romantic loves most what is least accessible. Hence, most banal and most true of clichés, the British love the sun. These images of the Kings Road catch some reflected sunlight of a single Saturday afternoon.' – Victor Burgin, *Some Cities*

theoretical writings about visual culture, in his photographs and in his art works, is not only this simultaneity, but above all the productive transactions between the two. This traffic between urban fabric, representation and imagination fuzzies up the epistemological and ontological distinctions and, in doing so, produces the city between, the imagined city where we actually live.

It is this city between that I attempt to map in this book. I do not pretend that it is an undiscovered city. On the contrary, it is the city that has, in the twentieth century, fascinated modern sociologists and cultural theorists as well as novelists and poets.

The figure who stands for the sociological articulation of this fascination is Georg Simmel. He taught Robert Park that the city is a state of mind, and that the city is both the location and embodiment of modernity. In his famous 1903 lecture on 'The Metropolis and Mental Life', Simmel offers a prescient attempt to grasp the uneasy urban space between physical and imaginary produced by the destabilizing dynamic between subjective space, the outside world, and social life.[15] How, he asks in effect, does the outside of the metropolis become the inside of mental life?

> An enquiry into the inner meaning of specifically modern life and its products, into the soul of the cultural body, so to speak, must seek to solve the equation which structures like the metropolis set up between the individual and the supra-individual contents of life. Such an enquiry must answer the question of how the personality accommodates itself in the adjustments to external forces.[16]

One of the surprising things about 'The Metropolis and Mental Life' is that it offers no description of its city, nor any detailed observation of places or people. It is already a largely unreal city. We only know that Simmel has Berlin primarily in mind when he muses about what would happen if all its clocks stopped at once, although he is also happy to refer to London when it serves his turn. The contrast between the abstraction of Simmel's sociological impressionism and the particularity of Dickens's novelistic realism is not just aesthetic or generic. It entails a different objective. Simmel does not want to conjure up the *this* metropolis now. Rather, he wants to understand *the* metropolis as the conceptual location of a split between subjective culture and objective culture produced by the money economy and the division of labour.

> The individual has become a mere cog in an enormous organisation of things and powers which tear from his hands all progress, spirituality, and value in order to transform them from their subjective form into the form of a purely objective life. It needs merely to be pointed out that the metropolis is the genuine arena of this culture which outgrows all personal life. Here in buildings and educational institutions, in the wonders and comforts of space-conquering technology, in the formations of community life, and in the visible institutions of the state, is offered such an overwhelming fullness of crystallised and impersonalised spirit that the personality, so to speak, cannot maintain itself under its impact.[17]

In some ways, I wish that there were a bit more Dickens in Simmel, that he had been more explicit in cataloguing exactly which institutions and formations produced the *newness* experienced in the metropolis. As two of Simmel's other pupils,

Siegfried Kracauer and Walter Benjamin (whom we shall meet again) were to document, the changed nature of time and space was no abstraction. They described the new technologies of gas lamps, arcades, trains, telephones and telegraphy, they catalogued the rebuilding of Europe's great metropolitan centres, and they observed new forms of mass spectacle and mass entertainment, including sport and cinema. More recently, post-Foucault, historians have shown how institutions of the state both responded to and helped to shape the reality of the great cities.

Simmel's great virtue was not detailed reportage. Rather, it was his ability to perceive the metropolis as a structure or field of social forces, and to convey the experience of that city with unprecedented clarity. His city is an overwhelming series of events and impressions, a representational space within which a mass of transitory, fleeting and fortuitous interactions take place. How are these events, impressions and interactions translated into an inner, emotional life – into a state of mind? In two ways. As their senses are bombarded, as urban life becomes increasingly mediated and as fellow citizens become, of necessity, more self-interested, suggests Simmel, individuals resort to stratagems of inward retreat and social distance. A blasé, intellectualising attitude is one such strategy for self-protection. This reflects less indifference than a reserve cultivated to contain the aggression inherent in urban relations: 'a slight aversion, a mutual strangeness and repulsion, which will break into hatred and conflict at the moment of a closer contact.'[18] Even though distance and deflection may appear to be forms of disassociation, they actually help to neutralise this propensity to violence.

That elementary form of defensive sociation is just one difference from the culture of small towns. There, you know who you are because everyone else knows who you are: 'frequent and prolonged association assures the personality of an unambiguous image of himself in the eyes of the other.' In the metropolis, fleeting contacts and transient relationships make it difficult to assert your own personality. This problem then produces a more expressive, and again specifically modern, reaction. It manifests itself in an aesthetic of self-creation, which can verge on being a parody of individuality.[19] In the city, 'man is tempted to adopt the most tendentious peculiarities, that is, the specifically metropolitan extravagances of mannerism, caprice, and preciousness.'[20]

Metropolitan man has become genuinely 'free' (the scare quotes are Simmel's) in the sense of being liberated from 'the pettiness and prejudices which hem in the small-town man'. This freedom from the constraints of community has to be exercised, however, in the crowded and claustrophobic space of the city. It is not a freedom without costs. Its consequence is physical closeness offset by mental distance.

> It is obviously only the obverse of this freedom if, under certain circumstances, one nowhere feels as lonely and lost as in the metropolitan crowd. For here as elsewhere it is by no means necessary that the freedom of man be reflected in his emotional life as comfort.[21]

The uncomfortable freedom of the metropolis is the key lesson to be learned from Simmel. He does not see in the city only the manifestation of a power that oppresses the individual. Rather, he suggests how individual agency is enacted within the field of possibilities realised by this real-imagined environment: its space, its population, its technologies, its symbolisation. The city may remain inescapably strange and

opaque. It is often oppressive. Yet it provides the texture of our experience and the fabric of our liberty. The city is the way we moderns live and act, as much as where.

That is an axiom that runs through the cultural history of twentieth-century Europe, from the Surrealists to the Situationists and beyond. Linking those two movements, and giving a different twist to many of Simmel's perceptions, is the work of that engaging and idiosyncratic observer of modernity and everyday life, Henri Lefebvre. In *The Production of Space*, Lefebvre, like Simmel, is concerned with the interplay between the space of the city and the mental life of its citizens. But Lefebvre is less concerned than Simmel with the impact of the metropolis on mental life. Simmel asks how the outside of the metropolis becomes the inside of mental life. Lefebvre is more interested in the way that mental life is projected outwards. Looking back from the period after 1968, when he wrote the book, Lefebvre links his vision to that of the surrealists.

> The leading surrealists sought to decode inner space and illuminate the nature of the transition from this subjective space to the material realm of the body and the outside world, and thence to social life.[22]

For both Lefebvre and Simmel, however, the key to understanding the dynamic (as a marxist Lefebvre would say dialectic) between social space and mental space is the *transition*. What Lefebvre takes from the surrealists is the model of a circuit running through imagination, representation, the body, the social, and the spatial.

What makes this circuit work, according to Lefebvre, is not the nature of space, but the spatial consequences of what people do. The space we experience is the material embodiment of a history of social relations. But we *conceive* space as well as perceive space. We map space, we calculate it, we control it, we exploit it – or at least the 'scientists, planners, urbanists, technocratic subdividers and social engineers' among us do, along with 'a certain type of artist with a scientific bent'. (He presumably means architects.) Through a process of abstraction and conceptualisation, they produce 'representations of space'. This is in turn different from the 'representational space' in which we actually live. Representational space is 'the dominated – and hence passively experienced – space which the imagination seeks to change and appropriate. It overlays physical space, making symbolic use of its objects.'[23]

This is Lefebvre's version of my imagined city, the city between mental space, social space, and physical space. The strength of his approach lies in his determination to show *how* the texture of this imagined space is produced. His view is that it happens in the 'lethal zone' of language, signs and abstraction. Because language is inherently metaphorical, it becomes possible – or inevitable – for meaning 'to escape the embrace of lived experience, to detach itself from the fleshly body'. In a move that is 'inextricably magical and rational', the representational space of our imagined reality comes into being.[24]

Although Lefebvre's account of the *production* of representational space has the operations of language at its very heart, it represents a polemical alternative to what he saw as the inflated claims about the *language-like* nature of space in structuralism and post-structuralism.[25] That is why he insists on the *texture* of space, and why he is so reluctant to allow that it has any *text-like* qualities. If we *read* the city, as Lefebvre accepts we do, our reading is pragmatic rather than semiotic.

Georg Grosz, Berlin, 1923 (© Viscopy)

Now, it may or may not be necessary to draw that distinction as firmly and exclusively as Lefebvre does. I suspect that it is not. Nevertheless, his insistence on the production and consequences of both representations of space and of representational space remain essential in any attempt to understand how we imagine the city.

Another influential perspective on these questions, and one much more sympathetic to the linguistic analogy, is that of Michel de Certeau. Despite this basic difference of emphasis, there are resonances between Lefebvre's account of the way we appropriate urban space and de Certeau's chapter 'Walking in the City' in *The Practice of Everyday Life*. There, de Certeau offers another dual perspective for mapping urban space.[26] Echoing Lefebvre's 'representations of space', he first describes the New York cityscape visible from the World Trade Centre. This leads him to meditate on the temptation inherent in such a panorama. It offers the perspective of a *dieu voyeur*, the promise of a Concept City to be found in 'utopian and urbanistic discourse.' This representation is the fantasy that has motivated planners and reformers in their desire to make the city an object of knowledge and so a governable space. They dream of encompassing the diversity, randomness and dynamism of urban life in a rational blueprint, a neat collection of statistics, and a clear set of social norms. Theirs is an idealised perspective, which aspires to render the city transparent. The city would become, as de Certeau puts it, '*un espace propre*': its own space and a purified, hygienic space, purged of 'all the physical, mental and political pollutions that would compromise it.' It would be the city of benign surveillance and spatial penetration. Institutions like hospitals, schools and prisons, carceral and pastoral at the same time, would provide constant oversight of its population. Its dwellings and settlements would be designed on therapeutic principles. Its lungs and arteries would be surgically opened up to allow the controlled flow of air, light, waste, traffic, and people.[27]

Against this panoptic representation de Certeau poses a representational urban space – what he calls the *fact* of the city. The city that people inhabit is a labyrinthine reality which produces 'an 'anthropological', poetic and mythic experience of space.' In the recesses and margins of the city, people invest places with meaning, memory and desire. We adapt the constraining and enabling structures of the city to an ingenious or despairing rhetoric. 'Beneath the discourses that ideologise the city,' writes de Certeau, 'the ruses and combinations of powers that have no readable identity proliferate; without points where one can take hold of them, without rational transparency, they are impossible to administer.'[28] For de Certeau, then, the city figures the labyrinth as well as transparency. Rather as Simmel drew a distinction between the 'enormous organisation of things and powers' and the 'forms of motion' in mental life, de Certeau (like Lefebvre) attempts to gauge the material consequences of the projection of that motile inner life: 'a *migrational*, or metaphorical, city thus slips into the clear text of the planned and readable city.'[29]

The imagery of de Certeau's battle between the tower and the street has often been criticised for its melodramatic opposition between power and resistance, between social and individual, between theory and practice. Meaghan Morris, for one, has objected that the model recuperates the heterogeneity that de Certeau celebrates in his invocation of the streets by pulling it back into an all too familiar grid of binary oppositions. The tower, Morris concludes, 'serves as an allegory of the structural necessity for a politics of resistance based on a bipolar model of power to

Ira Martin, New
York, 1929 (Courtesy
Vanity Fair.
Copyright © 1929 by
The Condé Nast
Publications, Inc.)

David Vestal, West
22nd Street, New
York, 1949 (© David
Vestal 1998)

maintain the imaginary position of mastery it must then endlessly disclaim.'[30] De Certeau himself acknowledges the historical contingency of his imaginary map. The tower has had its day. The heroic age of planning and building our way out of the problems of modernity has passed.[31] 'The Concept-city is decaying,' writes de Certeau, with no apparent sign of regret.

Nevertheless, despite his own caveats, the way that de Certeau's image of a mythical struggle between creative tactics and an abstracting vision of power has been taken up has tended to sustain a generalised and sentimental conception of 'resistance'. This is certainly Tony Bennett's objection. Because he fails to discriminate between different types of resistance, de Certeau provides no basis for political (or policy) action. De Certeau's description of the profane arts of the city is simply too poetic to be useful.[32] I see the strength of Bennett's argument. It is undeniable that de Certeau is not going to help much if you are trying to improve the street lighting, to encourage rational recreations in parks, libraries and museums, or to create well-ordered public spaces conducive to active and pleasurable citizenship. But then, why should he? De Certeau was not a policy-maker *manqué*.

What he does offer, however elliptically, is an attempt (again like Simmel and Lefebvre) to understand and explain how the imaginative appropriation of space is linked to mental life. What Bennett fails to spot, I think, is the psychoanalytic rationale for the steps by which de Certeau traces the creativity of metaphorical space to the intensity of dreaming and ultimately back to the re-enactment of 'the joyful and silent experience of childhood'. That experience is, like being both here and elsewhere, '*to be other and to move toward the other*' in a place.[33] Even if he does not altogether deliver it, de Certeau suggests the need for a sociological elaboration of styles of urban spatial appropriation that are expressed at their most intense and, yes, poetic in images like Joyce's Bloom walking the streets of Dublin or Dorothy Richardson's heroine 'tingling to the spread of London all about her, herself one with it, feeling her life flow outwards, north, south, east, and west, to all its margins.'

So de Certeau's alleged poeticism does not worry me as much as it does Tony Bennett. I interpret it less as an irresponsible disavowal of the reality principle, than as a sober acknowledgement that the city we actually live in is poetic in Vattimo's sense. In the subjective life of the city dweller, there is no possibility of defining clear-cut boundaries between reality and imagination: 'Haunted places are the only ones people can live in.'[34]

De Certeau's comment may sound like more throwaway poeticism. It foreshadows, though, Jacques Derrida's invocation of the figure of the *spectre* in his attempt to capture the 'elusive pseudo-materiality' of our everyday reality. The spectre is another refusal of the opposition between reality and the immaterial. 'There is no reality without the spectre,' argues Slavoj Zizek in his gloss on Derrida; 'the circle of reality can be closed only by means of an uncanny spectral supplement.' What does Zizek mean by this, and how might it help us to understand the real/imagined space of the city? To go back a few steps, I have argued that we never experience the space of the city unmediated. The city we do experience – the city as state of mind – is always already symbolised and metaphorised. The problem, though, is that the symbolisation never quite gets the measure of the real (understood as a formal, pre-ideological matrix onto which various ideological formations are grafted). What remains, says Zizek, is an unsettled, unredeemed symbolic debt.

And the non-symbolised part of reality then 'returns in the guise of spectral apparitions'.[35]

What appeals to me about this account of the haunted city is that it manages to give weight to the force of both the real and the imaginary. In doing so, it suggests how the real makes its presence felt in the imaginary, and so offers a model for the production of the actual or experiential. It avoids saying that the city is *purely* a social or a textual or a symbolic construction, without denying that it is all those things as well.

> To put it simply, reality is never directly 'itself', it presents itself only via its incomplete-failed symbolisation, and spectral apparitions emerge in this very gap that forever separates reality from the real, and on account of which reality has the character of a (symbolic) fiction: the spectre gives body to that which escapes (the symbolically structured) reality.[36]

How do we inhabit this spectral space of the city? One answer might be suggested by the angels in Wim Wenders's film *Wings of Desire*. Themselves invisible, to these benign and omniscient spectres Berlin is wholly transparent. They hear the inner speech of its inhabitants with infinite empathy. They see with tragic resignation all history sedimented into the most apparently banal spaces, and especially those spaces in pre-1989 Berlin rendered superficially meaningless yet historically meaningful by the presence of the Wall. Their ability to see all and hear all – to experience the city raw, as the thing itself – would, of course, drive us humans instantly mad. We are able to operate in urban society only *because* the surface of the city and the people in it (including ourselves) are opaque, historically contingent, complexly determined, but also in some ways and to some degree legible. And, agreeing here with Lefebvre, that legibility requires less the angelic skill of perfect reading than the human powers of imagination.

In deference to my sceptical and pragmatic readers, and to the sceptical pragmatist in myself, let me attempt a brief audit of what these powers are, and how they work. Their first and most important feature is that they involve a creative *act* of appropriation or meaning-making, rather than the mental reproduction or representation of a thing external to the mind.[37] Imagining is neither simple reflection nor pure projection. The lesson of Simmel, Park, Lefebvre and de Certeau – as well as the poets – is that imagination is always a creative but also constrained interchange between the subjective and the social.

Phenomenologists give a particular gloss to this premise. They see the act of imagining less as a translation from the sense-data of empirical experience into the movies in our minds, than as a way of intuiting the essence of things and then projecting alternative possibilities of how things *might* be. We do not just read the city, we negotiate the reality of cities by imagining 'the city'.[38] This suggests a broader lesson: that imagination precedes any distinction between fiction and truth, between illusion and reality. It is imagination that produces reality as it exists.[39] The question then is the degree of freedom of action that is opened up for the citizen of this constituted reality.

Imagination is neither a delusory nor a solipsistic act, even though it registers in its full force the reality of unconscious drives and fantasies. However idiosyncratic our imaginations and their flights of fancy may be, the *terms* of imagining are transindividual. This is the axiom that Cornelius Castoriadis builds on when he talks about a *social* imaginary. By this he means the power to create out of nothing the figures and forms of everyday social and historical life, the symbolic reality instituted as language, narrative, ritual, tradition, and myth.

Whether you look at it from a phenomenological or a psychoanalytic angle, the conventional hostility towards imagination as a luxury of idle fancy, especially as it shades into fantasy, makes little sense. On the contrary, imagination emerges as an instrument of truth.[40] The *value*, and not the limitation, of imaginative truths is that they are poetic, that they transgress the boundaries between social and psychic. They thereby sustain a fourth dimension of 'space-time', which is where the dynamic between unconscious and corporeality, between desire and the social, between pleasure and Law, is played out.[41]

Imagination is concerned with the exploration of possibilities, not merely the record of what is. Imagination is not limited to the mimesis of images sanctioned by the Law. Imagination is inherently ethical insofar as it always operates in the register of *as if*: as if I were another, as if things could be otherwise. As a political gesture, imagination has the power to offer what Sue Golding calls 'a kind of practical romanticism rooted in an 'as if' and fractured by the unequivocal perversity of the body itself.'[42]

THE MODERN CITY

Once, when I was presenting a paper based on a chapter from this book, I was asked, politely but subversively, whether my argument would stand up if I were to remove all reference to modernity and the modern from it. Certainly the concept needs to be justified. As the topic of modernity has been discussed almost to death in social theory, cultural criticism, and postmodern geography, its inflated status has understandably produced a backlash.

Shouldn't we pause, critics are quite properly asking, to reflect whether the attempt to identify the forces that have shaped the present necessarily entails or even needs a conception of modernity? Aren't the costs of using the concept – its implication of a progression from pre-modern to modern and possibly beyond, its tendency to assume a modernised, rational *us* in the west and an inadequately modernised, irrational *them* everywhere else – greater than the value of any insights it allows?[43]

One tactical response to such questions is to agree that there is no such thing as modernity, and never was – and then write a book about it. I shall resist the temptation.

I accept fully that 'periodising' modernity (or even modernism) is not in the end a very productive activity. (Did modernity really start at a certain hour on a certain day in 1910, as Virginia Woolf mischievously claimed? Did it end, as David Harvey reports, when a certain building in a certain American city was demolished in 1972?) I am not interested in modernity as an epoch – although I realise that that disavowal does not get me out of all the difficulties of the temporal baggage the concept brings with it. What intrigues me, especially when you bring modernity and the city together, is the consistency with which commentators, from Baudelaire through Le Corbusier to the postmodernists, end up saying that modernity too is a state of mind. I think that is right, although I do not see that 'state of mind' in terms of a mentality with a positive substance or content. It is something more elusive than that, something more akin to Raymond Williams's tantalising notion of a structure of feeling. Le Corbusier comes close to what I am trying to get at in one of the better jokes in *The City of Tomorrow*: an empty page with this box on it.

*Left blank for a work
expressing modern feeling.*

For Le Corbusier, 'modern feeling' is the undeliverable promise of a substantive answer to the question of what it means to live in modernity. That brings into focus what for me is the real issue: whether the category of modernity (or for that matter the category of the city) is a useful way of framing an answer to the question of how we live in the present.

This, of course, is Foucault's question, paraphrasing Kant in his late essays and lectures on the Enlightenment.

> What is happening today? What is happening now? And what is this 'now'
> which we all inhabit, and which defines the moment in which I am writing?[44]

What was novel in Kant's response, suggests Foucault, is 'the reflection on "today" as difference in history and as motive for a particular philosophical task.' This new approach to philosophy is what produces modernity as a state of mind. Foucault calls it 'a point of departure: the outline of what one might call the attitude of modernity.'

> And by 'attitude', I mean a mode of relating to contemporary reality; a volun-
> tary choice made by certain people; in the end, a way of thinking and feeling;
> a way, too, of acting and behaving that at one and the same time marks a
> relation of belonging and presents itself as a task. A bit, no doubt, like what
> the Greeks called an *ethos*.[45]

Modernity can then be seen as the term that denotes this critical reflection on the present. As I have suggested, however, some people who operate in this Foucauldian register argue that the term modernity has become so ideologically barnacled that it now actually inhibits that critical thought.

This sceptical case has been vigorously argued by Andrew Barry, Thomas Osborne and Nikolas Rose. They share the view that the fundamental problem with thinking the present as modernity and modernity as a comprehensive periodisation – 'an epoch, an attitude, a form of life, a mentality, an experience' – is 'an inherent impetus to totalisation.'

Where are the limits – geographical, social, temporal – of modernity? Is modernity a type of society, or an attitude or a mode of experience? Is modernity a functionalist, a realist, or an idealist concept? Where is modernity heading? What comes after modernity? Or perhaps – the greatest iconoclasm – we have yet to reach modernity at all?[46]

Part of the problem, for them, is a 'predictable' shift away from describing the empirical features of the present to speculating about the supposed transition to some new present epoch: postmodernity, late modernity, high modernity, super-modernity. Against this tendency to science fiction, Barry, Osborne and Rose defend the Foucauldian *ethos* of modernity as a way of orientating oneself to history.

Foucault was concerned to introduce an 'untimely' attitude in our relation to the present. Untimely in the Nietzschean sense: acting counter to our time, introducing a new sense of the fragility of our time, and thus acting on our time for the benefit, one hopes, of a time to come.[47]

The 'present' should be understood less as an epoch, or as the culmination of some grand historical process, than as an array of questions. Foucault's *ethos* thus leads to a methodological attitude based on a commitment to uncertainty in the permanent scrutiny of the present. It produces a version of Kant's 'pragmatic anthropology' – an attempt to produce perspectival analyses of the strategies and techniques which structure both our experience and our ethical certainties.

The strand in Foucault's thinking about the present which Barry, Osborne and Rose most value, and which their own work develops, is his concern with governmentality. They don't go quite as far as saying that all the rest is so much froth on the coffee, the overheated and apocalyptic rhetoric of boys who spend too much time strolling the shopping malls, reading detective stories, or watching *Blade Runner*.[48] But I think it is not unfair to say that applying their approach to the study of the city would mean spending more time understanding the logic and consequences of urban reform and welfare programmes and less time rhapsodising heroically about the voluptuous spectacle of the streets. Theirs is a rigorously de-poeticized reflection on the present.

Barry, Osborne and Rose have helped to illuminate 'some of the contingencies of the systems of power that we inhabit – and which inhabit us – today'. But in order to do that, is it necessary to drop the concept of *modernity* altogether? They look as if they are about to say that it does, but then they go silent, and leave its tattered remnants flapping in the breeze. The real issue, it seems to me, is less 'modernity or not' than the appropriate topoi and methods for a pragmatic anthropology of the present. If there is a disagreement, it is less about whether or not to call the critical attitude to the present 'modernity' than about the necessity or legitimacy of a poetic aspect to that attitude.

Rereading Foucault's essay 'What is Enlightenment?', which is where he discusses explicitly the present and modernity, reveals a curious blind spot in Barry, Osborne and Rose's argument. It is the missing figure of Baudelaire. They relate the ethos Foucault calls modernity to Kant and Nietzsche. They ignore his references to Baudelaire as the 'almost indispensable' exemplar of modernity, whose 'consciousness of modernity is widely recognised as one of the most acute in the nineteenth century.' In Baudelaire's comments on male dress, the painting of Constantin Guys and the subjectivity of modern man, Foucault sees key elements of the modern attitude: the 'ironic heroisation of the present', a 'transfiguring play of freedom with reality', and an 'ascetic elaboration of the self'. He also adds that, for Baudelaire, these have no place in society itself, nor in the body politic. 'They can only be produced in another, a different place, which Baudelaire calls art.'[49] This is not a way of cutting them down to size, so far as I can see. Rather, Foucault is acknowledging one of the most important modalities through which the relationship of the self to the present and of the self to the self have been kept under interrogation. To be sure, he dismisses any idea of modernity as 'a phenomenon of sensitivity to the fleeting present.' Modern art is a stern and inherently political discipline.

> For the attitude of modernity, the high value of the present is indissociable from a desperate eagerness to imagine it, to imagine it otherwise than it is, and to transform it not by destroying it but by grasping it in what it is. Baudelaire-an modernity is an exercise in which extreme attention to what is real is confronted with the practice of a liberty that simultaneously respects this reality and violates it.[50]

If Foucault's 'What is Enlightenment?' is read without censoring out Baudelaire, then a commitment to *imagining the city otherwise than it is* no longer appears incompatible with the *extreme attention to what is real* that Barry, Osborne and Rose demonstrate in their studies.

To illustrate what is at stake between a pragmatic reading of Foucault and one which accommodates the 'poetic' concern with the instability of boundaries reality and imagination, consider an example from their book which returns us to our Victorian starting point. In his essay on 'Drains, Liberalism and Power in the Nineteenth Century', Thomas Osborne attempts to pinpoint the place of drains and sewers in the emerging governmental rationality of the time. He plays down any symbolic or ideological connotations. Drains functioned, he insists, 'as the material embodiments of an essentially *political* division between public and private spheres.'

> What was at stake was not just a Victorian fetish for cleanliness, but a strategy of indirect government; that is, of inducing cleanliness and hence good moral habits not through discipline but simply through the material presence of fast-flowing water in and through each private household.[51]

Although his positive emphasis is no doubt right, neither the division between public and private nor what Osborne himself calls a *fetish* for cleanliness can be divorced from the sort of symbolic polarities identified by Peter Stallybrass and Allon White in their more poetic account of modernity, *The Politics and Poetics of Transgression*. The nineteenth-century division between private and public was not *just* political. It expressed an anxiety about the strength of boundaries between the two, about making the imagined space of 'the home' impervious to the *stink* of the unwashed and so to the contamination of their diseases. This meant also, suggest Stallybrass and White, the repression of certain types of knowledge and desire. They quote the image in Victor Hugo's *Les Misérables* of the sewer as a space of hidden truths unimaginable on the surface – 'the labyrinth below Babel.' For Hugo, the sewer was

John Thompson,
Public disinfectors,
London, 1876/77
(The Royal
Photographic Society
Collection, Bath,
England)

> . . . the conscience of the town where all things converge and clash. There is darkness here, but no secrets. . . . Every foulness of civilisation, fallen into disuse, sinks into the ditch of truth wherein ends the huge social down-slide, to be swallowed, but to spread. No false appearances, no white-washing, is possible; filth strips off its shirt in utter starkness, all illusions and mirages scattered, nothing left except what is, showing the ugly face of what ends.[52]

Or rather, this *had* been the nature of the sewer before their reform after the great European cholera epidemics of the eighteen thirties. 'Today,' according to Hugo, presaging Osborne's perspective, 'the sewer is clean, cold, straight, and correct, almost achieving that ideal which the English convey by the word "respectable".' But was this respectability achieved purely by the application of ameliorative social and political rationalities? Victor Hugo was no doubt right to say that: 'The sewer today has a certain official aspect.'[53] That is the often ignored or undervalued cue that Osborne picks up. In reality, though, at least in Zizek's sense of the real, the sewer was also haunted. Or rather, the respectability of the hygiene movement was haunted by a spectre: rats. It is not just that rats symbolise the reformers' disgust at its stink, their horror of the dark and subterranean. Moving between sewer and street, and even invading the home, the rat was the all too real surplus that revealed the impossibility of a society of non-corporeal communion (the ideal, purified, administered city). In the same gesture, though, the figure of the rat was also an attempt to close the circle of society's reality.

We have ended up again in Dickens's London, but now in the respectable but rat-infested sewers below ground rather than in the legible but implacably foggy streets above. To repeat, the point of introducing the drains has been to show that what is at issue between the perspective offered by Barry, Osborne and Rose and my approach is not really the ontological or historical status of modernity. If one accepts that the concept simply offers one way of telling the story of how we live in the present, and a limited, partial and loaded way of telling the story at that, then one can stop worrying about it too much and ask instead what gets left out from the official versions of that story. I happen to agree with Barry, Osborne and Rose that governmental rationalities have not been given their due weight in most accounts. But it does not follow that theirs are the only questions to ask about the city. They add considerably to an understanding of the pedagogy of the city. They have little to say, deliberately, about the power to imagine the city. I am interested in both. For all that they have been explored by poets and novelists and by sociologists and political theorists, I still think that there is more to be said about the haunted spaces of the city, and about their power to affect how we live in cities, and how we live together in cities. Holding onto both rationalities and spectres represents my attempt to confront 'extreme attention to what is real' with 'the practice of a liberty that simultaneously respects this reality and violates it'.

Charles Marville,
Boulevard Saint-
Martin, Paris, ca.
1874 (Bibliothèque
Historique de la Ville
de Paris)

chapter 2

Metaphor and Metropolis

If the city is an imagined environment, and modernity is an attitude more than it is an epoch, then what have been the dominant images and metaphors through which the modern city has been mediated? And, then, how have those images and metaphors shaped both the fabric and the experience of the modern city? The argument I make in this chapter is that ways of seeing and understanding the city inevitably inform ways of acting on the space of the city, with consequences which then in turn produce a modified city which is again seen, understood and acted on. It is not just that the boundaries between reality and imagination are fuzzy and porous. In the development of cities can be discerned a traffic between the two, an economy of symbolic constructs which have material consequences that are manifested in an enduring reality.

To exemplify this process, I trace one history of the modern city, from the rise of urban reformism in nineteenth century England to the faltering of what the architectural historian Anthony Vidler calls the 'therapeutic modernism' associated above all with the architect and planner Le Corbusier.[1] I look first at some of the concepts used by an emerging profession of social observers and reformers, and especially at the *organic* and *mechanical* metaphors that appear to have shaped their thinking. At the beginning of the nineteenth century, the problems of a rapidly growing industrial city like Manchester in the north west of England were conceived as a disease in one part of a body needing to be cured before the whole was affected, or as a faulty part making a machine inefficient. These ways of seeing the city determined the nature of urban policies. Taking Paris in the second half of the nineteenth century as an example, however, I argue that, when implemented, such rationalising plans had unexpected and unintended consequences. They produced a new way of imagining the city, a sensuous perception or experience of metropolitan life that was formalised in the new techniques of representation and the new artistic movements that came to be known (admittedly in a sweeping and catch-all way) as modernism. This modern sensibility and its modernist aesthetic often revealed the reformed cities to be not just more efficient and often more civilised, but also phantasmagoric, grotesque, and even inhuman.

This ambivalence of the metropolis meant that, by the turn of the twentieth century, debates about urban planning and architecture could not ignore *aesthetic* and *psychological* considerations as well as social and political ones. This argument is exemplified by looking briefly at the modernisation of Vienna and then at ideas about twentieth century urban life embodied in the utopian schemes of modernist architects and town planners. Enter Le Corbusier.

This may by now be quite a familiar story. I realise that it has become less novel, certainly, than when I first worked through the approach for myself in the early nineteen nineties.[2] I hope it bears retelling here nonetheless, if only to emphasise that the emergence and institution of certain governmental rationalities *is* an essential theme in the story of the modern city, even if it is not, for me, the whole story.

POLICING A POPULATION: MANCHESTER

In the early decades of the nineteenth century, many British towns and cities underwent a process of radical and often traumatic transformation. So did the ways in which they were perceived and represented. The emergence of industrial modes of production was accompanied by unprecedented population growth. At the same time, there was massive migration of rural populations into urban areas. These factors, in combination, led to the establishment of new class relations and new patterns of urban segregation in terms of work, residence, class, occupation and ethnicity.

Who were the first chroniclers of this unprecedented urban environment? Not novelists like Dickens, but rather two groups of investigators groping to find effective techniques for governing industrial town and cities. To begin with, these urban critics tried to make sense of this new problem by imagining it in familiar terms. They drew on the existing perspectives and explanations of natural theology, physiology and political economy, but they combined them in new ways and added distinctly new elements. As a by-product of their investigations, the reformers came up with new ways of reading the city. For the most part, they worked within an *organic* paradigm. That is, they saw the city as a *natural* system, and made sense of it in terms of interrelated ideas about the universe, the human body, and the body-politic.[3]

The first group of commentators adapted and extended the 'natural theology' of the eighteenth century theologian William Paley to the study of political economy and the urban environment. Paley had conceived of the universe as a benignly ordered system, with 'each part either depending on other parts, or being connected with other parts by some common law of motion or by the presence of some common substance.' In the eighteen thirties, in his *Introductory Lectures* as the Professor of Political Economy at Oxford, Richard Whately illustrated Paley's principle by considering the question of how London's population was fed. Imagine being a head commissionary responsible for this task, he suggested. The size of the city, the range of commodities, fluctuations in demand and the variability of supply would render the task impossible. And yet, Whately observed:

> ... this object is accomplished far better than it could be by any effort of human wisdom, through the agency of men, who think each of nothing beyond his own interest.... In the provisioning of London, there are the same marks of contrivance and design, with a view to a beneficent end as we are accustomed to admire (when our attention is drawn to them by the study of Natural Theology) in the anatomical structure of the body, and the instincts of brute creation.[4]

Such ideas also derived from Adam Smith's conception of the 'invisible hand' of the market. Those who espoused them belonged principally to the liberal section of the Church of England or the conservative wing of Dissent, and addressed themselves to 'the higher and more intelligent classes'. They seemed for the most part impervious to the brutal reality of poverty, crime and disease. These were generally treated as inevitable, if unfortunate, facts of nature.[5]

Less complacent (perhaps because more marginal socially) were an emergent group of professional administrators and reformers: men like Edwin Chadwick, who produced the influential *Report on the Sanitary Condition of the Labouring Population of Great Britain* in 1842, Thomas Southwood Smith, and Neil Arnott. Their strongest religious and philosophical affinities were with Unitarians and Benthamites. They had learned their economics from Malthus, and they took their model of society from contemporary physiology. They perceived urban ills as a disease – a more serious threat to the health of the body politic than the 'natural historians' acknowledged – and they believed in the power of human intelligence to diagnose and cure them. This group of investigators and reformers therefore devised new techniques of social observation and political calculation to tackle the perceived problems created by urbanisation.

Typical of these new administrators was a Manchester doctor, James Phillips Kay. (He later became Sir James Kay-Shuttleworth; I shall refer to him in this form.) He came from a nonconformist background in the industrial bourgeoisie. His family's capital was in cotton, calico, printing, and blacking. A founder-member of the Manchester Statistical Society, he became the city's chief public health officer, and, later, an Assistant Poor Law Commissioner. When he first moved to London he worked with Chadwick and, from 1839, he took on perhaps his most influential post, as the Secretary of the newly formed Committee of Council on Education.

From the start, Kay-Shuttleworth had set his medical researches in the context of broader political questions. In his 1877 autobiography, he reflects on his growing realisation that the causes of infectious disease, especially among the working classes, were linked to economic, social and environmental factors.

> I came to know how almost useless were the resources of my art to contend with the consequences of formidable social evils. It was clearly something outside scientific skill or charity which was needed. . . . Very early therefore, I began to reflect on this complex problem. Were this degradation and suffering inevitable? Could they only be mitigated? Were we always to be working with palliatives? Was there no remedy? Might not this calamity be traced to its source, and all the resource of a Christian nation devoted through whatever time, to the moral and physical regeneration of this wretched population? Parallel therefore with my scientific reading I gradually began to make myself acquainted with the best work on political and social science, and obtained more and more insight into the grave questions affecting the relations of capital and labour and the distribution of wealth, as well as the inseparable connection between the mental and moral condition of the people and their physical well-being.[6]

In 1832, Kay-Shuttleworth was senior physician at the Ardwick and Ancoats dispensary in a district of Manchester inhabited mainly by Irish labourers and textile workers. Early that summer, the cholera epidemic that had swept across much of

Europe hit the city, and Kay-Shuttleworth became the secretary of a special committee set up to co-ordinate the work of several boards of health dealing with the crisis.
This responsibility prompted him to investigate the social conditions of the slums at
first hand, and he reported his findings in his influential pamphlet *The Moral and
Physical Condition of the Working Classes Employed in the Cotton Manufacture in
Manchester*. Even a brief extract reveals how metaphors structure his way of seeing,
understanding and *narrating* the city and its problems. His scientific investigation is
imagined as a journey to the heart of darkness. The body politic is imagined as under
threat from the mutually compounding diseases of an impoverished environment
and political discontent.

> He whose duty it is to follow in the steps of this messenger of death [*cholera*],
> must descend to the abodes of poverty, must frequent the close alleys,
> the crowded courts, the overpeopled habitations of wretchedness, where
> pauperism and disease congregate round the source of social discontent
> and political disorder in the centre of our large towns, and behold with alarm,
> in the hot-bed of pestilence, ills that fester in secret, at the very heart of
> society.[7]

Although many evils afflicting the poor might 'flow from their own ignorance or
moral errors', Kay-Shuttleworth refused to dissociate these sufferings from external
factors. Among the social causes of misery he identified were appalling living conditions, wretched diets, inadequate or non-existent sanitation, the supposedly 'perni-
cious' moral example of Irish immigrants,[8] and the 'prolonged and exhausting
labour' which resembled 'the torment of Sisyphus' and deadened their minds.
These ills he attributed less to the commercial and manufacturing system as such
than to urbanisation. Kay-Shuttleworth believed that the natural tendency of capitalist industry was 'to develop the energies of society, to increase the comforts and
luxuries of life, and to elevate the physical condition of every member of the social
body'. This is why a pastoral or welfare strategy was not only ethically necessary, but
also offered a rational means of preventing potential damage to that system.

However conventional Kay-Shuttleworth's work may now appear in its emphasis
on the maintenance of social order, its proposed solutions were strikingly novel.
Here it is possible to see in nascent form those discourses and techniques which
eventually produced the modern conception of society as a knowable and governable object. Indeed, that concept only became a possibility within these new
techniques of observation, calculation, and writing. The city as a problem of
administration had to be rendered as 'text' – not in any metaphorical sense, but
through pamphlets like his, and increasingly in official reports and commissions – to
bring it into the ambit of government. How was this translation achieved?

It required a method of *reading* the city that produced a type and a scale of
knowledge that could form the target of this emerging political rationality. Again, the
analogy is with medical diagnosis. By attempting to isolate symptoms of disease in
the 'social body', reformers like Kay-Shuttleworth created both new techniques of
investigation, based primarily on the collection of statistical information about the
urban population, and new administrative apparatuses designed to impose norms of
conduct on that population. That is why Kay-Shuttleworth was concerned, not just
with the good order of the working class, but with the details of their health, literacy,
sentiments, domestic life, temperance, criminal propensities and sexuality – and

with the statistically significant relations he discerned between them. The problem, and the solution, came to be defined in terms of *social welfare.*

The emerging sphere of *the social* involved both techniques of information-gathering and administrative agencies. These divided up the city into a grid of regulated spaces and, in doing so, identified both new 'social problems' and new objects of government. In his autobiography, Kay-Shuttleworth explains how these techniques were developed in Manchester at the time of the cholera outbreak.

> Boards of Health were established, in each of the fourteen districts of Police, for the purpose of minutely inspecting the state of the houses and streets. These districts were divided into minute sections, to each of which two or more inspectors were appointed from among the most respectable inhabitants of the vicinity, and they were provided with tabular queries, applying to each particular house and street.[9]

The diagnostic map of the 'social body' that emerged from this collection of statistics not only enabled the reformers to promote norms of individual conduct, but – perhaps more effectively – norms for public health, decency, cleanliness and sanitation. Government became a question of welfare as well as surveillance and discipline. It attempted to manipulate the urban environment so as to remove the sources of infection and corruption.

To grasp what this new logic entailed, it is useful to spell out a little more fully the practical implications of a term that Kay-Shuttleworth uses in the quotation above: that is, the notion of 'police'. In the eighteenth century, this had had a broader meaning than the one we normally associate with it; it also prefigured many of the later reforms discussed in this chapter.

In a 1979 lecture, Michel Foucault explained the type of rationality implemented in the exercise of power by modern states. This rationality, he argued, is determined by the need to articulate two elements: political power wielded over legal subjects and pastoral power wielded over live individuals.[10] Its rationale was formulated in two sets of doctrine from the sixteenth century onwards. One was concerned with *reason of state*, the other with the *theory of police*.

Reason of state concerns those arts of governing which are concerned not with enhancing the power a prince can wield over his domain, but with reinforcing the state and its institutions as such. This therefore entailed the need for concrete, quantifiable and precise information about the strength of the state. The generation of this knowledge was then called political *statistics* or *arithmetic*. The vogue for statistics towards the end of the first half of the nineteenth century among reformers like Kay-Shuttleworth reflects this logic. Or, rather, it was a precondition for putting that logic into practice. Statistics were not just about counting what already existed. The new science was, as Ian Hacking puts it, about *making up people*. On the one hand, this meant producing an archive of information about the members of a *population* who had previously constituted a homogeneous and opaque mass. On the other hand, and at the same time, it meant giving an individual identity to the members of that population. This identity was, however, defined by the categories of conduct and attributes favoured by those doing the counting. People were thus made up of statistically measurable and significant characteristics: their geographical distribution, their conduct, their capacities, their morals, their rates of fertility and mortality, and their susceptibility to contagion. As Hacking emphasises, you cannot count without using categories to decide what it is you are counting: 'you can't just print numbers. You must print numbers of objects falling under some category or other.'[11] The selection of categories – health, literacy, criminality, sexuality, and so forth – is what produced new categories of people. These symbolic categories then had real consequences for the people being counted and categorised. They constituted an identity imposed on them. They operated as *normative* and not just descriptive categories. They were increasingly translated into governmental definitions of the normal and the pathological, and so also shaped people's social self-understandings.

Hence the importance of statistics for what was meant by 'the police'; that is, a technology of government which defined the domains, techniques and targets of state intervention. Police, in this sense, involved cataloguing the resources of a state, both material and human, in minute detail. This made it possible to identify that new object, a population, as the central concern of government. The population became the target of both surveillance and welfare. Foucault refers to *Elements of Police*, a work by the German author Von Justi, to draw out the central paradox of this combination.

> The police, he says, is what enables the state to increase its power and exert its strength to the full. On the other hand, the police has to keep the citizens happy – happiness being understood as survival, life, and improved living. He perfectly defines what I feel to be the aim of the modern art of government, or state rationality: viz., to develop those elements constitutive of individuals' lives in such a way that their development also fosters that of the strength of the state.[12]

This approach then produces:

> . . . a grid through which the state, i.e., territory, resources, population, towns, etc., can be observed. Von Justi combines 'statistics' (the description of states) with the art of government. *Polizeiwissenschaft* is at once an art of government and a method for the analysis of a population living on a territory.[13]

If you read Kay-Shuttleworth's pamphlet on Manchester – or perhaps even more Chadwick's *Sanitary Report*, with its statistical tables of mortality and disease juxtaposed against first-hand reports from doctors and medical officers – it is just this combination of analysis and policy prescription that you will find.

The underlying logic of the nineteenth-century strategy was by no means unique to Britain. The 1832 cholera epidemic had much the same effect in Paris. It provoked a more rigorous analysis of the urban milieu, focusing on *conditions de vie* (conditions of life) that included local biological and social variables. Although the attempt to imagine, implement, and co-ordinate macro- and micro-reforms was initially ineffective, it provided the catalyst for the emergence of an apparatus of finely grained observation of the social body: supervised by physicians aided by architects, and backed by the police, in the service of the health of the population and the general good.[14]

In his Foucauldian history of these developments, Paul Rabinow too suggests how this statistical grid of investigation produced a new social scientific conception of society that in turn informed the physical structure of the city.

Society was becoming an object *sui generis*, with its own laws, its own science, and eventually its own arts of government. If the individual's normality and pathology were a function not of his independent moral state but rather of his place within a social whole, then it made little sense to try to reform him separately from reforming the social milieu within which his actions were formed and normed. . . . The use of statistical approaches to social problems posed the problem of finding forms through which to present this understanding, just as the century-long search for new architectural forms was perplexed about the norms of modern society that these forms were supposed to embody and represent.[15]

Although, looking back at the nineteenth century with the hindsight of history, Rabinow seems to identify a development that was at least Europe-wide, strategies for social welfare and administrative reform took on quite distinct inflections at different times and in different national contexts. In Britain, they bore the marks of nonconformism, Benthamite utilitarianism, and the medical metaphors of the body-politic and the city. In France, the intellectual impetus came from the rationalism of Saint-Simon and his followers, and shaded more quickly into something like social engineering.

Nor did the dominant paradigms go unchallenged. Just ten years after Kay-Shuttleworth's pamphlet, another account of Manchester was published. This saw the city less as an organism to be modified than as a historical phenomenon to be interpreted, and its working class population less as an object to be taxonomised and normalised than as a force for radical social change. It attempted to synthesise Kay-Shuttleworth's pragmatic, and perhaps characteristically British, commitment to detailed empirical observation with a much more explicit philosophical framework based on the dynamics of social and economic relations. Its author was a young German businessman sent by his father to learn the cotton trade in England. His name was Friedrich Engels.

Engels was a diligent student of British writers like Kay-Shuttleworth, Chadwick and Southwood Smith, and he drew widely on their research in his book *The Condition of the Working Class in England in 1844*. Nevertheless, he was a Hegelian in his thinking and a revolutionary socialist in his politics, not a Benthamite reformer. That difference is apparent not just in his denial of the supposed virtues of capitalism or a providential social order but also in his rejection of the British urbanists' representation of the city as an organism or a natural system.[16] Instead, as Steven Marcus has argued, Engels managed to read the 'illegible' industrial city by showing that its 'apparently unsystematic and possibly incoherent' form could be 'perceived as a total intellectual and imaginative structure'.[17] And the method he used to achieve that encompassing vision was to go for a walk around Manchester with his eyes peeled.

Engels begins by mapping out the overall shape of the city. In doing so, he outlines an interpretation of the relation between districts in terms of a determining but implicit social dynamic. He describes how Manchester's commercial heart, with its offices and warehouses, is linked by new and efficient roads to its prosperous suburbs.

And the finest part of the arrangement is this, that the members of [the] money aristocracy can take the shortest road through the middle of all the

Jacob Riis, Mulberry
Street, New York, ca.
1890 (Museum of the
City of New York)

labouring districts to their places of business, without ever seeing that they are
in the midst of the grimy misery that lurks to the right and left. For the
thoroughfares leading from the Exchange in all directions out of the city are
lined, on both sides, with an almost unbroken series of shops, and are so kept
in the hands of the middle and lower bourgeoisie, which, out of self-interest,
cares for a decent and cleanly external appearance and *can* care for it. True,
these shops bear some relation to the districts which lie behind them, and are
more elegant in the commercial and residential quarters than when they hide
grimy working-class dwellings; but they suffice to conceal from the eyes of the
wealthy men and women of strong stomachs and weak nerves the misery and
grime which form the complement of their wealth.[18]

In contrast to someone like Kay-Shuttleworth, Engels does not conceive the poverty of Manchester as a sickness to be cured or a malfunction in the machinery of
production. He sees it as an inevitable consequence of the forms of production that
produce this spatial organisation. Poverty is what makes the display of wealth possible.

Having identified this coherence at the level of the city's macrostructure, Engels
records his explorations of its micro-structures. Starting at the twelve o'clock
position on the compass, he walks around the city in a clockwise direction, systematically penetrating the screens behind which increasingly squalid courtyards and
back alleys fester.

Immediately under the railway bridge there stands a court, the filth and horrors of which surpass all the others by far, just because it was hitherto so cut
off, so secluded that the way to it could not be found without a good deal of
trouble, I should never have discovered it myself, without the breaks made by
the railway, though I thought I knew this whole region thoroughly. Passing
along a rough bank, among stakes and washing lines, one penetrates into this
chaos of small one-storied, one-roomed huts, in most of which there is no
artificial floor; kitchen, living and sleeping-room all in one. In such a hole,
scarcely five feet long by six broad, I found two beds – and such bedsteads and
beds! – which, with a staircase and chimney-place, exactly filled the room. In
several others I found absolutely nothing, while the door stood open, and the
inhabitants leaned against it. Everywhere before the doors refuse and offal;
that any sort of pavement lay underneath could not be seen but only felt, here
and there, with the feet.

Engels's method of social and semiotic mapping enables him to impose a spatial
and narrative unity in his account of the 'unplanned wilderness' of Manchester. In
his exposition, he repeatedly attempts to pre-empt accusations of exaggeration by
insisting that his words are inadequate to the reality he discovered.

Such is the Old town of Manchester, and on re-reading my description, I am
forced to admit that instead of being exaggerated, it is far from black enough
to convey a true impression of the filth, ruin, and uninhabitableness, the
defiance of cleanliness, ventilation, and health which characterise the construction of this single district . . .

It is not the passion with which he denounces the conditions in which people are forced to live that is new, however, nor his narrative structure of a journey to the lower depths. Where he differs from an investigator like Kay-Shuttleworth is in the explanation he begins to offer of why these conditions exist.

On the one hand, he sees confident wealth. On the other, at the heart of darkness he finds the poorest of the working class living in shit. What is the link? Engels explains these urban social relations neither in terms of an organism nor of a machine, although he invokes elements of both. Rather, he discerns a *structure* which functions as a complex, concrete totality, and whose parts have meanings that are only decipherable in relation to all its other parts. The key insight is that this structure is a *dynamic* one. The whole thing is in motion. This movement does not represent the unfolding of divine or natural laws, but the interaction between the forces and the social relations of production.

> Everything which here arouses horror and indignation is of recent origin, belongs to the *industrial epoch*. The couple of hundred houses, which belong to old Manchester, have been long since abandoned by their original inhabitants; the industrial epoch alone has built up every spot between these old houses to win a covering for the masses whom it has conjured hither from the agricultural districts and from Ireland; the industrial epoch alone enables the owners of these cattlesheds to rent them for high prices to human beings, to plunder the poverty of the workers, to undermine the health of thousands, in order that they *alone*, the owners, may grow rich.

It is this dual focus on deciphering a systematic *economic structure* to urban social relations and interpreting it *historically* that embodies the powerful Hegelian insight in Engels's chapter.[19]

In some ways, Engels's reading of Manchester is more revealing than Kay-Shuttleworth's. Its conceptualisation of the city as the spatial embodiment or manifestation of economic relations points forward to the type of explanation of why cities are like they are offered by many of today's marxist geographers and urban sociologists. But what does it suggest in the way of policies for changing the city? Engels's approach to the problems of industrial cities implies rather different solutions from those of a Chadwick or a Kay-Shuttleworth. In contrast to the British pragmatists, his philosophical analysis offers little in the way of specific proposals for improvement. Indeed, he sees their plans as part of the same dynamic structure that produced the problems of industrialisation and urbanisation in the first place. He therefore ends up with little to say about the possibility of changing cities. If cities are the effect of an underlying structure, then Engels tends to insist that, in the end, it is that structure which needs changing if significant change is going to happen in actual cities. In that sense, for all its insights and sensitivity to details and connections, Engels's account of Manchester still entails the imposition of a grid of explanation onto the complex phenomena we call the city.

Let me offer an analogy. Given the investigative and statistical techniques they used, and their concern for surveillance as a means to both social discipline and individual welfare, it is not unreasonable to think of the new class of social scientists and administrators typified by Chadwick and Kay-Shuttleworth as policemen. For, whatever their function in crime novels and *romans policier*, the task of the police is not primarily to solve mysteries, but to uphold and impose the law. Rotten elements and bad influences have to be dealt with. Social relations have to be subjected to reason: hence the new nineteenth-century conception of 'the social' as an object of regulation.

If this is the logic of urban reform, then the Engels who patiently pursues his investigation by reading the apparently illegible clues of Manchester's topography seems to follow the logic of the detective. The detective starts not from the dictates of reason but from the inherently enigmatic nature of reality. The comforting serenity of a perfectly administered city will always be disrupted by conflict, by violence, by the unexpected and the irrational. It is not the police who solve the mysteries of a befogged London, but Sherlock Holmes. He does so by identifying clues, and deducing from them the sequence of events and combination of forces that produced the initially baffling event. In a similar way, Engels deciphers the social surface of Manchester and then names the villain responsible for the crime of poverty and misery.

The point of this contrast is simply to underline the consequences of adopting one set of metaphors and narratives for conceptualising 'the city' rather than another. Benthamite police work led to new discourses of government, social administration and social science, and to new practices of piecemeal and reactive social regulation which were increasingly embodied in the concrete form of architecture and planning. Engels's ingenious Hegelian detective work, on the other hand, produced a sophisticated critique of the capitalist city without indicating any obvious techniques for acting on, let alone improving, the lives of those who lived in such cities – other, that is, than the apocalyptic fantasy of revolution.

THE CITY IN EVIDENCE

My metaphors of policing and detection may be a bit fanciful. Yet they are at least true to the concern – sometimes almost the obsession – of nineteenth-century urban administrators with the amassing of *evidence* about the city. I have mentioned the question of statistics. Equally fascinating is the use of new technologies of reproduction to lend greater credibility to their evidence: the authority of vision.

John Tagg has studied the use of photographs as evidence for an administrative reading of the city in one especially revealing case: the campaign towards the end of the nineteenth century to have the Quarry Hill slums in the Yorkshire city of Leeds demolished and rebuilt.[20] When Tagg came across a folio of photographs of the district in a local library, he did not accept them simply as documentary representations of the city. Instead, he wanted to reconstruct the *uses* to which the photographs were put, and the *consequences* of those uses.

> Why were photographs of working-class subjects, working-class trades, working-class housing, and working-class recreations made in the nineteenth century? By whom? Under what conditions? For what purposes? Who pictures? Who is pictured? And how were the pictures used? What did they do? To whom were they meaningful? And what were the consequences of accepting them as meaningful, truthful or real?[21]

The tale Tagg tells about Quarry Hill is a familiar one after reading Kay-Shuttleworth and Engels on Manchester. It is the same story of appalling conditions, cholera epidemics, the gradual accumulation of an archive of information, and political struggles around rents, rates, and housing conditions.

Unknown
photographer, Yard
off St Peter's Square,
Leeds, 1896
(Brotherton Library,
University of Leeds)

Unknown
photographer, Yard
off Harrison's
Buildings, Leeds,
1896 (Brotherton
Library, University
of Leeds)

The particular interest of this case is the way that, towards the end of the century, the city was turned not just into a textual archive but into images that were supposed to have the power to authenticate both the facts and the moral outrage contained in that archive. Tagg recounts what is known about the preparation of these images. In addition, he explains how they were presented to a Select Committee of the House of Commons in 1896 and 1901, which was considering whether or not to allow the clearance. The Medical Officer of Health for Leeds, Dr James Spottiswoode Cameron, seems to have been responsible for the initiative. It was certainly he who took the leading role in schooling the committee in how they should interpret the photographs.

When charged that he was doing no more than 'rout people up with postcards', Cameron responded with all the pedantic authority of the archivist or archaeologist. Referring to different pictures, he insisted on the systematic and exhaustive nature of the evidence they provide – in this case about the condition of a public house.

> E is the front of it; F is the yard behind it; G is the back of the house taken from that same yard; H is the north end of Riley's Court adjacent to it; I is another view of the same court.[22]

As Tagg points out, however, Cameron, unlike some of his predecessors a decade or two earlier, did not assume that photographs of slum conditions spoke for themselves. On the contrary. Under cross-examination before the Select Committee, he constantly attempted to establish his professional expertise in defining what images meant. He would also invoke technical issues to back his own interpretations when it suited him, or link his preferred meanings to other kinds of evidence about people and places. Tagg quotes Cameron's response in 1896 to a question about a photograph of a yard off Harrison's Buildings. It may seem redundant in its detail, but, claims Tagg, it 'unobtrusively tied the Committee to the realism and evidential value he was seeking to establish for his folios of images.'

> ... on the right hand side, that is the back door of the common lodging house – this yard is 25 square yards in area – the photograph is taken from a narrow entry, and the only way into that yard from the other side in that yard is on the right hand side, the window and back door of the common lodging house, and on the left hand side two small two-storied buildings let off in furnished apartments, and then in front that wall with the line of light shown upon it is the wall of the 'Yorkshire Hussar', and the 'Yorkshire Hussar' prevents the only day light that might possibly get into these buildings on the left hand side from getting into them.[23]

Cameron also claimed the right to establish how his images could evoke other spaces, their grimness imaginable even if – or perhaps because – the spaces were themselves unrepresentable in a photographic image. 'I should like to have shewn you a Photograph of some of these places,' remarks Cameron, 'but the difficulty is that the yards are not big enough to allow the camera free scope.'

This case of the Quarry Hill photographs helps to establish the status of visual images in my argument. The pictures do not simply represent the city. Rather, in the way they were used, they constituted a certain claim to knowledge. They were part

Charles Marville,
Avenue de l'Opéra,
Paris, ca. 1877
(Bibliothèque
Historique de la Ville
de Paris)

Charles Marville,
Boulevard
Haussmann, Paris,
ca. 1876
(Bibliothèque
Historique de la Ville
de Paris)

of an attempt to establish normative techniques for observing and recording the city, and commentaries on them attempt to anchor that pedagogy yet more firmly in rules of interpretation. It is not that the images are over here, on the noumenal side of representation and text, as opposed to the phenomenal space of the city over there. The reality of the city emerges from the interplay between them.

The argument is not limited to images claiming to record and expose the reality of urban conditions in England. A nineteenth-century city can be seen emerging from the light and shadow of photography across a variety of places and genres. In some ways, the work of Charles Marville in Paris shared Cameron's 'documentary' imperative. His task, however, was not to make a case for the reconstruction of the city. It was to celebrate the transformation of Paris overseen by Baron Haussmann in the eighteen fifties and sixties. Haussmann wanted an archive of the bad old days in order to commemorate the obvious superiority of the modern Paris he was creating. In the early eighteen sixties, Marville had begun informally photographing rebuilding projects. Once he had joined Haussmann's team of historical researchers as the city's official photographer, he spent fifteen years producing clinical before-and-after shots of districts waiting to be broken up by Haussmann's relentless new boulevards.[24]

Later, around the turn of the century, while Dr. Cameron was presenting his folios of Quarry Hill, in Paris photography began to be put to a different use by Eugène Atget. Haussmann's modernisation had produced a preservationist reaction in many parts of Paris, and with it a voracious nostalgia for the old architecture. It was this new market that Atget's images first tapped into. He was one of the first visual archivists of the city as heritage. The primary purpose of his photographs was to provide a reference work for professional illustrators, but in 1899 he also found a willing buyer in Marcel Poëte, chief librarian at the Bibliothèque Historique de la Ville de Paris (and also a zealous guardian of Marville's images). This archival impulse meant that Atget was more concerned to produce a catalogue of urban *space* of the city, than to record the *life* of the city. Christine Boyer notes how this archaeological approach explains the comparative absence of people or activities from his mute images of scenery and structures.

> Historical buildings, ornamental motifs, and vernacular streetscapes were for Atget merely surface images devoid of a symbolic or ritualistic context. These empty stage sets were to be viewed as desolate relics and transitory landscapes . . . By juxtaposing, in his photographic compositions, objects against empty space, stressing contrasts between black and white, the three-dimensional and the flat, the curved and the straight, Atget continually set up a melancholic play between the present and the past, the intangible and the real, the timeless and the transient.[25]

It is important to underline that any such connotations were more a by-product of Atget's disenchanted, taxonomic perception of space than the expression of an aesthetic vision. It is also important to realise that this interpretation of Atget is a reading back through the retrospective enthusiasm of the Surrealists, who took up Atget and his work in his last years.

This is also the perspective that Walter Benjamin, during his infatuation with Surrealism, brought to bear in his comments on Atget. Here we are back to my metaphors of policing, detection, and evidence. Atget, for Benjamin, photographs the deserted streets of Paris like scenes of a crime. 'The scene of a crime, too, is deserted; it is photographed for the purpose of establishing evidence.' But what sort of evidence, and evidence of what? 'With Atget, photographs become standard evidence for historical occurrences, and acquire a hidden political significance.' I am not sure what that *standard* implies. It is not, apparently, that the photographs are evidence that certain events took place, nor do they embody the sort of claim to evidential authenticity and authority that Dr. Cameron was claiming before his Commons Committee. Rather, Atget's pictures seem to be evidence for something that had happened to the status or currency of images: that their cult or auratic value had given way to their value as evidence, although evidence in general rather than in particular. What is at stake, in other words, is a certain way of reading photographs.

> [Atget's photographs] demand a certain kind of approach; free-floating contemplation is not appropriate to them. They stir the viewer; he feels challenged by them in a new way.[26]

Benjamin links this new legibility – disenchanted, distracted, somatic – to two related phenomena. One is the visual world of picture magazines and films, with their pedagogies of captions and montage.[27] The other is, again, the city conjured up in Atget's photographs.

> He sought the forgotten and the neglected, so such pictures turn reality against the exotic, romantic, show-offish resonance of the city name; they suck the aura from reality like water from a sinking ship.[28]

Benjamin claimed that, in prefiguring Surrealist imagery, Atget 'disinfected the sticky atmosphere' of contemporary photography, and so 'established a healthy alienation between environment and man, opening the field for politically educated sight'.[29] Well, maybe. For me, the main interest of these comments lies in the way Benjamin mixes together metaphors of detection – unmasking guilt in the city, amassing evidence of unnamed crimes – with metaphors of visibility and health associated with new ways of looking at images of the city. Here, for once, Benjamin reveals himself to be a modernist on the side of the planner Haussmann rather than, or at least as well as, the poet Baudelaire.

RATIONALITY AND ENCHANTMENT: PARIS

We find ourselves in the Paris of the second half of the nineteenth century. Or, rather, we find ourselves in the shadowy, textual Paris whose foundations were laid by Walter Benjamin in the researches he undertook in the Bibliothèque Nationale for his Arcades project (*Die Passagen-Werk*).[30] This aspired to offer nothing less than a pre-history of modernity through the imaginative recreation of nineteenth-century Paris. It was an attempt to conjure forth Baudelaire's mythical Paris in order to understand the logic (if that is the right word) of the poetic experience of everyday life in the modern metropolis that I introduced in the previous chapter. Benjamin's ruse was to show that the transformation of the city into spectacle and phantasmagoria was as closely linked to the logic of capitalism as either the concept city of urban reformers or planners like Haussmann, or the hidden misery and squalor

Eugène Atget, Rue
Saint-Rustique,
Paris, 1922 (The
Museum of Modern
Art, New York)

uncovered by Engels in industrial Manchester. His touchstone for understanding the consequences of capitalism for both the fabric and the experience of the metropolis was therefore not the slums, but the arcades: glass-covered, gas-lit 'fairy grottoes' of consumerism that prefigured today's shopping malls. These, Benjamin saw as 'the original temple of commodity capitalism'. Their shop windows displayed luxurious commodities like icons in niches. Food, drink, roulette and vaudeville shows were abundantly on offer, and, in the first-floor galleries, sexual pleasures could be bought: 'The windows in the upper floor of the Passages are galleries in which angels are nesting; they are called swallows.'[31]

Although never completed, and perhaps too sprawling in its ambition ever to be so, the project's sketches, fragments and ruins have in recent decades become the site of a creative if sometimes frenetic archaeology and architecture. A shanty town of conceptual structures has sprung up among them. In the ramshackle laboratory of *modernity*, the historical consequences of processes of social reconstruction (*modernisation*) are studied: not just new economic practices and political arrangements, but the new techniques of government and even the notion of 'the social' itself that I traced in the first part of this chapter. Close by, and possibly linked, stands the sleek playhouse of *modernism*. Here are staged both artistic practices and new forms of social commentary which stand in some critical relation to that modernity.[32] Milling around these edifices is a noisy throng of social historians, cultural geographers, sociologists, literary theorists, art historians, feminist critics, and other assorted academic tourists like myself.

Inescapably, we come to this Paris through texts. But Paris also comes to us as already a text. That is not least because its representative figures – and maybe this is one of the things that makes them modern – had themselves already begun to think about the city in that way. Some of these new urbanites and urbanists self-consciously *read* the city to decipher its enigmatic meanings; others attempted to reshape the city to the text of their plans. These figures are social types – the *flâneur*, the administrator, the planner, the artist, the photographer, the detective – but we also ascribe their own names to them: Baudelaire, Haussmann, Manet,[33] Atget, and by now also Benjamin himself.

It is difficult not to be overwhelmed by the ever-growing heaps of text. To pick my way through them, I shall hold onto two threads in my story. One is the question of how the planned modernisation of Paris was conceptualised, and what often unintended consequences the rebuilding of the city has actually had. The other is more methodological: how is it possible to grasp these complex processes?

In attempting to answer either question, the *flâneur* is unavoidable. Even if the figure risks becoming a cliché – sometimes, it seems, little more than a way of claiming a frisson of outlaw glamour for the pedestrian tasks of the sociologist of urban culture – the *flâneur* remains a pivotal term in Benjamin's unfolding project and in his emerging perspective.

In part, the *flâneur* represents one of Benjamin's defining topics; or rather, the figure condenses a number of themes. It stands for a certain historical moment, a social type associated with the period from the Revolution of 1839 to the creation of Haussmann's boulevards and the opening of the first great department stores. It thus also denotes a certain relationship to an intensifying process of commodification. The *flâneur* is a creature first of the arcades themselves, but later, in his twilight, of the stores and the Great Exhibitions which were the commodity's first great cathedrals. But, as an author or journalist, as the writer of *feuilletons* and physiologies, the

flâneur is himself also locked into an especially insecure form of commodity production; and one that, in selling the urban crowd to a bourgeois audience as a repertoire
of vignettes, characters, and caricatures, colludes in the domestication of its dangers.
The *flâneur* thus occupies an uncertain social position: sometimes a dandy, an aristo-
crat or gentleman stylishly on the slide, sometimes a bohemian.[34]

Above all, the *flâneur* embodies a certain perspective on, or experience of, urban
space and the metropolitan crowd. In the anonymous ebb and flow of the urban
crowd, Baudelaire as *flâneur* felt himself able:

> To be away from home and yet to feel oneself everywhere at home; to see the
> world, to be at the centre of the world, and yet to remain hidden from the
> world. The spectator is a *prince* who everywhere rejoices in his incognito.[35]

The *flâneur* thus combined the passionate wonder of childhood with the analytic
sophistication of the man of the world as he read the signs and impressions of 'the
outward show of life'. He has to be something of a detective. Otherwise, *flânerie* is no
more than gawping.

> In the *flâneur*, the joy of watching is triumphant. It can concentrate on obser-
> vation; the result is the amateur detective. Or it can stagnate in the gaper; then
> the *flâneur* has turned into a *badaud*.[36]

Like other nineteenth-century detectives, Baudelaire adopted other perspectives
– or guises – in order to get the correct distance from, and closeness to, the city.
Among them were those of the dandy, the whore, and the rag-picker. In these
marginal, despised figures, living on their wits and for whom reading the signs of the
city right could be a matter of life or death, Baudelaire saw an image of the modern
poet's social location and role.

This is where the *flâneur* as historical figure shades into *flânerie* as critical method.
As his researches progressed, Benjamin increasingly narrowed his focus specifically
to Baudelaire – that is, a self-conscious theorist of *flânerie* when *flânerie* had already
become history – and to the *flâneur* as detective. This is only in part because, as
David Frisby argues, the *flâneur*/detective, together with the archaeologist/critical
allegorist and the collector/refuse collector, illuminates what Baudelaire was doing
when he was botanising on the asphalt of Paris. Above all, these figures are methodological metaphors for Benjamin's own way of working in the Arcades Project. Both
Baudelaire and Benjamin watched and interpreted the city: crowds moving through
space, architectural and human configurations, signs and images, the sounds and
tempi of everyday life. Both also transformed those styles of imagining into distinctive
types of texts: Baudelaire's lyrical and prose poetry, Benjamin's poetic journalism
and (for all his disavowals) his sociology of urban experience.[37]

What Benjamin shares with Baudelaire above all is not just a way of seeing the city
or a way of experiencing its newness, but a concern with the possibility of representing the space and the temporality of (to use Baudelaire's coinage) *modernité*. This the
poet perceived not in grand schemes or epochal changes, but in representational
spaces characterised by *le transitoire, le fugitif, le contingent* – what is transitory, fleeting, and contingent. His task as a modern artist was, he believed, to capture 'the
ephemeral, contingent newness of the present'. What was new was not the figure
of the *flâneur*. It was almost because he knew that the *flâneur* was already an

anachronism, because the figure was slightly out of synch with the new city, that it enabled Baudelaire to make sense of the traumatic moment of modernisation he was living through. As the Paris he had known was blasted apart and recreated by Baron Haussmann, he was less interested in predicting the future than in capturing the unintended and unexpected imaginative consequences of the changes.

Haussmann represents, in part at least, a new conception of the city. In the second half of the nineteenth century onwards, the modernisation of the great Western metropolises was characterised, physically, by the spectacular redesign of city centres and the growth of residential suburbs. An early embodiment of de Carteau's planner as *dieu voyeur*, Haussmann saw Paris largely as a space for economic exploitation – his projects fuelled a boom in property speculation on the grand scale – and a space that needed to be opened up for effective circulation and communication.

What impact did this way of seeing the city have on the physical fabric of Paris? Haussmann was appointed as Napoleon III's prefect of the Seine in 1853. By 1870, when he was dismissed for dodgy wheeling and dealing to finance his projects, he had got rid of the medieval walls that had surrounded the city, one-fifth of the streets in central Paris were his creation, and the acreage of the city had been doubled by annexation. At the height of the reconstruction, one in five Parisian workers was employed in the building trade. In the name of slum clearance, some 350,000 people (on Haussmann's own estimation) were displaced from the *quartiers* of old Paris to make way for his new boulevards, parks and 'pleasure grounds'. The boulevards, lined by the uniform facades of new apartment blocks, created unprecedented urban vistas which had in part a pedagogic purpose. They were interspersed by national monuments, which Haussmann had studiously excised from their original context and functions and placed strategically as ornamental fragments and focal points in the new landscape. Equally important was the creation of the physical infrastructure to sustain the new developments. A hundred miles from Paris, aqueducts were laid to improve the city's tap-water supply. New lenses were fitted on the gas lamps. The great collector sewer and a new morgue were opened. An outer circle of railways surrounded the city, and a ring of stations acted as city gates. Haussmann broke the monopoly of the cab company in 1866, and promoted that of the makers of street lamps in 1856.[38]

The purposes of Haussmannisation were, naturally, complex and sometimes contradictory. There was certainly an element of Saint-Simonian utopianism in the 'concept city' of Haussmann and Napoleon III. They wanted to create a clean, light and airy city protected by policemen and night patrols. They wanted to provide trees, schools, hospitals, cemeteries, bus shelters, and public urinals (for men at least). As I have suggested, though, the needs of commerce and social control were probably more powerful motives. What Haussmann understood by a modern city was one designed to allow the most efficient circulation of goods, people, money, and troops. Famously, the boulevards provided the shortest routes between the barracks and working-class districts.

What, then, were the social consequences of Haussmannisation? Insofar as Haussmann's schemes reflected the logic of the stock market and commerce rather than that of the factory and its disciplines, they were based on a static conception of both urban space and the social relations of the city. In that sense, they represented an already archaic reading of the city.[39] Although he could understand the political, economic and technological problems of Paris, Haussmann did not think in the emerging social terms of technocratic and administrative rationality. He did not understand the social logic of the concern with the welfare, morality and efficiency of an urban population which reforming administrators like Kay-Shuttleworth and Chadwick were already putting into practice in England.

One result was to intensify the misery of the population displaced by his schemes. However egalitarian the new public spaces of boulevards and parks may have appeared, the practical effect was to raze working-class neighbourhoods and shift the eyesores and health hazards of poverty to the suburbs. In Paris, Engels saw the division between bourgeois show and working-class squalor that he had observed in Manchester being repeated. In Manchester the split had been a by-product of capitalist industrialisation. Here it had become a matter of policy. He commented on 'the method called "Haussmann"' in his 1872 pamphlet, *The Housing Question*.

> I mean the practice, which has now become general, of making breaches in working-class quarters of our big cities, especially in those that are centrally situated.... The result is everywhere the same: the most scandalous alleys and lanes disappear, to the accompaniment of lavish self-glorification by the bourgeoisie on account of this tremendous success – but they appear at once somewhere else, and often in the immediate neighbourhood.[40]

Even for more bourgeois Parisians, the benefits of Haussmann's carefully planned upheavals were ambivalent. Many complained that he had created an artificial city in which they no longer felt at home. The boulevards, parks, and other new public spaces created a backdrop against which the worlds of rich and poor – supposedly cordoned off from each other – now became more visible to each other, if no more legible. Even his 'strategic beautification' proved of limited value when barricades appeared across his boulevards in the Paris Commune of 1870.

What fascinated Benjamin in this new city – and this is what he was trying to get at by adopting Baudelaire as his surrogate – was the way that the displacements brought about by Haussmannisation lent a fantastic and elusive quality to life in the city. The arcades may have been waning in popularity as the Second Empire progressed, but it was during this period that the urban phantasmagoria they represented burst out of these confines and spread across Paris. Giant advertising hoardings began to appear, creating a new layer of visual textuality in the city. Commodity displays became ever more grandiose and impossible to ignore.

This ostentation reached its public peak in a series of world expositions inspired by London's Crystal Palace in 1851. The Paris expositions were staged in 1855, 1867, 1889 and 1900. Industrial products and machine technologies were displayed like artworks. They were set off against ornamental gardens, statues, and fountains. Military canons were juxtaposed with fashion costumes in a dazzling fantasy world. The fairs also left permanent traces on the city landscape: the Grand Palais, Trocadero, and the Eiffel Tower were all built for them.

In these international fairs Benjamin saw the origins of a pleasure industry which developed advertising techniques skilfully calibrating spectacle and fantasy to the tastes and dreams of a mass audience. In a magnified version of the *flâneur*'s window shopping, their message was: 'Look, but don't touch.' The crowds were taught to derive pleasure from the spectacle alone. At these fairs, buying and selling were less significant than their function as fantastic metropolitan folk festivals of capitalism. Here mass entertainment itself became big business.[41]

A more enduring legacy of this realignment of urbanity as commodity fetishism

Unknown
photographer, Paris,
1900 (Roger-Viollet,
Paris)

was the department store. This has been presented as both the culmination and the final undoing of *flânerie*. One of the characteristics of the *flâneur*'s ambiguous relationship with streets and crowds, and one of the reasons for his affinity with the arcades, was that both entailed a blurring of boundaries between outside and inside. 'The appearance of the street as an *intérieur* in which the phantasmagoria of the *flâneur* is concentrated is hard to separate from the gaslight', writes Benjamin.[42]

> The crowd was the veil from behind which the familiar city as phantasmagoria
> beckoned to the *flâneur*. In it, the city was now landscape, now a room.[43]

The glass coverings and gas lamps of the arcades reclaimed for artifice a space which was nonetheless *outside* in the sense of being *public*. With the coming of the department store, however, the ambivalence between landscape and room, between exterior and interior that had defined *flânerie* in its pure form – which translates, although Benjamin does not confront this, as its masculine form – is resolved on the side of room, interior, commodity, the feminine.

> If the arcade is the classical form of the *intérieur*, which is how the *flâneur* sees
> the street, the department store is the form of the *intérieur*'s decay. The bazaar
> is the last hangout of the *flâneur*. If in the beginning the street had become an
> *intérieur* for him, now this *intérieur* turned into a street, and he roamed through
> the labyrinth of merchandise as he had once roamed through the labyrinth of
> the city.[44]

The department store was undoubtedly a symptom of the decline of the *flâneur*. No great cause for mourning there. But what if the stronger argument is right: that the department store was an institution created to invent the *flâneuse*? Does this make it possible to rescue a female version of the type from invisibility? Or does it confirm that the *flâneur* as historical figure was both empirically and axiomatically male, at least until new public spaces like the department store and the cinema enabled women to appear safely and respectably in public by reconfiguring the boundaries of outside/inside and public/private?[45] Put like that, it may not seem terribly important. What matters more, perhaps, is that the remapping of urban modernity around the spatialisation of sexual difference undercuts any easy equation between public, outside and masculine and then the opposition of this chain of equivalences to domestic/inside/feminine. That, in turn, does not mean that men and women have been able to move through urban landscapes and to occupy rooms in the same way. But it is less a question of barred spaces than gender-differentiated experiences of spaces and sexually inflected repertoires of public, private, or intimate behaviour and performance.[46]

What does the question of the sexually differentiated experience of space have to do with Haussmann's grand designs? My argument has been that, whatever their economic and social purposes, the effect of Haussmann's metropolis on the mental life of Parisians was to produce (as just one retrospectively comprehensible but unpredictable example) Baudelaire's spleen. Parisians did not necessarily grasp or accept the pedagogy of the boulevards. More significant, perhaps, were the exacerbated divisions between centre and suburb, and so between public and home. New means of transport, new modes of communication, and new forms of entertainment engendered perceptual and psychological changes through their reconfigurations of

Unknown
photographer,
Galeries Lafayette,
Paris, 1910 (Studio
Chevojon, Paris)

time and space. In such ways, the landscape, rhythms and dynamism of the city became internalised. Modern consciousness became urban consciousness.[47] Inner space cannot be securely separated from the space of the streets. And vice versa. That is why the experience of ourselves as sexual beings, supposedly our most intimate sense of ourselves, both inflects and absorbs the way we walk the streets.

This modernist conception of the self helps to explain the impossibility of governmentalist attempts to manage the conduct and welfare of potentially insurrectionary urban populations by reorganising and regulating space. Whenever modernisers have sought to impose the rationality of the 'concept city' on urban life, *flâneurs*, artists and the rest of us have systematically re-enchanted their creations: as comic parade, as sexual display, as hellish dream-world, or simply as home. This is one of the key lessons from Benjamin. He perceived enchantment not only in the spectacular or mysterious aspects of Paris. Myth even whispered its presence to him in the most rationalised urban plans that, 'with their uniform streets and endless rows of buildings, have realised the dreamed-of architecture of the ancients: the labyrinth.'[48]

RATIONALISM AND HISTORICISM: VIENNA

One consequence of the unignorable instability of the boundaries between reality and imagination in the modern city was that, at the beginning of the twentieth century, old images of urbanism had to change. Just as the medical paradigm had given way to the metaphor of social engineering, now a purely mechanical conception of planning was itself being called into question. Two new variables became evident in any concept city: the cultural and aesthetic values expressed in an architectural style or an urban plan, and their supposed psychological impact on the population.

This change can be seen in a debate about architecture and planning that raged in Vienna right at the end of the nineteenth century.[49] When the liberals won control of the Austrian capital for two decades after 1860, despite the fragility of their political base and in the face of the adamantine conservatism of the Hapsburg dynasty, they had reshaped the city in their own image. The centrepiece of this version of Haussmannisation was the Ringstrasse, a sweeping circular boulevard of municipal buildings and private dwellings that separated the old city centre from its suburbs. Typically, its creators had attempted to combine a historicist grandeur of style with rationality and efficiency in function. When Austrian intellectuals turned against the culture and values of liberalism, the Ringstrasse became the symbolic focus of their critique. Most relevant for my argument here are the polemics of two pioneers of modern thought about the city and its architecture. One, Camillo Sitte, was a nostalgic communitarian; the other, Otto Wagner, a thoroughgoing modernist and rationalist.

Sitte's objection to the Ringstrasse was that, although traditionalist in its aesthetics, traditional values were betrayed to the exigencies of modern life. By *modern* in this context he meant the technical aspects of city building – 'traffic, hygiene, etc.' – whereas he was interested in what makes certain forms of spatial organisation picturesque and psychologically satisfying. Against the geometric grids favoured by both speculators and rationalist planners, he exalted in the irregular streets and squares of ancient and medieval cities, and set out to recreate by deliberate artistic planning what earlier eras had achieved by spontaneous slow growth. Inspired by the idea of opera as a total work of art and committed to the traditions of artisanship, he envisaged the city planner as an inspired creator who remakes our lives by redesigning our environment.[50]

Otto Wagner's attack on the Ringstrasse was diametrically opposed to Sitte's. He denounced the masking of modernity and its functions behind the stylistic screens of history. Whereas Sitte evoked visual models from the communitarian past to counteract the anomie of modern urbanism, Wagner sought new aesthetic forms to express the values of the hectic capitalist urbanity he joyfully embraced. He wanted to celebrate new materials and the functional rationality of buildings. 'Art,' he proclaimed, 'has the task of adapting the face of the city to contemporary humanity.' Architects and city planners should therefore 'make visible our better, democratic, self-conscious and sharp-thinking essence, and do justice to the colossal technical and scientific achievements as well as to the fundamentally practical character of modern mankind.'[51]

How does this Viennese dispute illuminate my history of the metaphors through which people have made sense of the city? As a traditionalist, Sitte saw the city in organic terms, although now as an historically evolving organism: an entity with a natural process of growth that can be stunted or perverted by insensitive attempts at planning and social engineering. Wagner, in contrast, saw modern man as a radically new, self-created being. He therefore sought progressive styles of architecture and city planning adequate to a machine age. Sitte wanted to recapture the human scale of the past, Wagner to create the city of the future. In both cases, the old explanatory metaphors had been rearticulated as architectural and urban *aesthetics*. They no longer merely provided a guide to reading the city, but principles for redesigning it. The competing claims to authority of the nostalgic and progressive models were now based on assumptions about how the urban environment affects people's psychic well-being. Elements from the organic and mechanical metaphors were still very much in play. But the city had also become a work of art and a human laboratory.

THE MIDDLING OF MODERNISM

By the turn of the twentieth century, the discipline of urbanism – the management of urban populations – combined spatial planning with political power and social scientific knowledge. Planners and architects like Sitte and Wagner had learned to be alert not only to historical and aesthetic considerations, but also to the psychological impact of cities that Simmel analysed in 1903 in 'The Metropolis and Mental Life'.

Over the next fifty years, it was progressivists like Wagner rather than traditionalists like Sitte who defined the terms and set the tone for urbanism. The archetypal figure here was Le Corbusier, who, part prophet and part salesman, poured forth models for ideal cities during this period.[52] Le Corbusier remains a perplexing and controversial figure, who can all too easily be caricatured as the wicked wizard of hubristic modern planning. That is partly his own fault, given his propensity for apocalyptic hyperbole. Even though Henri Lefebvre's pithy judgement is surely right – that Le Corbusier was 'a good architect but a catastrophic urbanist'[53] – it is still important to understand how he thought about the modern city, and why he thought about it that way.

First, then, let's acknowledge the sophistication of his conception of modernity. Like Baudelaire and Benjamin, he realised that modernity was a state of mind to do

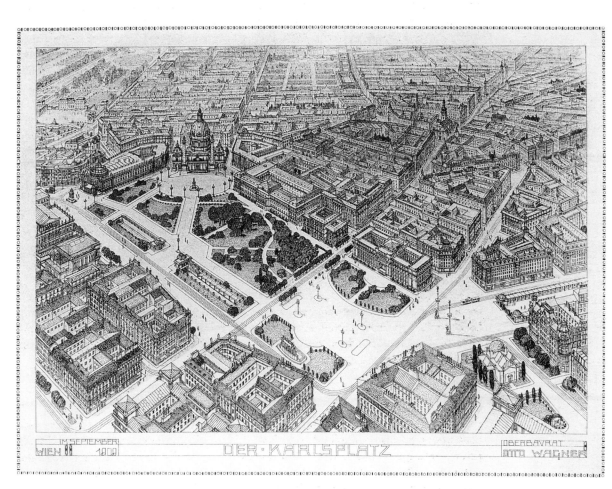

IM SEPTEMBER
WIEN 1909

DER · KARLSPLATZ

OBERBAVRAT
OTTO WAGNER

Otto Wagner, Plan
for Karlsplatz,
Vienna, 1909
(Museen der Stadt
Wien)

with accommodating *newness*, with adapting to an insistent tempo of new sensations often mediated through the ephemeral products of new mechanical forms of reproduction and communication.

> At every moment, either directly or through the medium of newspapers and reviews, we are presented with objects of an arresting novelty. All these objects of modern life create, in the long run, a modern state of mind.[54]

Le Corbusier understood that, with modernity, space, and the temporality of spatial experience, had been transformed through the mass media. The huge horizontal windows in his buildings, for example, in effect turned the outside world into an unfolding cinematic spectacle, and so structured into his architecture modernist uncertainties about outside and inside, about public and private.[55]

Le Corbusier also shared, in a practical way, something of Simmel's conception of modernity. The architect like the sociologist saw that in the metropolis all practices and relations tend to be reduced to *calculation*. For Simmel, this was an effect of the money economy, in which qualitative differences are expressed in purely quantitative terms, thus producing the defensive self-interest of the blasé attitude. For Le Corbusier, it was an effect of the triumph of engineering over architecture.[56]

> The city is profoundly rooted in the realms of calculations. Engineers, nearly all of them, work for the city. And through them the necessary equipment for the city will come into being. This is the essential thing for that part of it which is utilitarian and consequently ephemeral.
>
> But it is the city's business to make itself permanent; and this depends on considerations other than those of calculations.
>
> And it is only Architecture which can give all the things which go *beyond* calculation.[57]

In his response, Le Corbusier espoused what seems on the surface to be quite a different modernism, the modernising imperative of Haussmann and Otto Wagner. Le Corbusier's faith was that the forces which had created the urban problem of modernity could be transformed into a power capable of solving it. The first machine age – the age of the Industrial Revolution – had in the nineteenth century created dehumanised and chaotic cities. In the new machine age, the progressivists argued, architecture would solve that problem. It would not do so by turning back to premodern values and urban landscapes. Le Corbusier was justifiably scathing about such archaeological nostalgia: 'The Pack-Donkey's Way has been made into a religion. The movement arose in Germany as a result of a book by Camillo Sitte on town-planning, a most wilful piece of work.'[58] On the contrary, it was the destiny and the responsibility of architecture to create a more orderly, more efficient and more egalitarian metropolitan fabric. But the way in which that was to be achieved itself reflects the abstraction and quantification identified by Simmel. It was by translating those qualities into their plastic equivalent: abstract geometrical form, and Le Corbusier's cult of the straight line and the right angle.[59]

Second, given that this style of thought is anathema to our present scepticism about planning, let's remind ourselves that Le Corbusier was neither an idiot nor a crypto-Stalinist,[60] even though (in my view) his taste for polemics led him to say some fairly daft things and he was willing to flirt with odious political regimes if he thought it would help him to get his buildings built. The problem is not that he did not *want* to create better cities and to free people from the miseries of existing urban life, but the way he imagined it could be done. Here again it is the way of seeing the city, the metaphors through which his vision of the city was mediated, and so the way of conceptualising the city as a problem to be solved, that is the issue. Le Corbusier's way of thinking about cities appears to have been riven by a number of unstable oppositions: between calculation and aesthetics, between polemical plan and normative model, between empirical and ideal, between industrial methods and architectural values, between engineer and artist. This dualistic cast of mind characterised all Le Corbusier's work and in the end, the architect and critic Alan Colquhoun has argued, undermined it: 'he never satisfactorily reconciled his search for the timeless human values of architecture with his belief that modern technology and the structures of modern capitalism provided the means whereby these values could be re-established in a new form.'[61]

Third, then, it is perhaps worth separating Le Corbusier's often extremely acute diagnosis of the problems of modern cities – it is difficult not to have sympathy for a man who so loathed motor cars – from his proposed remedies. Both aspects of his thinking are evident in his curious account of a moment of revelation on the Champs Élysées in the early evening twilight on the first day of one October in the nineteen twenties. After the quiet of summer, the fury of the traffic was growing again.

> To leave your house meant that once you had crossed your threshold you were a possible sacrifice to death in the shape of innumerable motors. I think back twenty years, when I was a student; the street belonged to us then; we sang in it and argued in it, while the horse-'bus swept calmly along.

That seems reasonable enough. It is the sort of thing that Richard Rogers says all the time about London in the nineteen nineties. The worries start with Le Corbusier's brain wave. Suddenly he sees that the power embodied in this traffic is not just the problem, but will have to provide the solution.

> Motors in all directions, going at all speeds. I was overwhelmed, an enthusiastic rapture filled me. Not the rapture of the shining coachwork under the gleaming lights, but the rapture of power. The simple and ingenuous pleasure of being in the centre of so much power, so much speed. We are a part of it. We are part of that race whose dawn is just awakening. We have confidence in this new society, which will in the end arrive at a magnificent expression of its power. We believe in it.[62]

Of course, the cult of speed was part of the aesthetic of modernism in the early part of this century. But that is part of the difficulty with Le Corbusier, not an excuse. His solutions to political problems are not themselves political. Rather, they are a curious and dangerous combination of a modernist structure of vision, industrial techniques, and an avant-garde aesthetic.

By vision, I mean both a way of seeing and a way of giving expression to that way of seeing. Le Corbuiser's was, paradigmatically, the abstracting vision which de Certeau talks about in his account of the *dieu voyeur* looking down on the city from the skyscraper. This view from on high, whose inhumanity de Certeau decried, was

Germaine Krull,
Place de l'Etoile,
Paris, 1926 (Centre
Georges Pompidou)

exactly what Le Corbusier aspired to. For him, the skyscraper could never be high enough. To see through the miasmic chaos of existing cities, and to be able to imagine their transformation, what was needed was the perspective from an aeroplane.

> Take an aeroplane. Fly over our 19th century cities, over those immense sites encrusted with row after row of houses without hearts, furrowed with their canyons of soulless streets. Look down and judge for yourself. I say that these things are the signs of a tragic denaturing of human labour. They are proof that men, subjugated by the titanic growth of the machine, have succumbed to the machinations of a world powered by money.[63]

Le Corbusier's own damning judgement was often expressed in familiar metaphors and images of the city as a sick body. The slums of industrial cities were *cesspools* of tuberculosis and cholera, spreading *contagiously* and destroying the surrounding countryside *like a disease*. In place of the strong skeleton of a *healthy organism*, the sprawling metropolis displayed morbid symptoms: its circulation clogged, suffocating for lack of air, its tissues decaying in their own noxious wastes.[64]

Le Corbusier admired Haussmann as a *surgeon* who had tried to decongest the arteries of Paris and to endow the city (in Haussmann's own words) with 'space, air, light, verdure and flowers, in a word, with all that dispenses health'. Le Corbusier and other modernist planners went further than Haussmann in two decisive ways, however. One was in proposing new forms of public expropriation of land in order to allow planners a free hand and to disentangle regeneration from speculation. The other, more relevant here, was again at the level of metaphor.

Although Le Corbusier used organic metaphors of disease when describing existing cities, his prescriptions were always couched in terms of the city as machine. For architects of his modernist ilk, this was not just a metaphor. They proposed, quite literally, to organise and recreate the city as a machine, as 'a working tool'. They therefore adopted a functionalist, engineering approach.

> The machine, that vast modern event, will be seen for what it really is, a servant and not a ruler, a worker and not a tyrant, a source of unity and not of conflict, of construction and not of destruction.[65]

According to *The Athens Charter*, in which many of the progressivists' principles were laid down: 'The keys to city planning are to be found in the four functions: housing, work, recreation (during leisure) and traffic.' The retooling of the city would entail the reconceptualisation and reorganisation of these functions. Each was to be specifically catered for so that it would mesh smoothly with the others to make the machine-city hum.

This was why Le Corbusier's desire to 'green' the city, de-densifying it by substituting for the old rows of houses detached high-rise units set in sunlight and greenery, had more to do with this rigorous separation of spheres than with environmentalism. Whereas in the old cities housing and other buildings were interspersed by parks and public spaces, in the progressivist city space would become the background in which vertical settlements would be set. Le Corbusier's dream was that: 'The city will gradually be transformed into a park.'

Pedestrians were to be completely separated from vehicles. This, along with the

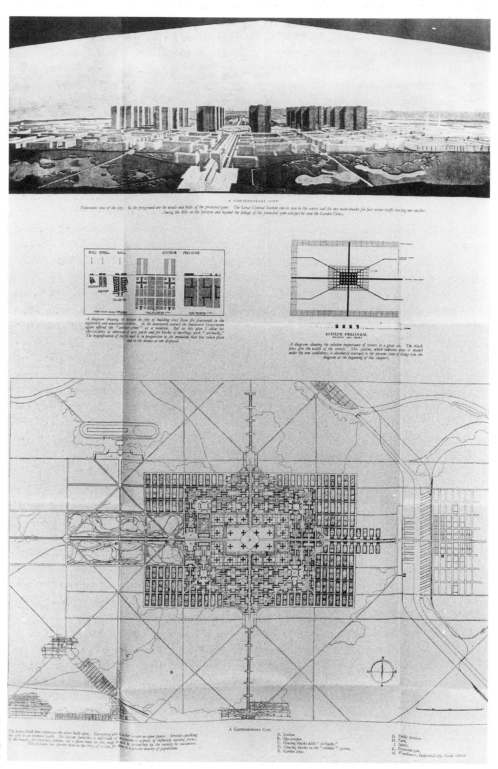

Le Corbusier, Plans
for a Contemporary
City, 1929
(© Viscopy)

disappearance of old forms of low-rise housing, pointed to the abolition of the street, and with it the type of crowd and the range of activities associated with it. The urbanism charted by Baudelaire was now regarded as a barbaric anachronism. In the modern master plan, residence, work, commerce, and recreation were to be hived off into designated zones. Right down to 'coffee-houses, restaurants, shops . . . remaining vestiges of the present street', everything must be 'given form or set in order, in a condition of full efficiency. Concentrated places for strolling and socialising.' These different zones were to be linked by new highways, themselves determined only by the terrain and 'perfectly independent of the edifices or buildings which happen to be in greater or lesser proximity' – another radical departure from the old idea of the street, here seen as 'the symbol in our era of the chaos of transportation'.

Behind all this social engineering lay an ambition far more audacious than the desire to manage the urban population that guided much nineteenth-century reformism. It was nothing less than the construction of a new framework of experience that would determine any possible social behaviour, and so create a new type of person. Like many avant-garde artists, their aim was to 'de-familiarise' the city, to make it strange and so to negate previous expectations.[66] Such changes in perception were a prerequisite for the imposition of a new urban order.

It is here that the brilliance of the progressivists' critique of the capitalist city and the heroic radicalism of their alternative vision is, in the end, vitiated by a dangerous naiveté. Dangerous, because their style of total social engineering can often turn out in practice to be, simply, totalitarian. Naive, because they fell into the trap of aesthetic formalism. They believed not only that their concept city could provide the basis for a more rational spatial organisation, but also that it could exhaustively determine how people would experience and respond to the city. From the premise that the built environment plays an important role in shaping and constraining how we live, they made the unwarranted deduction that *planned* changes in that environment would be sufficient to produce *predictable* changes in people's perceptions, mental life, habits and conduct.

'On the day when contemporary society, at present so sick, has become properly aware that only architecture and city planning can provide the exact prescription for its ills,' predicted Le Corbusier in an utterance that encapsulates the whole history of organic and mechanical metaphors of the city and at the same time the limits of his political imagination, 'then the time will have come for the great machine to be put in motion.'[67] Because there was simply no room in Le Corbusier's vision for the representational space of experience, symbol, myth and fantasy, his city remained the 'theoretically rigorous system' he offered it as, a sterile skeleton without flesh or life.[68] 'Nothing is contradictory any more' in Le Corbusier's utopia. 'Everything is in its place, properly arranged in order and hierarchy.'

Of course, it didn't happen like that. Perhaps it was never meant to. I still find it difficult to tell whether, or when, Le Corbusier took his metaphors at face value, and mistook them for achievable states. Maybe it is better, and certainly more generous, to treat his more visionary designs as just that: imagined cities designed as tools or metaphors for thinking with. In any case, very seldom were the large-scale plans put into practice wholesale. His blueprints have turned out to be more forlorn than monstrous.

So what is Le Corbusier's legacy? As an architect, in Alan Colquhoun's judgement, he can be celebrated for his creation of *fragments of the city*.

> If the dualism in Le Corbusier's thought produces an unresolved contradiction in his theory and a disembodied abstraction in his city, then in his building this dualism produces a dialectic in which aesthetic meaning is created. . . . Rather than trying to see Le Corbusier's buildings as an attempt to transform the real world, it seems more fruitful to see them as constituting a reflexive system of order, in which [these] contradictions are resolved at the level of metaphor. . . . As in poetic metaphor, the elements of contradiction are resolved without losing their independence.[69]

As a planner, his diluted visions turned out to be just one tributary to the emergence of what Paul Rabinow calls *middling modernism*. This was the version of modernism that came into existence in the middle ground between Le Corbusier's imaginative prophecies and the exigencies of political and economic reality. It is a useful term for something that is distinct from the public space of *la cité*, but which cannot be reduced to the rationalised, regulated, anonymous space of the suburban *agglomération*.[70]

A boosterish history of middling modernism might present it as an attempt to build a landscape for a welfare state, especially in Europe in the period of reconstruction after the Second World War. In Britain, for example, Le Corbusier's ideas were often mediated through a more nostalgic version of modernism: not Sitte's taste for medieval and Baroque towns, but the vision of 'garden cities' that pioneered by Ebenezer Howard and embodied in the development of new towns like Letchworth (1903) and Welwyn (1920). A less sanguine version would see modernist planning less as a failed utopia, than as the *cause* of many problems associated with cities in Britain and the United States in the nineteen sixties and seventies. The crisis of the inner city came to be attributed less to the endemic conflict between the cost of managing the urban environment on welfare state principles and political constraints on government expenditure, than to the very idea of planning. Anti-modernist critics began to claim that the failures and shortcomings of urban planning were inevitable, rather than contingent. The more lurid versions of the argument associated *any* idea of planning with what one urban sociologist has described as 'a stereotypical concoction of high-rise barracks, children without childhood, family disruption, noise, pollution, unemployment, crime, blackness and organised vice.'[71]

Of course, such Malthusian rhetoric is hardly unfamiliar. It echoes the denunciations of urban ills that run from Kay-Shuttleworth and Engels to Le Corbusier. What seemed to be new, as neo-liberalism came to dominance in the nineteen eighties, were the terms in which solutions were imagined. The paradigm of 'the social' lost its force. This new vision, however, itself turned out to be a throwback. In place of the social, we were offered a natural theology of the market. The temptation is then always to react by clinging on to the not quite so bad old days. Maybe there was something to be said for the old metaphors? Didn't therapeutic modernism, for all its hubris, on balance make cities better places to live for many (though by no means all) people?

For me, this is not a moral tale, a comforting denunciation of fools and villains. My account is a critique of a century of modern urban discourse, in the sense of trying to understand its components and its limits. To caricature, what emerged in the period of high modernism was a belief that if you could get space right, if you could organise all the bits of the city in the right configuration, then the social problems would go away. In the past couple of decades, that dangerous oversimplification has produced an opposite and equally damaging cliché: that the city, by analogy with the market, is a self-correcting system. The lesson I take from the century of modernism is less extreme. It is simply this. No aesthetic vision, however daring, can be a substitute for the worldly and piecemeal arts of government.

Henri Cartier-
Bresson/Magnum
Photos, Pershing
Square, Los Angeles,
1947

chapter 3

Light in Dark Spaces

Cinema and city

Wherever in this city, screens flicker
with pornography, with science-fiction vampires,
victimised hirelings bending to the lash,
we also have to walk . . . if simply as we walk
through the rainsoaked garbage, the tabloid cruelties
of our own neighbourhoods.
We need to grasp our lives inseparable
from those rancid dreams . . .

Adrienne Rich[1]

In this chapter I look at a different archive of urban images: the cities conjured up in cinema, and the way they render certain states of mind and styles of imagining. As a prelude, though, I shall consider briefly the role of cinemas in American and European cities in the first half of the twentieth century. What that history suggests is how the mass media during that period helped to shape the experience of the city. They provided, as it were, a mediating pedagogy between the reality of the metropolis and its imaginary place in mental life.

Why should such a pedagogy be necessary? When Georg Simmel wrote 'The Metropolis and Mental Life' soon after the turn of the twentieth century, the Wilheminian Berlin which was its largely unspoken point of reference was still in the throes of a period of remarkable growth. The city's population grew from 182,000 in 1800 to 1,840,000 in 1880 to 3,400,000 in 1910.[2] Berlin therefore provided an unfamiliar home for many new citizens, and one transformed and made more complex and speedy for all its citizens. How were they to learn the rules of this new metropolitan game?

One way was through the pedagogic role of the mass press. Newspapers constructed a 'word city' whose proliferation kept pace with Berlin's physical expansion. 'The city,' argues the historian Peter Fritzsche, 'simply could not be used without the guidance of newspapers.'[3] Many new titles appeared, and existing ones grew in circulation: the *BZ am Mittag*, the *Lokal-Anzeiger*, the *Berliner Tageblatt*, the *Berliner Morgenpost*. They advertised jobs. They listed sporting events and what entertainment was available. They packaged a view of the world which both mirrored and made sense of their readers' hurried and often anxious experience of the metropolitan landscape. Unlike Hegel, these readers did not treat the newspaper as 'a kind of realistic morning prayer', an exercise in the *Bildung* of active and responsible citizenship. For them, newspapers offered two things. One was a practical guide to surviving, exploiting and also enjoying the city. The other was a collage of fragmentary stories to be consumed distractedly at home, in the workplace, or on the move in tram or train between them.

Fritzsche's view is that the affinity between the medium of the press and the mental life of the metropolis in Berlin during these years was unique, and that it was diluted by the rise of the new media of cinema and radio, which 'lacked a specifically metropolitan focus.' Although he is right to say that 'mass broadcasting denied both the city and the text the cultural status they once enjoyed,' I take a different view of cinema.[4] The affinities between city and cinema may have been less pragmatic and less utilitarian, but they were equally strong and, in their own way, just as disciplinary.

It was certainly the case that in its early days – the period Fritzsche writes about – the cinema was almost exclusively an urban phenomenon. Both in Europe and the US, cinemas were first located in cities. In the US, they were mostly to be found in working-class and immigrant ghettos. Between the mid-nineteen tens and the nineteen thirties, the explosion in the number of cinemas, and their glorious transformation into picture palaces, took place not only in central entertainment districts but, especially, in the new suburbs springing up around major cities as mass public transportation made travel easier. The art of locating cinemas to attract the maximum possible audience, especially in the more affluent suburbs of cities like Chicago and New York, was to ensure that no potential patron needed to travel for more than half an hour to reach the theatre, and then to offer an experience not just of the film, but of stage shows, luxurious surroundings, air conditioning, and even baby sitting. Along with the national chains of department stores and grocery stores from which they learned many of their marketing techniques, the cinemas helped to give a sense of place to the growing suburban agglomerations around twentieth-century cities.[5] In the emerging geography of twentieth-century urbanism, the cinema thus plays a transitional role. In one sense, its theatres helped to sustain and reinvigorate entertainment districts in the city centre. But cinema also helped to consolidate the suburbs. It did so by bringing the experience of 'going out' to a way of life primarily built around 'staying in', a way of life mediated increasingly through a privatised experience of telephone, radio, and television.[6]

The cinema's own geography of exhibition was a key factor in making film a genuinely mass medium. It helped to extend its appeal beyond a working-class audience to one that incorporated the middle classes. ('A fellow of an Oxford college no longer feels an embarrassed explanation to be necessary when he is recognised leaving a cinema,' commented an English report on *The Film in National Life* in 1932 with an almost audible sigh of relief. 'A growing number of cultivated and unaffected people enjoy going to the pictures, and frequent not merely the performances of intellectual film societies, but also the local picture house, to see, for instance, Marlene Dietrich.'[7] But the *mass* nature of cinema was not just about selling itself to a market far larger and less socially discriminated than before. It also implies a homology between cinematic spectatorship and urban experience, with both being characterised by distraction, diffusion and anonymity.[8]

How and why did this come about? One premise of my whole argument is Simmel's observation that the dramatic changes to the great nineteenth-century

European cities had an impact on what he called mental life. Established forms of perception were disordered and reconfigured. We have already seen the causes, or at least some of them: new methods of industrial production; new cityscapes and the anonymity of the crowds encountered in them; new techniques of government and social regulation; new means of transport, especially the unprecedented and dis-orientating speed of the railway and the automobile; and instant, long-distance communication through telegraph and telephone.

It is possible to discern at least two responses to the undermining of stable or enduring structures of perception by the saturation of sensory stimuli. Some people saw it as a danger to social order and industrial efficiency. Others saw it as a new marketing opportunity.

One result was the emergence of new human sciences like scientific psychology whose purpose was to impose a disciplinary regime of *attentiveness*. Distraction, a lack of attentiveness, was seen as a threat to efficient industrial production and an incipi-ent social problem. At the same time, though, as Jonathan Crary suggests, there was quite a complicated relationship between this imperative and the commercial exploitation of distraction in new spheres of consumption like mass entertainment. 'It's possible to see one crucial aspect of modernity as a continual crisis of attentive-ness,' observes Crary: 'a crisis in which the changing configurations of capitalism push distraction to new limits and thresholds, with unending introduction of new organisations of sensory experience, new sources of stimulation, and streams of information, and then respond with new methods of regulating but also productively harnessing perception.'[9]

From its beginnings in the eighteen nineties until the end of the silent era towards the end of the nineteen twenties, cinema learned to exploit the desire of urban audiences for distraction. It did so by regulating their perception, by setting in place the norms of spectatorship associated with the classical Hollywood style roughly in the decade between 1907 and 1917. As Miriam Hansen (and others) have shown, this institutionalised mode of narration made it possible 'to anticipate a viewer through particular textual strategies, and thus to standardise empirically diverse and to some extent unpredictable acts of reception.'[10]

The consequences of this change can be seen in terms that recall my discussion of the implications of Benjamin's account of the decline of the arcades and the rise of the department store in the nineteenth century. The argument of feminist historians and critics like Hansen and Anne Friedberg is that cinema too produced a major shift in the topography of public and private domains, and one which differed most dra-matically from earlier formations 'with regard to the position of women and the discourse on sexuality.'[11] By the mid-nineteen twenties, for example, the packaging of Rudolph Valentino's star persona, and the sadistic display of his torso in *The Son of the Sheik* (1926), indicates the creation of a new public space of consumption specific-ally for women: 'Valentino becomes an emblem of the simultaneous liberalisation and commodification of sexuality that crucially defined the development of American consumer culture.'[12] The publicness of the cinema, like the domesticated publicness of the department store, was, Hansen acknowledges, primarily geared to the communal pleasures of commodity consumption. Nonetheless, she insists that it also established a certain *distance* (however absentminded or distracted) from exist-ing social and cultural norms. In doing so, it offered its consumers an *alternative horizon of experience*.[13]

Miriam Hansen's argument is that, in this sense, cinema created a new type of public space in the modern city. In Weimar Berlin, in the nineteen twenties and early thirties, cinema offered 'the single most expansive discursive horizon in which the effects of modernity were reflected, rejected or denied, transmuted or negotiated.'

> It was both part and prominent symptom of the crisis as which modernity was perceived, and at the same time it evolved into a social discourse in which a wide variety of groups sought to come to terms with the traumatic impact of modernisation.[14]

For Hansen it is Siegfried Kracauer – more than his friend Walter Benjamin – who in essays like 'The Cult of Distraction' (on the picture palaces of Berlin) and 'The Mass Ornament' (on the Tiller Girls dance troupe) perceived what was, at least potentially, public about the new forms of popular culture. Whereas others denounced them as inauthentic because of their mechanised nature or because they invited a distracted, mass response, Kracauer took a different view. For him, their significance lay in their address to the masses as (in Hansen's words) 'a specifically modern form of collective'. There is no point in bemoaning the 'inauthenticity' of mass culture, because 'authenticity' is no longer an option: 'the mass media might be the only horizon in which an actual democratisation of culture was taking place'.[15]

Cinema, Kracauer insists, *is* the paradigm of public life in the modern metropolis, insofar as it does provide some basis for critical self-reflection on a mass basis. That is why he had no truck with the 'petit bourgeois reproach' that Berliners are 'addicted to distraction'. At least the penchant for distraction, and the craving for 'the display of pure externality' it engenders, have the virtue of being *sincere*.

> It is not externality that poses a threat to truth. Truth is threatened only by the naïve affirmation of cultural values that have become unreal and by the careless misuse of concepts such as personality, inwardness, tragedy and so on – terms that in themselves certainly refer to lofty ideas but that have lost much of their scope along with their supporting foundations, due to social changes. . . . In a profound sense, Berlin audiences act truthfully when they increasingly shun [anachronistic and pretentious] art events . . ., preferring instead the surface glamour of the stars, films, revues, and spectacular shows. Here, in pure externality, the audience encounters itself; its own reality is revealed in the fragmented sequence of splendid sense impressions. Were this reality to remain hidden from the viewers, they could neither attack nor change it; its disclosure in distraction is therefore of *moral* significance.[16]

As if to confirm Kracauer's observations in Berlin, although in a different register, the novelist Dorothy Richardson was at the same time engaged in her own informal ethnography of cinema in London. In her regular contributions to the influential film journal *Close Up*, and rather against the grain of its avant-garde allegiances, she prefigured Hansen's argument about the new public space cinema provided for understandably distracted women.[17] She describes a visit to a picture palace in North London.

> It was a Monday and therefore a new picture. But it was also washing day, and yet the scattered audience was composed almost entirely of mothers. Their

August Sander,
Berlin, 1929 (The
J. Paul Getty
Museum, Los
Angeles)

children, apart from the infants accompanying them, were at school and their
husbands were at work. . . . Tired women, their faces sheened with toil, and
small children, penned in the semi-darkness and foul air on a sunny afternoon.
There was almost no talk. Many of the women sat alone, figures of weariness
at rest. Watching these I took comfort. At last the world of entertainment had
provided, for a few pence, tea thrown in, sanctuary for mothers, an escape
from the everlasting qui vive into eternity on a Monday afternoon.[18]

As she tracked cinema's presence across London, Richardson saw it fulfilling a
variety of functions for different urban audiences: not just providing a haven for
women in the suburbs, but offering entertainment in the West End, and acting as a
'civilising agent' in the slums. To her cinema suggested a public, a community of
spectators, being educated for modernity: Everyman, 'at home in a new world',
thanks to the movies. 'They are there in their millions, the front rowers, a vast
audience born and made in the last few years, initiated, disciplined, and waiting.' To
this new mass public, this congregation, cinema offered:

School, salon, brothel, bethel, newspaper, art, science, religion, philosophy,
commerce, sport, adventure; flashes of beauty of all sorts. The only anything
and everything. And here we all are, as never before. What will it do with
us?'[19]

What *did* it do with 'us'? Cinema's function in providing a mediated, distracted
public space for critical self-reflection and imagination has undoubtedly decreased.
It has been first tempered by radio and then probably displaced by television. They
too constitute a public space, and a more pervasive one. But this is more a suburban
space than an urban one. The genius of John Reith at the BBC was to see in
broadcasting another potential for redrawing the boundary between public and private. This time, in contrast to cinema, it did not open up communal and public
spaces to women, to working class audiences, or to migrants in the ghettos of the
great metropolitan cities. On the contrary, it found a way of disseminating public
events and discourses into the home, thus quite literally domesticating it and turning
the home into a centre of this form of consumption to an unprecedented degree. Of
course, commercial broadcasting has pushed that logic to apply to other forms of
consumption too. That history tells us a great deal about how we experience public
space and publicness, and about the changing relations between public and private.
But I still insist that even if broadcasting is often more civic than cinema, it is much
less urban.

One thing cinema – or at least film – has continued to do since the nineteen
twenties has been to teach its audiences across the globe ways of seeing and so
imagining the modern city, whether or not they live in one. The imagined landscape
of the city has become, inescapably, a cinematic landscape. But the city in cinema
does not operate just as a backdrop. Nor is the representation of the city really the
issue. To use Lefebvre's term, film presents urban space as itself representational, as
simultaneously sensory *and* symbolic. It thus provides a paradigm for understanding
how and why we experience the real-imagined space of the city as haunted. It
establishes distraction as an ontological norm.

Margaret Morse has updated the use of distraction by Benjamin and Kracauer in
order to reflect on the reality of an urban landscape and a suburban experience

dominated by the freeway, the mall, and television. These, she suggests, are 'the locus of an attenuated *fiction effect*, that is, a partial loss of touch with the here and now.'[20] They are the physical, technological and discursive extensions of the ability to be both here and elsewhere that are described in the fiction of Joyce and Richardson. Morse is very persuasive about these post-modern, sub-urban forms of distraction. In the rest of this chapter, however, I explore a cinematic space that remains defiantly urban and modern in its melding of the cognitive and the spectral.

THE URBAN UNCANNY

Flash forward sixty years or so from Kracauer's Berlin to an imagined Chicago in 1992. In Bernard Rose's horror movie *Candyman*, we are offered almost a tutorial on contemporary perceptions of the city. The film is punctuated by aerial shots of Chicago's townscapes: the circulation of traffic on freeways, barrack-like housing, monumental but silent amphitheatres. From that God's eye view, the city presents a dehumanised geometry. People are as invisible, or as insignificant, as they appeared to Harry Lime in the Ferris wheel high above post-War Vienna. But this abstracted view is not the film's dominant perspective. From below, on the streets, the black underclass who live in the housing projects make sense of the city's irrationality and alienation in terms of myths and sub-cultural legends: tales of miscegenation, racial murder, and the avenging undead. Urban space, then, is doubly textured. It is concrete, but just as brutally it is fantastic.

There is nothing new about the juxtaposition between panorama and myth as styles of imagining the city, nor about the sense that there is something edgily disturbing in the mismatch between the two. Inevitably, the panorama/myth couplet recalls de Certeau's contrast between the transparent abstraction of the concept city and a densely textured urban imaginary which produces 'an "anthropological", poetic and mythic experience of space.'[21] In the recesses and margins of urban space, people invest places with meaning, memory and desire. As they strike out on the town or plod the joyless street, they adapt the constraining and enabling structures of the city to an ingenious or despairing rhetoric.

Setting the mood for his speculations on the 'architectural uncanny' to be found in this labyrinthine city, Anthony Vidler provides a context for viewing *Candyman*.

> The contemporary sensibility that sees the uncanny erupt in empty parking lots around abandoned or run-down shopping malls, in the screened trompe l'oeil of simulated space, in, that is, the wasted margins and surface appearances of post-industrial culture, this sensibility has its roots and draws its commonplaces from a long but essentially modern tradition. Its apparently benign and utterly ordinary loci, its domestic and slightly tawdry settings, its ready exploitation of an already jaded public, all mark it out clearly as the heir to a feeling of unease first identified in the late eighteenth century.[22]

What is the nature of this disquiet provoked by urban space? How to think about it? How does it relate to the ways of imagining the city I have considered in previous chapters?

One of the great figures for this confrontation between the transparent, readable city and the obscure metropolitan labyrinth is the detective. From Dickens and

Balzac and Baudelaire to Benjamin and *film noir* and beyond, the detective story stages the city as enigma: a dangerous but fascinating network of often subterranean relationships in need of decipherment. The detective embodies knowledge of the city's secret lore and languages, and the daring to move at will through its society salons, its ghettos and its underworld. *Candyman* gives a novel twist to this convention. Its heroine is an anthropologist, and so placed ambivalently in relation to the visibility of the city. Although Helen Lyle is a scientist and an investigator, she has no ambition to normalise or purify the city, to reduce it to a concept. Rather, she wants to understand its mythical texture by getting inside its legends, its fears and its phobias. She has to make herself vulnerable to its powers of horror, and in doing so she is seduced by their irresistible force.

In this, she reminds me of another anthropologist, Jeanne Favret-Saarda, who, setting out to study witchcraft in contemporary France for her book *Deadly Words*, soon found that the available models of explanation – irrationality, peasant credulity, atavism, or whatever – were beside the point. What matters about myth and magic is not their truth, but their effectiveness. As she was inevitably drawn into the drama of witchcraft, the question Favret-Saarda was asked – and asked herself – was not whether she was clever enough or rational enough, but, '*Are you strong enough?*'[23]

In the end, Helen Lyle both is and is not strong enough. She is killed as she destroys the Candyman, dragged down into the dark space of an urban imaginary. But then she finds her way back as the angel of that deadly myth.

Candyman is a knowing movie, perhaps a little too knowing in its references to the legacy of boyish academic enthusiasm for collecting and taxonomising the city and its mythologies. Nevertheless, it does prompt the question of whether, and how, critical investigation might avoid the twin dangers of rationalism and prurience. When looking at the experience of the city – any city – the distanced concern for interpretation and evaluation with which we might view a work of art would be inappropriate, and even to observe this or that city with an historical eye for architectural style and meaning would seem curiously partial and eccentric. We are too much part of the landscape, too involved as actors, for that. But it is equally clear that our experience of urban space involves some more pragmatic state of mind, an imagination that is somehow bound up with our contemporary sense of agency as much as with our powers of observation.

Here we might follow a lead from the figure of Helen Lyle, and recall again the notable tradition of urban anthropologist-detectives which appeared alongside the emergence of the modern metropolis – roughly between the industrial revolution and the first World War. We have already seen how Engels, Baudelaire and Simmel all fall within this category. Although radically unlike each other in all sorts of ways, their writing is united by an attempt to balance the distance of the detective and the being in the thick of it of the city dweller. It is this disjunctural perspective that enables their investigations and their insights to transcend the generic confines of politics, poetry and sociology. An enduring image of the city emerges from their texts. Immersing themselves in the dangerous labyrinth, they articulated a novel experience of the modern city, and in so doing mediated it as both problem and possibility.

Let's recall briefly how each of them conducted their investigations, and how they attempted to make themselves strong enough to survive the adventure.

In his reading of Manchester in the 'Great Towns' chapter of *The Condition of the Working Class in England in 1844*, Engels wanted to make visible the truths hidden by the city's imposing public facades. Armed with the shield of reason and the burning torch of revolution, he descended into a nightmare of working-class immiseration and alienation in order to expose the brutal reality of capitalist social relations which sustained the bourgeois industrial city. Like the British urban reformers, Engels tried to turn the unhealthy and immoral city into a text: a report, an irresistible accumulation of facts and statistics, a programme for action. For the reformers this translation was a precondition for governing the city and policing its population through the imposition of social norms. Engels's vision was more apocalyptic. He wanted to shame the bourgeoisie and to rouse the masses. Shedding light on the urban labyrinth was for him the prelude to the real solution: the destruction of the bourgeois city and its transfiguration into a classless and just metropolis.[24]

Baudelaire had no illusions about rendering the city transparent. Rather than bringing the light of reason to illuminate the metropolitan labyrinth, he bent to the currents of the Paris streets, with their unpredictable pleasures and dangers. His protection was the opacity of the *flâneur* and (like Sherlock Holmes) a mastery of disguise. He hid behind vagrant, marginal perspectives. But Baudelaire also saw himself as a metaphysical fencer. That is how he defended himself against the psychical mutilation the city can inflict. Losing yourself in the crowd, he knew, could mean losing your *self*, cutting adrift from the familiar co-ordinates of identity and community. *Flânerie* requires a certain protective distance. Whereas Engels lets his readers know where they are in Manchester's back streets and obscure courts with the same meticulous precision that he catalogues the evils he uncovers, Baudelaire's rendition of the city's secrets is more poetic, more abstract. He respects its opacity. His Paris is reassembled according to a symbolic architecture of memory, association and desire. He mentions a boulevard, a park, a street. He gives no name and few details. Although his Paris is not yet a purely imaginary city, the implication is that what happened here could have happened on any other street, perhaps in any other city.[25] The city is allowed to retain its mystery. The case has no solution.

It is the uneasy space between the physical and the imaginary intuited by Baudelaire that Simmel explored in 'The Metropolis and Mental Life'. His city remains inescapably strange, opaque, and often oppressive. The abstraction of Simmel's vision may itself be read as a symptom of what he attempts to describe: the ways in which modern citizens make themselves strong enough, or at least protected enough, to withstand the city's intellectual shocks. Yet Simmel is also clear that the city provides the texture of modern experience and the fabric of modern liberty. This tension suggests one of the questions posed by the modern city. What does it mean to live in this world where all social relations are reduced to calculation and yet, at the same time, our experience remains that of a phantasmagoria? How can such a bewildering and alien environment – the city as unsolvable enigma – provide a home? The disquieting slippage between a place where we should feel at home and the sense that it is, at some level, definitively unhomely links Simmel to Freud, or at least to his premise that that the uncanny, the *unheimlich*, is rooted in the familiar, the *heimlich*.[26] That suggests why it is necessary to make sense of the individual in the metropolis not only in terms of identity, community, and civic association, but also in terms of a dramaturgy of desire, fascination and terror. This uncanny city defines the architecture of our apparently most secret selves: an already social space, if often a decidedly *un*civil form of association.

To understand the logic of the urban uncanny that emerges from the anthropology of Engels, Baudelaire and Simmel, it may help to return to de Certeau's all too

tantalising and elliptical account of the psychic processes involved in our migrational, metaphorical and poetic negotiations of urban space. In attempting to explain
the psychological mechanisms through which cognitive mapping actually works, he
asserts that we should bring these negotiations 'back down in the direction of oneiric
figuration'. In other words, we should think about them in terms of the imagery and
logic of dreams. But what is the nature of this dream-work on the city? De Certeau
suggests 'three distinct (but connected) functions of the relations between spatial
and signifying practices.' They are:

> . . . the *believable*, the *memorable*, and the *primitive*. They designate what
> 'authorises' (or makes possible or credible) spatial appropriations, what is
> repeated in them (or is recalled in them) from a silent and withdrawn memory,
> and what is structured in them and continues to be signed by an in-fantile
> *(in-fans)* origin.[27]

What is going on in these three 'symbolising kernels'? In the *believable*, de Certeau
is no doubt alluding to the everyday tactics and discourses through which we construct the reality of the city for ourselves, as our own. By *memorable*, I take him to
refer to the Freudian commonplace that what appears to come from outside is often
the return of what we have projected onto that outside – something drawn from a
repository of repressed memories or fantasies. But what can de Certeau mean by the
primitive, that which is 'signed by an in-fantile *(in-fans)* origin'?

That insistence of the hyphen presumably stresses the infantile as the inability to
speak, and so points to some pre-symbolic residue within the symbolic. De Certeau
does not elaborate on the notion himself, but he does return to it in the final sen-
tence of the chapter:

> . . . the childhood experience that determines spatial practices later develops
> its effects, proliferates, floods private and public spaces, undoes their readable
> surfaces, and creates within the planned city a 'metaphorical' or mobile city,
> like the one Kandinsky dreamed of: 'a great city built according to all the rules
> of architecture and then suddenly shaken by a force that defies all
> calculation.'[28]

This formulation, with its emphasis on an experience that returns as an irresistible
force, leads us straight back to the uncanny. It seems to have no place in attempts to
rationalise the city and in the process (to repeat) to 'repress all the physical, mental
and political pollutions that would compromise it'. And yet now the force has
become irrepressible. This uncanny is not a piece of grit to be expunged from the
urban machine. On the contrary, it is, in Mladen Dolar's words, 'a fundamental
dimension of modernity.' From the outset, the uncanny has represented the internal
limit of modernity, the split within it.[29]

The uncanny then indicates too not only the split, but also the relationship,
between Weber's modernity of rationality, bureaucracy and disenchantment, and
Baudelaire's *modernité* of *le transitoire, le fugitif, le contingent*. These are not alternatives. The one exists within, and is an effect of, the other. Remember that, in
Benjamin's reading at least, Baudelaire grasped the effects of this ambivalence in
aspirations to rationalise the city. While many of his contemporaries lamented that
Paris would lose the element of mystery and chance as a result of Haussmannisation,

and so also the charm of *flânerie*, Baudelaire seems to have taken the view that, however regimented the emerging city, its social texture was becoming more hospitable than ever to the *jeu du hasard*.[30] This is the key perception which Benjamin picked up and elaborated in the *Passagen-Werk*. However rationalised and disenchanted modern societies may become, at an experiential level (that is, in the unconscious) the new urban-industrial world had become fully *re*-enchanted — not just in the surreal and dream-like imagery of arcades, billboards, stores, and streets, but even in the very uniformity of its anonymous rows of identical buildings. Paradoxically, it is the attempt to render urban space transparent that *produced* the phantasmagoric city of modernity.[31]

The uncanny specific to the modern metropolis arises in the disquieting distinction between the city as object of government and the city as frame of mind. On one side of this paradox is de Certeau's Concept City: the will to visibility evident in the history of architectural schemes and dreams that runs from Bentham to Le Corbusier. What motivated Bentham's commitment to 'universal transparency' as the paradigm and mechanism of governmental power was an Enlightenment terror of darkened spaces, the illegibility of men and things. The aim of this tradition has always been to eradicate the domain of myth, suspicion, tyranny and, above all, the irrational. The logic of this politics of transparency, surveillance and social pedagogy has become familiar since it was meticulously unpicked and reconstructed by Foucault. And yet, suggests Anthony Vidler, even Foucault may have underplayed the other side of the paradox. He failed to spot how intractably the fear of darkened spaces and the opacity of the social marked Enlightenment conceptions of space. What is important is not that power works through surveillance, but the extent to which the pairing of transparency and obscurity is essential for power to operate.

> ... it is in the intimate associations of the two, their uncanny ability to slip from one to the other, that the sublime as instrument of fear retains its hold — in that ambiguity that stages the presence of death in life, dark space in bright space. In this sense, all the radiant spaces of modernism, from the first Panopticon to the Ville Radieuse, should be seen as calculated not on the final triumph of light over dark but precisely on the insistent presence of the one in the other.[32]

This modern uncanny, imagined as the labyrinth, always returns to haunt the City of Light.

FACTORY OF FACTS

If the city stages dark space in bright space, cinema projects a bright light in a dark space. To bring the two together by looking at some of the ways in which the city has been presented in cinema is not wholly arbitrary or tangential. In 1896, the Lumière brothers first showed their films in Paris. Only seven years later, Simmel published his essay on the modern metropolis. The juxtaposition between the modern city and the technology of cinema provides more clues as to the way we experience the city as psychic space: the way we imagine the city. As Benjamin observed in 'The Work of Art in the Age of Mechanical Reproduction', 'the camera introduces us to unconscious optics as does psychoanalysis to unconscious impulses.'[33]

Many modernists were quick to see analogies between the urgent rhythms of the metropolis and the constructed reality of film. 'The life of the village is narrative,' observed Ezra Pound. 'In the city the visual impressions succeed each other, over-lap, overcross, they are cinematographic.' Without making the link, Simmel had already in 1903 seen metropolitan culture in strikingly cinematic terms. He describes the individual being overwhelmed by 'the rapid crowding of changing images, the sharp discontinuity in the grasp of a single glance, and the unexpected-ness of onrushing impressions.' This experience of remorseless visual stimuli is what, for Benjamin, created the *need* for the new medium. In cinema, 'multiple fragments . . . are assembled under a new law.' It is thus with the coming of film that 'perception in the form of shocks was established as a formal principle'. Cinema goers and city dwellers alike become Baudelaire's man of the crowd: 'a *kaleidoscope* equipped with consciousness'.[34]

For artists, the challenge was to give formal expression to this kaleidoscopic con-sciousness. How could they render the overlapping discontinuity of the metropolitan glance in a single image? For a start, the image would have to be multiperspectival. Cubists like Picasso, Braques, and Delaunay exploded the illusions of spatial homo-geneity and depth created by the conventions of linear perspective. In their treat-ment of urban space, and that of Paris in particular, they would incorporate different views of a building at the same time, introduce buildings from different districts (as in Delaunay's studies of the Eiffel Tower), and over-ride outside/inside boundaries by showing interiors in landscapes. Grosz, too, gave a nightmarish intensity to the onrush of visual impressions in his street scenes by piling image upon image and caricature upon caricature. Secondly, the image would have to incorporate the elem-ent of temporality, a sense not only of newness but also of accelerated rhythm. The multiplication of perspectives was a way of acknowledging the existence of simul-taneous realities and also the condensation and intensification of time in the street, the automobile, the train, and the newspaper.[35]

What was the 'new law' that made it possible to combine multiple perspectives with a complex, multilayered temporality in order to capture the unique texture and rhythm of the modern metropolis? It was the third, and most important, characteristic of the modernist aesthetic: *montage*. As the Harvard psychologist Hugo Münsterberg noted in his pioneering study of film spectatorship in 1916, cinematic editing allowed the viewer to have the experience of being 'simultaneously here and there.' In Paul Citroën's crammed photographic collage of Paris, for example, the sense of being overwhelmed is produced not only by the massive proliferation of buildings, but also by their simultaneity. Inevitably, the concern with temporality chafed against the restriction of the still image: the push towards the explosive potential of cinema was intense. A limit case can be found in *Dynamic of the Metropolis*, a film project sketched in 1921–22 by László Moholy-Nagy. He aimed to 'bring the viewer actively into the dynamic of the city' by knitting together different elements – factories, buildings, big city traffic – on the basis purely of their visual and optical relationships. In his storyboard, he attempts to give graphic representation to the cinematic tempo of this dynamic, a tempo determined above all by the sequence and duration of proposed shots, but also by the placing and movement of the camera.[36]

Citroën's collage and Moholy-Nagy's storyboard are also symptomatic of a widespread enthusiasm for the possibilities opened up by new technologies for reproducing reality: photography, film, audio recording. This was associated with a distrust, even contempt, for fiction and all forms of aesthetic illusionism. The prin-ciple of *factography*, as it was termed by the LEF group in the Soviet Union, was set

Paul Citroën,
Metropolis, 1923
(University of
Leiden; © Viscopy)

against all attempts to beguile the reader or viewer. The new objectivity sought not to domesticate or beautify reality, but to make the visible world strange by the jolt of shocking and enlightening juxtapositions.

In *The Film Sense*, Sergei Eisenstein condenses many of these themes when discussing how the audio-visual composition of film according to the principles of montage requires both a synthesis of techniques from different arts, especially pattern from graphics and rhythm from music, and also a new, or renewed, aesthetic of temporality. Acknowledging that there is nothing new in this *principle* – the classic architecture of 'Roman squares and villas, Versailles' parks and terraces could be 'prototypes' for the structure of classical music' – he notes one modern manifestation of the principle in the current affinities between jazz, architecture, cubism and the experience of the New York cityscape at night.

> The modern urban scene, especially that of a large city at night, is clearly the plastic equivalent of jazz. Particularly noticeable here is . . . the absence of perspective.
> All sense of perspective and of realistic depth is washed away by a nocturnal sea of electric advertising. Far and near, small (in the *foreground*) and large (in the *background*), soaring aloft and dying away, racing and circling, bursting and vanishing – these lights tend to abolish all sense of real space, finally melting into a single plane of coloured light points and neon lines moving over a surface of black velvet sky. . . . Headlights on speeding cars, highlights on receding rails, shimmering reflections on the wet pavements – all mirrored in puddles that destroy our sense of direction (which is top? which is bottom?), supplementing the mirage above with a mirage beneath us, and rushing between these two worlds of electric signs, we see them no longer on a single plane, but as a system of theatre wings, suspended in the air, through which the night flood of traffic lights is streaming.[37]

What interests Eisenstein here is not just 'the correspondence between musical and graphical arts', but above all 'the idea that these arts, fused together, correspond to the very *image of an epoch and the image of the reasoning process* of those who are linked to the epoch.'[38] The aesthetic of montage not only responded to, but self-consciously *used*, the experience of fragmentation that characterised the *modernité* of the city. This was, no doubt, what prompted Benjamin's declared methodological ambition 'to carry the montage principle over into history. That is, to build up the large structures out of the smallest precisely fashioned structural elements.'[39] This commitment to montage helps to explain why, in the 'Work of Art' essay, Benjamin does not condemn cinema as part of modernity's dream world. But nor does he see it as a public space for mass self-reflection and critical imagination. Rather, he sees it in more epistemological terms. It is an analytic light that can reveal the labyrinthine constraints of the ordinary, of commonsense knowledge, and so expand the spectator's field of possibilities.

> Our taverns and our metropolitan streets, our offices and furnished rooms, our railroad stations and our factories appeared to have us locked up hopelessly. Then came the film and burst this prison-world asunder by the dynamite of the tenth of a second, so that now, in the midst of its far-flung ruins and debris, we calmly and adventurously go travelling.[40]

Which cinema is Benjamin talking about? Although he was writing in 1935, possibly the strongest case for the cinema's epistemological power to explode and recompose the familiar fragments of modern urban experience might be made by looking at the avant-garde 'city symphony' films of the nineteen twenties. Taking actuality footage and editing it to capture the complex, syncopated rhythm of the metropolitan day, they at least aspired to a similar end. The first in the cycle was *Manhatta* (1921), a Whitmanesque celebration of New York by the photographer Paul Strand and the painter Charles Sheeler. European examples were Alberto Cavalcanti's *Rien que les heures* (1926), a more humanistic portrait of Paris based around the fictionalised lives of two 'ordinary people', *À propos de Nice*, Jean Vigo's first film in 1930, and Manoel de Oliveira's study of Oporto, *Douro, Faina fluvial* (1931). Another American example was Herman Weinberg's *City Symphony* (1930).[41]

Two of the best known films, often compared with each other, are Walter Ruttmann's *Berlin: Symphony of a Great City* (1927) and Dziga Vertov's *The Man with the Movie Camera* (1929). Both use the 'day in the life of a great city' structure. Both attempt to capture a dynamic of traffic, machines, work, and leisure. Vertov describes his Cameraman being hurled into 'a whirlpool of interactions, blows, embraces, games, accidents'.[42]

In transforming this maelstrom into a structured portrait, Ruttmann worked with the same affinities between urban architecture and traffic, the rhythmic manipulation of time, and a cubist aesthetic of space that Eisenstein discussed in *The Film Sense*. He concentrated on three elements.

First, there is the film's self-consciously formalist perception of objects and its graphic presentation of relationships between them. In part, this reflects a delight in the aesthetic serendipity of abstract shapes and formal juxtapositions. But it is also a principle of construction. The film opens, for example, by cutting from the horizontal patterns on the surface of a lake to analogous patterns of railway tracks and telegraph lines, and then to a point of view sequence from a train heading into the city.

Second, and equally formal, is the organisation of time and space to create the 'film city' of Berlin. The film lays out a *montage mapping* of Berlin. It conveys the accelerating tempo of a Berlin day through the rhythmic principles of its editing. (As if in reference to Simmel's essay, periodic shots of clocks punctuate the film.) It eschews any temptation to offer the encompassing view of the *dieu voyeur* or the aeroplane pilot. Instead, it presents urban space as fragmented and socially differentiated. This space is rendered meaningful, however, in part through the events which take place within it, and in part by the experience of movement between spaces – hence (as in Dickens) the film's emphasis on networks of communication, transport, circulation and exchange.[43] In the modern city, space is experienced as time. As the geographer Wolfgang Natter comments in his study of *Berlin*, 'speed effects and incarnates the spatialisation of place.'[44]

Both these elements – abstraction and the construction of space over time through montage – Ruttmann had learned from his earlier abstract films. In *Berlin*, he now added to them a third element: an almost voyeuristic record of the little human dramas of public life. In part this represents an attempt to encompass the class differences and divisions that make up the social relations of the metropolis: a montage city which in some ways recalls the word city of the popular press in the early years of the century. Ruttmann cuts between the different ways (and times) that

people get to work: by bicycle at dawn, by public transport, by chauffeured limousine at a more leisurely hour. He cuts between the works canteen and the downtown restaurant, and highlights the different mores and manners to be found in them. He cuts between different forms of entertainment: consumer sports like boxing and indoor cycling, the *flânerie* of window shopping, variety shows, Josephine Baker, a symphony concert. It is the class inflected nature of the events that take place in them as much as the aesthetics of the architecture that distinguishes the elegant Kurfürstendamm from the dowdy Scheunenviertel.[45] But, as I have suggested, events are portrayed not just as social commentary. They render the space of the Berlin day, and the temporality of its streets. Children go to school, people chat in cafés, men get into a fight, a policeman helps a little boy across the road, a prostitute plies her trade,[46] street performers appear in silly costumes, a woman commits suicide.

If Ruttmann's vision of Berlin remains broadly Cubist, Vertov's aesthetic is Constructivist and Futurist. His city is no one place, but more strictly a product of the imagination and of the editing table. His city – a combination of footage of Moscow and of a number of locations in the Ukraine – provides a metaphor, a projection, for the structure of vision and perception embodied in the 'eye' of cinema. *The Man with the Movie Camera* thus becomes a reflection, both utopian and critical, on the dynamic interaction of life and technology, and on the persistence of contradictions, in the construction of the new Soviet society. What cinema brings to this process is the power to reveal these possibilities and problems – its power of epistemological detonation, to use Anne Friedberg's phrase. In this, Vertov not only presages Benjamin, he also follows Mayakovsky's faith in poetry. In his poem 'A Conversation with the Inspector of Taxes about Poetry', written in 1926, Mayakovsky used imagery that foreshadowed Benjamin's.

> A rhyme's
>
>   . . .
>
> a barrel of dynamite.
>
>   A line is a fuse
>
>   that's lit.
>
> The line smoulders,
>
>   the rhyme explodes –
>
> and by a stanza
>
>   a city
>
>   is blown to bits.[47]

Vertov's film should be seen neither as a record nor a portrait but, following the precepts of formalism, as an *analysis* which makes our normal perceptions of the city strange by laying bare the device of cinema. Vertov described his aims in these terms:

> The film is the sum of events recorded on the film stock, not merely a summation of facts. It is a higher mathematics of facts. Visual documents are combined with the intention to preserve the unity of conceptually linked pieces which concur with the concatenation of images and coincide with visual linkages, dependent not on intertitles but, ultimately, on the overall synthesis of these linkages in order to create an indissoluble organic whole.[48]

Walter Ruttmann, *Berlin: Die Sinfonie der Großtadt*, 1927 (Courtesy of BFI Stills, Posters and Designs)

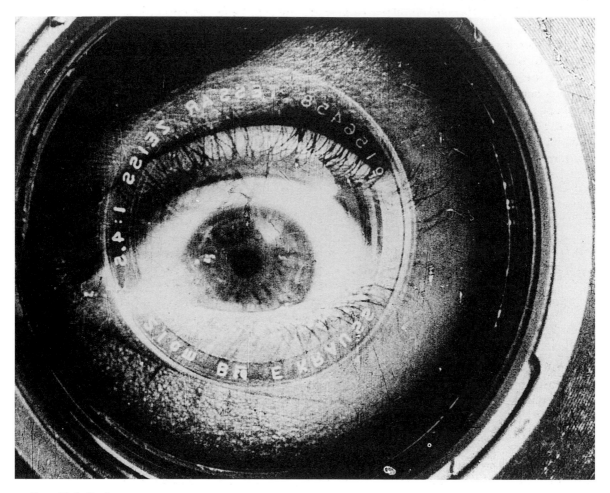

*Man with the Movie
Camera*, 1928/9
(Courtesy of BFI
Stills, Posters and
Designs)

The facts which the film reworks are not just those of work and leisure, people and technology, marriage and divorce, or even birth and death. Above all, they are the facts of filming, editing, and viewing in cinema. We see Vertov's brother Mikhail Kaufman at work filming (often using techniques of superimposition, stop frame, and so forth), and his wife Elizaveta Svilova editing sequences that return in their diegetic context later in the film. The constructed temporality of film is emphasised through the use of techniques like freeze frame, slow motion, and accelerated motion. Space too is manhandled, as the screen is divided, and buildings made to collapse in on themselves.

When *Berlin* and *Man with the Movie Camera* are compared and contrasted, it is usually to the detriment of Ruttmann's film. In his study of German cinema in the inter-War period, *From Caligari to Hitler*, first published in 1947, Siegfried Kracauer accuses Ruttmann of indulging in aesthetic formalism at the expense of political critique. It is not just that Ruttmann offers too restricted a cross-section of Berlin – Kracauer bemoans the absence of 'the Berlin of the worker, the white-collar worker, the shopkeeper, the upper bourgeoisie, each of which according to professional and human categories occupies a definite radius, definite segments.'[49] When he does show social contrasts, it is as 'formal expedients' rather than as 'social protests'. Ruttmann can only reflect 'a shapeless reality, one that seems to be abandoned by all vital energies.' Vertov, in contrast, 'the son of a victorious revolution', portrays 'a reality quivering with revolutionary energies that penetrate its every element'.

> In his lyric enthusiasm, Vertov stresses formal rhythms but without seeming indifferent to content. His cross sections are 'permeated with communist ideas' even when they picture only the beauty of abstract movements. Had Ruttmann been prompted by Vertov's revolutionary convictions, he would have had to indict the inherent anarchy of Berlin life. He would have been forced to emphasise content rather than rhythm. . . . Ruttmann's rhythmic 'montage' is symptomatic of a withdrawal from basic decisions into ambiguous neutrality.[50]

It may be the wisdom of hindsight to remark that Kracauer sells short Ruttmann's montage mapping, which from today's perspective prefigures contemporary ways of imaging the spatialisation of social relations and so the production of space.[51] I think it is fair to say, however, that the tone of Kracauer's criticism, which was equally evident during the period of revived cinematic avant-gardism in the nineteen seventies, takes on a hollow ring, if not worse, when one reflects on the way the 'victorious revolution' first marginalised Vertov, not least by exploiting Eisenstein's accusation of 'formalist jack-straws and unmotivated camera mischief', and then wrote him out of Soviet history.

More to the point, by making his critical yardstick the commitment of the film-maker and the progressiveness of the text, Kracauer seemed to rule out of court the concern for ambivalence and the uncanny that must be central to the unconscious optics of modernism. In doing so, he lost sight of the central point he made in his original review of *Man with the Movie Camera* as the film critic of the *Frankfurter Zeitung* in 1929. There it was not the celebration of technology or the revolutionary perspective of the film that Kracauer highlighted, but its affinity with states of dreaming and dying. Kracauer praised Vertov as a 'surrealist artist who registers the colloquy that the died-away, disintegrated life holds with the wakeful things'.[52] This earlier, perceptive, emphasis suggests that *Berlin* and *Man with the Movie Camera* might be compared more usefully, not in terms of a reductionist political criticism, but in the light of de Certeau's oneiric perspective on the city and Benjamin's unconscious optics of cinema. Without denying their powerful use of montage to capture the city's dynamism and fragmentation, do the films also convey a sense of the urban uncanny, of the city's dark spaces?

In *Berlin*, something like the uncanny makes a disconcerting appearance at the heart of the film, in the suicide of the woman throwing herself off a bridge. It is a curious episode. Who is this woman? Is she one of the women we have seen before, and if so which one? Even after several viewings, it difficult to be sure. And what is it that drives her to suicide? In keeping with the film's rejection of dramatic narrative and novelistic characterisation, we are given no psychological clues. In her discussion of female *flânerie* in the film, however, Anke Gleber points to a formal logic that begins to make sense of the event. Early in the film, Gleber notes, the first group of human figures on which the camera comes to rest is a shop window of mannequins displaying women's erotic underwear. From this display of dolls, there is a cut to the first image of water running under the bridge where later the drowning will take place. And after the spectacle of the suicide – a drama staged for an audience whose avid attention is underlined in the film – the action cuts to models parading the catwalk in a fashion show. The connections Gleber rightly draws out are between display, commodification, objectification, and death.

She also notes as an aside that this chain of connotations around the appearance of women may be linked to some notion of the uncanny: 'Their walking down the street opens a space for the female *flâneur*, develops the presumably nonexistent, improbable and uncanny presence of a woman in the street *as in a photograph . . .*'[53] What sort of photograph might this be? No doubt prompted by Gleber's emphasis on shop-window displays in *Berlin*, and their similar prominence in *The Man with the Movie Camera*, what first comes to my mind are Atget's images of mannequins in the stores of Paris. Here the sense of the uncanny inherent in the ambiguity of doll-women (Olympia in Hoffmann's *The Sandman* and then in Freud's own essay on the uncanny, as one obvious example) is given an additional twist by the nature of their representation. For in these photographs what Atget documents with elegiac precision is neither event nor place, but the display of *artifice*.

It is this ambivalence that resurfaces in *Berlin*'s *mise-en-scène* of the suicide and that, in doing so, unsettles the whole film. The problem is not just that its very obvious actedness casts doubt on the authenticity of the film's other vignettes. Rather, it is the formal irruption of artifice and fiction into a cinematic space avowedly dedicated to the fact-based truth of the New Objectivity. The sequence violates what were emerging as the generic rules of documentary film. More to the point, the intrusion of an overtly melodramatic event and an equally melodramatic staging is disruptive because it interpolates a superficially quite different vision of the city to be found in the contemporary German genre of 'street films'. In these, Berlin's mysteries were imagined as feminine through the figure of the prostitute. The pivotal positioning of this spectacle of the enigmatic woman places Ruttmann's film in the tradition which, Patrice Petro argues in *Joyless Streets*, makes a metaphorical equation between the city and modernity, between modernity and the feminine, and so between the city – its commoditised social relations, its pleasures and its dangers – and the feminine. In all these ways, the feminine and the uncanny are closely aligned in *Berlin*.[54] As the film repeatedly demonstrates, in part through

Eugène Atget, Paris,
n.d. (Julien Levy
Collection, © The
Art Institute of
Chicago)

this uneasy and uncertain rendering of the different truths of fiction and documentary, the street is an unhomely space for women – even, the suicide suggests, a terrifying and unbearable one. And perhaps this female experience is then displaced for the male (or normative) spectator *onto* the figure of the woman in the street, thus rendering it uncanny: something familiar, something that embodies both desire and threat, something that seems out of place there now.

Vertov's case is trickier. The uncanny returns in his film not as a residue, but as a potential, even a threat, implicit in his commitment to a dialectical conception of the city. For Vertov, as for Benjamin, cinema was the liberating light that could destroy imprisoning social relations by rendering them transparent once and for all. 'I, a machine, am showing you a world, the likes of which only I can see,' wrote Vertov, identifying himself with the camera. 'My road leads toward the creation of a fresh perception of the world. . . . I decipher, in a new way, a world unknown to you.' This is the utopian will to visibility that Dziga Vertov and Benjamin seem to share with Le Corbusier, whose visions of the machine-based, machine-like cities of a perfected future at this period show the same audacious vision as *Man with the Movie Camera*. Vertov's dream that cinema would 'open the working masses' eyes to the links (neither of the love story nor the detective story) uniting visual phenomena' recalls Le Corbusier's faith that existing habits of perception could be disrupted and cleansed by 'de-familiarising' the city. Both envisaged a new, technological and harmonious framework of experience that would determine social behaviour, and so create a new type of person. 'Our artistic vision departs from the working citizens,' proclaimed Vertov, 'and continues through the poetry of the machine toward a perfect electrical man.'[55]

For Le Corbusier, establishing a new social order required the absolute repression of all traces of history, memory and desire from the city. There was nothing to celebrate in its messy dynamics. In New York he could see nothing but grandiose and cataclysmic chaos, in Paris a dangerous magma. Remember Le Corbusier's prophecy, or maybe I should say his fantasy: 'On the day when contemporary society, at present so sick, has become properly aware that only architecture and city planning can provide the exact prescription for its ills, then the time will have come for the great machine to be put in motion.'

Inevitably, I have argued, the uncanny architecture of experience, symbol, myth and fantasy returns to expose the limits and bathos of Le Corbusier's paranoid city of absolute transparency. Does Dziga Vertov fall into the same trap as Le Corbusier? However exhilarating his cinematic imagination, however heroic his faith in the possibility of social transformation, Vertov's belief in the transformative power of film must now seem hubristic, even tragic. Like Le Corbusier (and *pace* Benjamin), Vertov's politics remain formalist and aestheticised – not aestheticised in the kitsch of fascism, but in a romantic ethic of personal and social perfectibility. True, Vertov acknowledges the persistence of history and desire in his constructed city, but the narrative image that lingers from *Man with the Movie Camera* is that of the Cameraman looming over the crowd and filming it. Who is this but the *dieu voyeur*? He prefigures less the emergence of the 'new man' – and more problematically the 'new woman' – than the city of total surveillance.

Man with the Movie Camera, 1928/9 (Courtesy of BFI Stills, Posters and Designs)

DREAM FACTORY

To Benjamin, modernity was 'a store of dialectical images' bearing contradictions which are capable of development, but which are now frozen in 'dream images'.[56] Vertov's Constructivist cinema – his Factory of Facts – pushes that dialectical development as far as it can go, and yet still ends up confronting the constitutive uncanny of modernity, the split between the will to visibility and the irredeemable opacity of the social. To understand the persistence of the labyrinthine city, perhaps we should turn away from the modernist visions of the city symphonies, and take once more the route of dream work and 'oneiric figuration'. This would mean following *Candyman*'s Helen Lyle into the underworld of urban dream images, the Dream Factory of mass produced fantasies. One thing we find there is a psychic space that can be given physical substance only through the architecture of the film studio and the ingenious artifice of its special effects.

These are perhaps most spectacularly evident in the anti-documentary representation of urban space that runs from *Metropolis* and *King Kong* to *Blade Runner*, *Brazil*, the *Batman* films, and the Manga animation of *Akira*. In this tradition, says Peter Wollen, 'the city is perceived as a kind of dream space, a delirious world of psychic projection rather than sociological projection'. However excessive or unsubtle their dystopian visions may be, however much at odds with the idea of a dialectical cinema, the anxieties these films project may offer some profane illumination of what goes on in our everyday experience of the metropolitan dreamworld. 'Le Corbusier ultimately failed to impose his will on the twentieth-century city,' as Wollen observes. 'André Breton's *Nadja* was nearer the mark.'[57]

Wollen traces the architectural imagery of the films to its sources in grandiose and often unrealised schemes from the early decades of the century – the Futurist cities of Sant'Elia, Hugh Ferris's vistas of an imaginary Manhattan, Harvey Wiley Corbett's landscapes of multilevel arcades and vast bridges across urban abysses – as well as in comic-book urban dystopias and the tradition of science fiction that culminated in cyberpunk. Inspired by his first visit to New York in 1924, for example, Fritz Lang's *Metropolis* (1926) can be read as a critique of the cult of the machine endorsed by both Vertov and Le Corbusier. Metropolis is, in effect, Le Corbusier's zoned city turned on its side to reveal its implicit hierarchy. Its gilded youth play in Elysian pleasure gardens above the streets and towers of a dehumanised public sphere. Beneath both, sustaining them, is the subterranean world of slave labour. Similarly, the critique of postindustrialism in Ridley Scott's *Blade Runner* (1982/ 1992) is rendered by an imagined Los Angeles built in a hodgepodge of architectural styles from different periods, an aesthetic of disintegration and decay appropriate to a city in ruins.[58]

However compelling, we should not be mesmerised by the look of the films. If fantasy is the *mise-en-scène* of desire, the next step should be to consider the narratives acted out in these imaginable but unbuildable cities. What do we find?

The Futurist architecture of *Metropolis* provides the backdrop for an Expressionist tale about sentimental love confronting the combined Oedipal forces of Reason and Magic, as well as the political message about the relationship between capital and labour which rightly worried Kracauer and other critics. But the most compelling narrative strand concerns forces which, once unleashed, have an unmanageable capacity for destruction. One is the proletarian mob, that Frankenstein's monster which, however biddable, always threatens to run out of control and destroy its creator. The

Antonio Sant'Elia,
La Città nuova, 1914
(Civic Museum,
Como)

Metropolis, 1926
(© F.-W.-Murnau-
Stiftung, Wiesbaden/
Transit-Film GmbH,
Munich. Courtesy of
BFI Stills, Posters
and Designs)

technology that enslaves the mob is also seen to harbour atavistic powers of destruction.[59] Most dangerous of all is an untrammelled female sexuality. It is the mechanical vamp built to mimic the real, virtuous Maria who leads the workers to rebellion and disaster. This robot, the false Maria, thus conflates characteristic modern anxieties about sexuality, technology and the mob at the same time as combining two figures of the uncanny – the automaton and the double. (Alternatively, you can take a more optimistic view of the robot Maria as a subversive sex machine, a prototype of Donna Haraway's cyborg-woman.)[60]

In *King Kong* (1933), it is less technology that runs out of control, than a primitive (and so, for the modernists, uncontaminated and redemptive) nature abused and offended by explorers, by scientists, by film-makers and by showbiz entrepreneurs. Kong, like the mob in *Metropolis*, is enslaved and exploited in the city – not as a proletariat, though, but as a spectacularly fetishised commodity. In the final section of the film, he goes marauding through New York until, swatting against aeroplanes as he clings to the Empire State Building, even his brute strength proves inadequate against the violence of technology. This image has become iconic not only of New York, but also of Baudelaire's vision of the modern uncanny as 'the savagery that lurks in the midst of civilisation', the primitivism that haunts Le Corbusier's modernist skyscraper.

The rebellious replicants in *Blade Runner* come to the forbidden city, not to destroy it but to pose some Kantian questions to their maker. They want to find out what they are, to demand a history as well as a fate, and to learn what they can hope for. Like Kong, Roy Batty and his colleagues are dangerous but sympathetic, and ultimately martyred, outsiders – more sympathetic, at any rate, than those who exploit and then destroy them: 'More Human Than Human', to use their creator's slogan. In the 1992 version of the film, the director's cut, it is made clear that Deckard, the blade runner, is himself a sophisticated replicant. In a new twist of the uncanny, his self-perception as human, and his anxiety that he may be a cyborg, turn on the question of whether his dreams express a repressed childhood memory, or an implanted unconscious.

In *Batman* and *Batman Returns*, the infantile nature of the fantasies underlying all these scenarios of origins and boundaries is made grotesquely overt. Gotham City is threatened by an evil genius more powerful that Fredersen in *Metropolis* or Tyrrell in *Blade Runner*. To combat the Joker or the Penguin, our mild-mannered superhero dons his cape and leaps into his Batmobile to do battle for right. . . . Doesn't the very infantilism of this imagery ring a bell? For me, at least, it recalls de Certeau's tantalising remarks about the primitive city.

De Certeau suggests that the primitive city, which might as well be Gotham City, is the product, or projection, of a symbolising kernel that continues to be marked by its infantile origin. It returns as a force that defies all calculation, the archaic force that can suddenly shake a great city built according to all the rules of architecture. On the cusp of terror and absurdity, these films tell of conflict with the claims of authority and the bonds of community, and also of the unfixing or uncertainty of identity. They play on the fragile, shifty boundaries between human and technology, between human and nature, or between adult and infant. They remind us of that ineradicable unease about who we are and where we belong that also haunts the very way we walk the streets of the modern city.

King Kong, 1933
(Courtesy of BFI
Stills, Posters and
Designs)

Blade Runner, 1982
(© Warner Brothers.
Courtesy of BFI
Stills, Posters and
Designs)

ANGELS

The city is not a place. That is neither to deny the actuality of cities, nor to trivialise the social problems associated with cities today. The problems of homelessness are more pressing than theoretical debates about the *unheimlich*.[61] Racial injustices cannot be solved by noticing how a clever horror movie like *Candyman* comments on the equation of the non-white with the archaic and the monstrous without quite escaping that racialised urban discourse. Nevertheless, in making sure that we have extricated ourselves from the modernist political imagination that is the legacy of people like Le Corbusier and (I reluctantly have to admit) Dziga Vertov, there is some point in continuing to insist that the unifying concept of 'the city' should not be used to authorise lazy and damaging fantasies of total social transformation. 'The city', I have tried to suggest here, may be better understood at least in one of its aspects as a historically specific mode of seeing. It names a structure of visibility that incorporates not only the analytic epistemology theorised by Benjamin and achieved by Vertov, but also the primitive fantasies hypothesised by de Certeau and realised in the fantastic cities of Ufa, Hollywood and Manga.

A sensitivity to this ambivalence in the state of mind that is the modern city may prefigure a new urban imagination, a new structure of visibility, that transcends de Certeau's manichean opposition between the Concept City of power and a pedestrian poetics of resistance. Its contours are hinted at in the delirious architectural narratives of Rem Koolhaas as well as in Guy Debord's maps of a psycho-geography. Whatever emerges, it is already clear that both 'the city' and 'cinema' are in any case slipping into history. Spatial organisation is increasingly determined by global information flows. The analytics and oneirics of cinema are becoming less powerful than the apparatus of visibility inscribed in and by television, video and multimedia.

Those changes may provoke a modernist nostalgia. And if we are living, as usual, in a transitional period, then morbid symptoms are to be expected. But there may also be grounds for optimism, even in the gore of *Candyman*. Although Helen Lyle returns (quite reasonably) to eviscerate her husband, she died saving a baby from the Candyman. She is an angel of mercy as well as the angel of death. Perhaps we should take hope from that, for she may also be the angel of history. Why, asks Christine Buci-Glucksmann, do we always see the uncanny in demonic images of 'dismembered limbs, severed heads, gouged eyes, people buried alive, animated puppets'?

> To be sure, in relation to the Father and castration anxiety, the uncanny is thoroughly enmeshed in violence. But there is never any question of that other violence, more female than paternal, more androgynous than phallic, more seraphic than Luciferian: the violence of the Angel. Not, that is, unless we follow Lacan's suggestion of 'another side' to sexual pleasure [*jouissance*], a more female side in which the uncanny [*l'étrange*] merges with the angelic [*l'être-ange*].[62]

For Buci-Glucksmann, this beauty coming from the abyss can only be found in the metaphors of femininity and redemption embodied in the *Angelus Novus* that haunted Benjamin's work. But also, maybe, it is in cinematic cities that we hear the quiet yet insistent rhythm of the wings of desire.

Ted Croner, *Sharpie*,
New York, 1947
(© Ted Croner,
Courtesy Howard
Greenberg Gallery)

chapter 4

The Citizen and the Man about Town

O. Henry was an American writer of meretricious but, in their turn-of-the-century day, hugely popular short stories. In the late nineteen fifties or early nineteen sixties, a television series was based on them. One episode has always stuck in my mind. It was called 'Man About Town'. Intrigued by the persistence of this screen memory, wondering how I may have creatively misremembered it, but having no access to the programme, I decided to check the original story.[1] To my surprise, it matched my recollection almost exactly.

The narrative tells of O. Henry's wish to find out what a Man About Town is. He asks a number of people around New York: a reporter, a barman, a 'Salvation lassie', and a critic. They offer him a variety of more or less helpful, more or less inconsequential suggestions. Inspired by these, he determines to meet a Man About Town face to face. 'I am going to find my Man About Town this night if I have to rake New York from the Battery to Little Coney Island.'

> I left the hotel and walked down Broadway. The pursuit of my type gave a pleasant savour of life and interest to the air I breathed. I was glad to be in a city so great, so complex and diversified. Leisurely and with something of an air I strolled along with my heart expanding at the thought that I was a citizen of great Gotham, a sharer in its magnificence and pleasures, a partaker in its glory and prestige.

So absorbed is the narrator in his search that he steps absentmindedly into the road, and is run over. When he wakes up in hospital, a young doctor shows him a newspaper report of the accident.

> I read the article. Its headlines began where I heard the buzzing leave off the night before. It closed with these lines:
> '– Bellevue Hospital, where it was said that his injuries were not serious. He appeared to be a typical Man About Town.'

From the mass of tacky television tales that I absorbed in childhood, why should this one stay with me? If I could not measure my investment in the story by what I had added to it or altered in it, what could be the fascination?

One explanation is obvious enough. I too would like to find out that I am the Man About Town. In my fantasy world, His Majesty the Ego can often be observed roaming the metropolis 'with something of an air.' Much of my life has been happily wasted in reading about tough detectives braving the cliché of those mean streets, and in watching movies about doomed, Promethean gangsters or flawed heroes ensnared by fatal *femmes*. Even in my academic work, as this book betrays, I am also repeatedly drawn to the asphalt jungle as the locus of modernity. Although equally interested in the rationalised urban environment of planners and reformers, what fascinates me despite myself is the enigma of modernity represented by the city. What possibilities of public life and worldly self-creation does it embody, and what ineradicable dangers are to be found in the metropolitan labyrinth? The reassuringly familiar location of New York, tonight, with its cast of stock characters is no doubt part of the appeal of O. Henry's story. But that cannot be a sufficient explanation. There must also be something about its narrative structure to which I respond.

I certainly feel an affinity with the dissonance between image and self-image at the heart of the story. It plays on my non-transparency to myself, the tantalising impossibility of seeing ourselves as others see us, and my frustrating sense of a self which is not me, but a reflection of the world's perceptions of me. It is on the specularity and alterity of male subjectivity that the story's twist turns.[2] The narrator conducts himself as a Man About Town, he exhibits all the habits and characteristics of the Man About Town, and yet he cannot recognise himself as the person he is obsessively searching for. Inside, he simply does not feel like the image he projects.

Not only does the story appeal to a pattern of imaginary identification in me, then, to the fantasy of being seen as a Man About Town. It may also plug into a symbolic identification with an assumed position from which I could be identified and judged. There again you can see the attraction of the symbolic space of the city as a topic of study. *The city* provides an imagery for the way we represent ourselves as actors in the theatre of the world, and for what it feels like to act out that drama of the self on that stage.

I have considered in earlier chapters how the mediated, metaphorised, spectacularised and narrated city of experience produces disconcerting shadows and obscurity in the rational City of Light. But somewhere in the imagination of modernity there is a third city in play, in addition to the city of *flânerie* and the planned technological city. This is the *republican* city, the city which since Aristotle at least has been supposed to provide the forum for debates about what constitutes the good life and for the non-violent resolution of conflicts arising from the sheer difficulty of people living together in the shared space of the city. This ideal of civilisation, the creation of society and the formation of self made possible only through the *civis*, may appear sometimes in surprising and profane forms (like the cinema) even if it is forever betrayed by the grimy reality of an alien and unhomely environment.

These days, there is a renewed interest in thinking about questions of citizenship, republicanism and the possibilities of a radical democratic political culture based on difference and passion rather than consensus and technical solutions. That is why the city as a place of politics – axiomatically, the *polis* – has returned to haunt and reanimate political theory and philosophy. My question here is whether the imagined city of the man about town can shed any light on the political imaginary shaping current thinking about citizenship.

CITIZENS

If I ask, 'who is the citizen?' I may end up like O. Henry's narrator. After scurrying around quizzing those who ought to know where I might track down such a creature, I could just be told to look in the mirror. I have my passport, my driving licence, and no doubt soon I shall have an identity card. I have done jury service. I am sent my voting card at election time, and my tax demand once a year. These rights and obligations confirm my status as a member of the state. What more do I want to know? What's the problem?

The problem, of course, is that this legal status as citizen does not feel as though it has anything much to do with my sense of self. It tells me what I am, not who I am.

Let me illustrate what is at stake in that distinction by examining what seems to me the central flaw in Habermas's contribution to the citizenship debate: his eminently sensible argument that a nation of state-citizens whose affective loyalties were expressed in a *constitutional patriotism* would be the best hope for a mature and sustainable democracy.[3] Here the problem takes this form: Could any set of institutional arrangements, however rational and just, really plug into libidinal structures of the self with the same peremptory authority as the claims of *nation* and *people*? Could they command our loyalty or solicit our desire?

If the answer is no, does that mean we are doomed forever to slide back from the political aspiration to a civilised democracy into the pre-political loyalties of nationalism and ethnic exclusivism? It is easy to sympathise with Habermas's desperate concern, writing in Germany during the throes of reunification, to challenge traditional versions of identity. He makes a powerful case for a post-traditional identity which exists 'only in the method of the public, discursive battle around the interpretation of a constitutional patriotism made concrete under particular historical circumstances.'[4] Here Habermas shows his determination to pre-empt the re-emergence of any idea of Germany as a community of fate. Membership of a cultural or ethnic community should never be the grounds for having or not having rights. No one should be disbarred from having rights. Constitutional patriotism, as expressed in the discursive battle to defend and proliferate rights, would be the measure of citizens' commitment to that principle.

The trouble with Habermas's formulation is that his horror of traditional identity leads him to conflate different questions about citizenship that are better kept apart. One is the question of who, under particular historical circumstances, does and does not bear the rights entailed by full membership of the state. That is, *who are* citizens – and, by the same token, who are not? A second question concerns individuals' self-understanding as belonging to a collectivity. This comes closest to my question, *who is* the citizen? Habermas narrows it down, though, or, rather, wants a sociological answer to a philosophical question. What he wants to know is, what would it be like to be a post-traditional citizen of a reunified German state? I would prefer to separate this aspect out as a third question. This concerns the *practice* of citizenship understood as the formation of opinion and the self-definition of a community within civil society. In other words, *what are* citizens? What do people *do* when they are being citizens?

Almost as if recognising that the notion of constitutional patriotism is incoherent, Habermas insists in principle on the need to distinguish between *demos*, the political sovereignty of the people, and *ethnos*, filiation to an imagined cultural community. The conundrum is whether *civic* identity, the membership of this or that state, can ever be extricated from *national* identity, self-recognition as a member of a *nation* state. In his book on *Citizenship and Nationhood in France and Germany*, Rogers Brubaker suggests that history gives a thumbs down. 'The politics of citizenship today,' Brubaker concludes, 'is first and foremost a politics of nationhood. As such, it is a *politics of identity*, not a *politics of interest* (in the restricted, materialist sense).'[5] He contrasts the French and German traditions of citizenship and nationhood. In the former, since even before the Revolution, the nation has been understood politically, in relation to the institutional and territorial frame of the state. Even so, this political and secular conception has still had cultural implications. The cost of universal citizenship is always and inevitably cultural assimilation. A unitary state cannot tolerate alternative centres of value legitimation and loyalty.[6]

In Germany, on the other hand, the nation emerged out of a cultural nationalist aspiration to define and embody the specificity and destiny of a *Volk*.

> Since national feeling developed before the nation-state, the German idea of the nation was not originally political, nor was it linked to the abstract idea of citizenship. This prepolitical German nation, this nation in search of a state, was conceived not as the bearer of universal political values, but as an organic cultural, linguistic, or racial community – as an irreducibly particular *Volksgemeinschaft*. On this understanding, nationhood is an ethnocultural, not a political fact.[7]

Habermas is, of course, entirely aware of these histories, and his argument is only partly that the Germans need to be a bit more like the French. More fundamentally, he tries to cut through Brubaker's citizenship/ethnicity knot by arguing for a sense of identity that should forever be up for grabs in the 'daily plebiscite' of democracy. This is his attempt to reanimate the virtues and disciplines of the republican city. The reflexivity of its citizens, and the evanescence and instability of any consensus, are what, for him, makes an identity post-traditional. Such identity is not handed down from the past, but constantly scrutinised, challenged and remade here and now.

Although that sense of democracy as a noisy, fractious, and routine negotiation is both attractive and persuasive, why does part of me remain unconvinced? The answer probably lies in my O. Henryish nosiness. Habermas asks the question, what bonds will be both democratic and effective in tying the legitimate members of the state to its constitution? His answer provokes in me a different question: Where might I find a post-traditional democratic state-citizen and how would I recognise her? Habermas is still trying to give the legal *status* of citizenship a cultural *identity*, even though this post-traditional identity will supposedly have had all traces of ethnicity bleached out of it. He knows that *Gesellschaft* is all there is or should be, but he still wants it to feel like *Gemeinschaft*.

Although Habermas tries to break the equation of state-membership with ethnic identity, he does not ask the prior question. Must bearing the rights and obligations of state-membership necessarily entail a cultural identity, whether traditional *or non-traditional*? Does it not make more sense to argue that, on the contrary, the very principle of universality inherent in the idea of citizenship means that this status cannot be colonised by any claim to define it in cultural terms? The premise would then be that 'the citizen' can have no substantial identity. Intuitively, that matches my own experience of the status as citizen making little impact on any sense of identity. More importantly, it suggests a stronger political and theoretical argument. The position of the citizen *must not* have a substance. Any claim to identify citizenship in terms of cultural identity – even, I would say, the identity of post-traditional constitutional patriotism – undermines democratic popular sovereignty and the rights of citizenship by drawing a line separating those who are members of this political community from those who are not.

My argument is therefore that 'the citizen' should be understood in the first instance not as a type of person (whether German nationalist or constitutional patriot) but as a position in the set of formal relations defined by democratic sovereignty. Just as 'I' denotes a position in a set of linguistic relations, an empty position which makes my unique utterances possible but which can equally be occupied by anyone, so 'the citizen' too denotes an empty space. It too can, in principle, be occupied by anyone – occupied in the sense of being spoken from, not in the sense of being given a substantial identity.

To say that (for example) only white male property owners can be citizens is therefore like saying that (for example) only people six foot two in height with green eyes and a red beard can speak from the position 'I'. That is why Slavoj Zizek equates 'the subject of democracy' with 'the Cartesian subject in all its abstraction, the empty punctuality we reach after subtracting all its particular contents.'

> . . . there is a structural homology between the Cartesian procedure of radical doubt that produces the *cogito*, an empty point or reflective self-reference as a remainder, and the preamble of every democratic proclamation 'all people *without regard to* (race, sex, religion, wealth, social status).' We should not fail to notice the violent act of abstraction at work in this 'without regard to'; it is an abstraction of all positive features, a dissolution of all substantial, innate links, which produces an entity strictly correlative to the Cartesian *cogito* as a point of pure, nonsubstantial subjectivity.[8]

Rather than fill the position of citizenship (or the subject of democracy) with a post-traditional content, as Habermas does, I would follow Zizek and insist on the substancelessness of citizenship. The logic is, in part, that the universality of rights should be instituted as a regulative ideal in the daily plebiscite of democracy, even if that ideal cannot be realised in practice. This move has, of course, often been criticised by Marxists and feminists. They dismiss the idea of a desirable but unachievable universality as an alibi for ignoring, or even colluding in, actual inequalities and domination. Their scepticism is neither surprising nor ill-founded. Hypothetical green eyes and red beards are not at stake: the oppression and exploitation suffered by real people in the real world are. It seems indecent, almost perverse, to worry about democracy always being a formal link between abstract subjects, instead of righting such wrongs.[9] So why is it important nonetheless?

My case is that it is only the *symbolic* relationship between subjects instituted by the category of rights that makes it possible to mediate the social relations between people through the third term of Law. Even if any and all actually existing laws were to inscribe inequalities of race, gender, class, age or whatever, *still* I would say that it remains essential to retain this principle of Law. Only this makes it possible to articulate the needs of oppressed or exploited groups and individuals as demands or claims. Only Law makes it possible for their wrongs to be assessable as injustices. That is absolutely not to say that the laws in an imperfect world will guarantee that social disputes will be arbitrated justly. Of course not. It is to insist, however, that the absence of the principle of Law leaves only the clash of forces, the assertion of power, and no hope of anything else. It is only the principle of universality inherent in citizenship (and so its *identitylessness*) that makes it possible to articulate the fact of a denial of rights or an exclusion from state membership as an injustice that demands redress. It creates the perspective from which (for example) the injuries of patri-archal domination can be discerned, identified as contrary to declared rights, and so called to account. It defines the space, not the substance, of the *res publica*.

Having established that democratic relations have their basis in a symbolic order, I can now rephrase my doubts about Habermas. Even though he wants to displace ethnic identity in favour of loyalty to a constitution, Habermas's new version of rational patriotism and provisional identity still envisages an *imaginary* identification. To experience yourself as a constitutional patriot would be to recognise yourself in a constitutional patriotic interpellation: 'Yes, that state-citizen is me!' The underlying question in Habermas's daily plebiscite would still be, 'Who are we?' I agree with Claude Lefort. It is the wrong question. What matters is less the imaginary identity of the citizen, than the *symbolic* order of citizenship rights. Democracy is founded on '*the legitimacy of a debate as to what is legitimate and what is illegitimate* – a debate which is necessarily without any guarantor and without any end.'[10]

The citizen as empty space or as pure Cartesian *cogito* may seem a pretty anaemic answer to the question, 'who is the citizen?' But it drives home one point: that the status of citizenship is contingent on an operative symbolic order that needs to be distinguished from any claims to a cultural identity for the citizen. To *become* a citizen is therefore to become a subject within this symbolic order, to be subjected to it, just as we are forced to take up the empty space of 'I' when we become speaking subjects.[11] This citizen-subject has no identity other than that produced by the Law. That is not to say that subjectivity is merely a facsimile of the Law. On the contrary, assigned identities are transformed and recreated as individuals negotiate the Law's play of power. But it is the lack of any primordial identity that produces the *need for identification*: 'the subject attempts to fill out its constitutive lack by means of identi-fication, by identifying itself with some master-signifier guaranteeing its place in the symbolic network.'[12]

This fantasy structure of identification shows why citizenship inevitably becomes enmeshed with questions of national belonging and communal self-definition. Without question, Brubaker is right to see one history of citizenship as the history of parties, sects and movements attempting to occupy the empty place of popular sovereignty, to give community a fixed and exclusive identity, to speak for and through the citizen. On the other hand, teasing out the logic of the connection between the symbolic and the imaginary as I have, explains how the desire for identification is produced, but without reducing either the symbolic order of citizen-ship or the habits and rhetorics it generates to the absolutism of identity politics. The desire for identification means that politics is centrally concerned with the *question* of community and publicness. Politics is about the always-to-be-achieved construction of a bounded yet heterogeneous, unstable and necessarily antagonistic 'we'.[13]

MASKS

Some obvious questions follow from this. How does the symbolic relation of citizenship get translated into the imaginary, and so culturally differentiated, identities of everyday life? If the subject of democratic citizenship is the substanceless *cogito*, how can citizens actually make an appearance in the urban forum of public life? How does the political question of community relate to the creation of an identity in the social interactions of the city? Descartes himself gives us at least a clue about the nature of a public self. In his earliest extant jotting, he wrote:

> Actors, taught not to let any embarrassment show on their faces, put on a mask. I will do the same. So far, I have been a spectator in this theatre which is the world, but I am now about to mount the stage, and I come forward masked.[14]

Descartes, presumably, was referring to the need to take up a position within discourse in order to participate in philosophical debate. Nevertheless, it is striking how frequently the metaphors of drama and masquerade recur in attempts to capture the nature of selfhood and citizenship in metropolitan life.

In his famous Huxley Memorial Lecture of 1938, the anthropologist Marcel Mauss sketched a history of 'the notion of person' and 'the notion of "self" ' as 'a category of the human mind.' The central argument is that the structure of personality we experience as the most fundamental and the most psychologically implacable fact of life is not a biological given. It is contingent. It has a history. Mauss therefore looks beyond cultural identities to their subjective conditions of existence. In a profoundly radical turn, he tells a story of how the various elements in our specific organisation of 'being a person' were set in place.

He starts in ancient Rome, with the original meaning of *persona*. It was, literally, a mask. Mauss sees 'the person' as the bearer of status and responsibilities beginning to emerge as the word's meaning expanded to incorporate the roles legitimately allowed to the wearer of a given mask and the bearer of a given name. In doing so, he claims, the category of the person became 'a fundamental fact of law'.[15] This turns on its head a common-sense assumption, as well as a Rawlsian fiction. These picture an original or pre-social state consisting of people, or persons, who would naturally seek to satisfy their various needs and desires. Only secondarily, as a calculated strategy to mitigate the dangers of this state descending into a war of all against all, would Law have emerged as a means of mediation and arbitration, as a codification of individual rights and mutual obligations. Mauss does not believe this scenario of persons first and Law second. Roman law not only defined but *produced* the category of the person. The person emerges as an effective entity when individuals were ascribed an identity in terms of membership of a family or clan, and then, on that basis, were granted the right to a say in the forum of politics. It was through this move that the *personal* character of the law was instituted. Equally, however, in this moment of its inception, the symbolic institution of personhood was engendered by, and has always remained contingent on, the existence of a particular legal and political order.

Being a person was not yet perceived to be a universal attribute of humanity, let alone experienced as a psychological reality. It was a status defined by law, ascribed to some and not to others in a ritual of naming, and enacted through a public dramaturgy of citizenship. (To underline the non-essential nature of the category, people who were slaves could not be persons, whereas, before the law, corporations and religious institutions could be.) The name and status that betokened personhood were of their nature exterior. This mask did not hide the true identity of its wearer. It declared who and what they were, and so made public discourse possible. It provided a role and bestowed the right to speak. Whether the performance entailed any characteristic sense of an inner life, it is impossible to know. We need not assume that it did, and it would certainly be wrong to suppose that it would have been experienced as an innate personality or an ethical substance moulded or repressed by the demands of citizenship.

That modern sense of self, for Mauss, only began to be appear with the rise of Christianity. First, a moral sense of personhood was added to the legal and political definition, 'a sense of a conscious, independent, autonomous, free, responsible being'.[16] To act as a person meant less putting on your mask of identity and performing a public role than searching your private conscience. Second, in the transition from the idea of man invested with a status to the notion of Man as a being with an ulterior inner nature, Christianity ascribed to personhood a new universality, a universal structure of individuation defined by the relationship between each person and a personal God.[17]

Read in this context, what is the significance of Descartes' image of a detached, observing, interior self emerging, masked and doubting, onto the stage of an exterior, discursive, public world? It suggests the final twist in Mauss's history: the emergence of the modern *category of the self*. In a slow but dramatic evolution, personhood no longer consists in the mask. It now exists as that abstracted position of ethical apperception which *lies behind* the public mask. Or rather, it appears to lie behind. It is in fact created retrospectively by the masquerade, yet as if it were not only topologically behind but temporally prior to the mask. Mauss ends by linking this modernisation of the self to Kant and Fichte. For Kant, individual consciousness was the sacred basis of Practical Reason. For Fichte, the 'ego' was the precondition of consciousness and science, of Pure Reason. Then, in an intriguing, almost throwaway conclusion, Mauss again picks up the intricate links between the psychological interiority of modern personhood and the socio-symbolic structures of citizenship. 'Since that time,' Mauss observes, 'the revolution in our mentalities has been achieved, we each have our own "self" or ego, *an echo of the Declarations of Rights which preceded Kant and Fichte.*'[18]

THE SUBJECT OF THE ENLIGHTENMENT

Mauss's assertion has itself been echoed by Etienne Balibar. Balibar too sees 1789 and the *Declaration of the Rights of Man* as marking a rupture from which there emerged a new category of subjectivity – a category which only makes sense in terms of the revolutionary citizen.

Although the *Declaration* proclaims the rights *of man*, Balibar sees them as being really the rights of man *as citizen*. The objective of the *Declaration* is the constitution of citizenship, but now a citizenship that demands not absolute loyalty and obedience to the monarch (subjection) but a new capacity for self-determined agency (subjectification) and so new forms of intersubjective *and* intrasubjective relationships. Democratic sovereignty requires a symbolic equality between all citizens, because all citizens are the nominal source of its authority, as well as being subject to that authority. The *sovereign equality* of democratic authority thus institutes citizenship as a certain kind of freedom, and anchors this liberty not in a relationship to God but in the nature of Man. The privileged civic freedoms and equality of antiquity, embodied in rights and roles granted by law, give way to an understanding of equality and freedom as natural and universal. When Rousseau proclaims that 'Man was born free, but he is everywhere in chains', he is asserting that freedom and equality are innate attributes whose denial is not only an injustice, but an affront to nature. The symbolic order of rights and the modern sense of a self embodied in an inner voice of nature are each a condition of the other's existence.

So the question ceases to be, as it would have been in ancient Rome, and continues to be in the formulation of nationality laws and immigration policies, Who is a citizen? (or: Who are citizens?). For Balibar, concerned with the production of subjectivity, the question now is, *Who is the citizen?*

> The answer is: The citizen is a man in enjoyment of all his 'natural' rights, completely realising his individual humanity, a free man simply because he is equal to every other man. This answer (or this new question in the form of an answer) will also be stated, after the fact: *The citizen is the subject*, the citizen is always a *supposed subject* (legal subject, psychological subject, transcendental subject).[19]

By a different, more historical route, Balibar reaches the same conclusion as Zizek. The citizen is the *cogito*; the citizen is the subject. But Balibar's gloss on this pure, nonsubstantial subjectivity emphasises less its emptiness than its perennial deferral. The citizen is always *becoming-a-subject* (*devenir-sujet*). The possibility of action is now mediated through a new sense of a primordial but incomplete self, the sense of a self in need of completion that is manifested in a psychic life of need, desire and guilt. To be a person now entails the remorseless aspiration to self-knowledge, self-expression, and self-fulfilment. The status, the rights, and the responsibilities of citizenship come to be experienced as somehow constitutive of a sense of self, as subjective.

But (to repeat) they are not experienced or recognised as an identity. On the contrary, it is the traumatic lack of fit between the impulses of a supposed inner nature and the demands of an external reality – their necessary non-identity – that produces the characteristically modern sense of the self as divided and incomplete. Schiller's *On the Aesthetic Education of Man* (1791), for example, articulates the romantic conception of this split as an opposition between natural feeling and 'all-dividing Intellect'.

> It was civilisation itself which imposed this wound upon modern man. Once the increase of empirical knowledge, and more exact modes of thought, made sharper divisions between the sciences inevitable, and once the increasingly complex machinery of State necessitated a more rigorous separation of ranks and occupations, then the inner unity of human nature was severed too, and a disastrous conflict set its harmonious powers at variance.[20]

At first sight this may sit oddly with Balibar's definition of the citizen subject as a person 'completely realising his individual humanity'. Remember, though, that Balibar sees this not as an achieved state of wholeness, but as the process of unendingly *becoming* a subject. That superficially paradoxical notion of the subject becoming a subject is vital. Taking up a position within the symbolic, because it is to occupy a necessarily empty position which makes it possible to articulate need as desire, always entails a sense of loss. It produces the sense of subjectivity as *lack* that motivates the compulsion to heal the wound of modern culture, the drive to recreate a harmony or fullness that feel as though they must once have existed.

If you want to hear that foundational myth of modern selfhood voiced with unrivalled vivacity and paranoid conviction, and to see how that myth is inextricably bound up with the question of the city, then you need only listen to Jean-Jacques Rousseau. Rousseau above all proclaimed the self to be the locus of a primordial nature, one subjugated to society but guided by a conscience which still 'speaks to us in the language of nature'.[21] That voice, he believed, can all too easily be drowned out by the noise of society, and especially by the babble and chatter of the city. The least worst city would therefore be the one which allows the nearest alignment of its codified principles of justice (Law) to the demands of nature (Conscience). It would allow a degree of authenticity in interpersonal relations, without disavowing the necessary deformation of the natural self entailed by the subject's entry into society. The artifice and theatricality of the city were to be deplored because they were incompatible with this striving for subjective authenticity. Not only did they lead to the corruption of morals and culture (*moeurs*), they were against nature. The question for politics was not just how to arbitrate between the public good and selfish hedonism, but, given the intractable conflict between nature and society, how to create good citizens.

In making the link between the public conventions, codes, and conducts of cities and the subjective repertoire of action and self-understanding available to citizens, Rousseau (as Richard Sennett reminded us in *The Fall of Public Man*) was one of the most insightful and probing early theorists of urbanism.[22] Yet he despised the cosmopolitanism of Paris, and the way that here people disguised their true natures as a matter of course. What he really could not stand was the impossibility of knowing for sure who is a citizen and who is a man about town.

> The men to whom one speaks are not at all those with whom one communicates. Their sentiments do not come from their hearts, their insight is not in their character, their speech does not represent their thoughts. Of them only their appearance is perceived, . . . Until now I have seen a great many masks; when shall I see the faces of men?[23]

His moral repugnance at the masquerade of the big city was no mere metaphor. Rousseau's most sustained assault on cosmopolitanism and his most passionate defence of a strict civic republicanism were provoked by the Encyclopaedist d'Alembert's suggestion that Geneva would benefit from having a theatre.

D'Alembert's argument was that civilised behaviour could be learned from the pedagogic example of theatrical performances. To Rousseau, the very thought was absurd and disgusting. The artifice evident in the performances of men (and especially women) about town – let alone the morals of actors and actresses! – implied not refinement but corruption. The presentation of self in the cosmopolitan world of Paris did not allow an interior nature to express itself. It was an obstacle to open intersubjective relationships. In this drama, honesty and authenticity were sacrificed for the tawdry prize of reputation.

> In a big city, full of scheming, idle people without religion or principle, whose imagination, depraved by sloth, inactivity, the love of pleasure, and great needs, engenders only monsters and inspires only crimes; in a big city, . . . *moeurs* and honour are nothing because each, easily hiding his conduct from the public eye, shows himself only by his reputation . . .[24]

To dispel this opacity and illegibility of others, Rousseau wanted to render social relations transparent. He would have liked all office holders to wear badges or emblems denoting their rank of position, so that at least there could be no doubt about *what* they were.[25] In the big city, he fretted, how can you know *who* strangers really are if you cannot take their courtesies, or even intimacies, at face value?

> People meet me full of friendship; they show me a thousand civilities; they render me services of all sorts. But that is precisely what I am complaining of. How can you become immediately the friend of a man whom you have never seen before? The true human interest, the plain and noble effusion of an honest soul – these speak a language far different from the insincere demonstrations of politeness (and the false appearances) which the customs of the great world demand.[26]

It was to counteract the city's masquerade of false appearances that Rousseau was willing to endorse the imposition of a quite tyrannical transparency. Every citizen should forever be subject to the surveillance of government, to the gossip of women's circles, and to the inner voice of conscience. In an exemplary republican small town like Geneva, 'the authorities have everyone under their eye.' Paradoxically, because 'individuals are always in the public eye, critics of one another from birth', they are freed from the pressure of 'public opinion' and so are better able to develop and grow.[27] Stripped of the masks of fashion, artifice, and anonymity, people are forced back on their natural inner resources, and this provides a more fertile soil for the cultivation of good citizens.

This, then, was the Rousseauian dream of a transparency of the self to the self and to others that revolutionised European politics.

> It was the dream of a transparent society, visible and legible in each of its parts, the dream of there no longer existing any zones of darkness, zones established by the privileges of royal power or the prerogatives of some corporation, zones of disorder. It was the dream that each individual, whatever position he occupied, might be able to see the whole of society, that men's hearts should communicate, their vision be unobstructed by obstacles, and that opinion of all reign over each.[28]

Foucault is no doubt right in this assessment of how Rousseau's will to transparency is related to the new phenomenon of governmentality. Techniques of surveillance, a pastoral concern with the capacities of a population, and the force of public opinion all helped to shape the social and political terrain of the nineteenth-century city.

And yet, despite the tendency to totalitarianism in the fantasy of absolute transparency, it would be wrong to see only the infancy of Big Brother (or Le Corbusier) in Rousseau's response to the city. For, contradictorily, and no doubt despite himself, Rousseau was also a man about town. However vehemently he denounces Paris and lauds Geneva, the story he tells in the *Confessions* is of a callow youth who leaves an emotionally and intellectually stifling provincial town, acquires his sentimental education through a series of adventures, and eventually makes his name in the capital city. Isn't this the blueprint for the *Bildungsroman* narrative of the nineteenth century? And doesn't it therefore entail a different image of the metropolis? Artificial and illegible it may be, but for many a young fictional hero, as for Rousseau, the big city offered a field of liberating possibilities. Here were the urbane pleasures of squares and cafés, the chance encounters with strangers, the frisson of amorous adventure and political intrigue, the opportunity to make your reputation in the community of letters or the world of theatre. Its anonymity could be cruel, its dark zones could harbour hidden dangers, but the city at least allowed the space for self-formation and self-creation, for experimentation and change.

Reading the *Confessions* is like riding a roller coaster, as Rousseau recounts his triumphs, his real or imagined slights, and his farcical and often self-inflicted humiliations. Could it be that these extraordinary vicissitudes are symptomatic of the way that Rousseau acted out, in all its ambivalence, the uneasy relationship between the citizen and the man about town? Each is a characteristically modern type, and each is by definition an urban type. But each seeks to heal or salve the wound of civilisation in a different way. The citizen, not without pain and sacrifice, embraces the ascetic comforts of civic virtue as a means to psychologically authentic personal relations. The man about town pursues a different, though not necessarily less demanding ethic: the increasingly aesthetic cultivation – and perhaps creation – of the self. Rousseau unquestionably committed himself, morally and intellectually, to the former. By the end of the nineteenth century, however, his idea of a primordial inner nature had to a significant degree been superseded by a new sense of interiority: not now a nature deformed by society, but the only defensible space of an authenticity threatened with obliteration.

MODERN MAN

An apparently trivial example can illustrate this shift. It is the question of how a man should dress about town. By his own admission, Rousseau was a slob. Typically, though, he defended his slobbishness in ethical terms. Excessive ornament and non-functional adornment – or 'garishness of dress' – he found not only offensive but inconvenient. It cramped his style. 'In order to retain all possible liberty, when I am among other men, I would want to be dressed in such a way that in every rank, I appeared to be in my place, and that I did not stand out in any,' he declared. 'In this way I would be more the master of my conduct, and I would put the pleasures of all stations always within my reach.'[29] Although this deliberate opaqueness in his own case may appear inconsistent with the transparency he would impose on others, it points forward to a later, modernist presentation of the masculine self. By 1908, for the Viennese architect Alfred Loos, Rousseau's eccentricity had become a norm.

> The person who runs around in a velvet suit is no artist but a buffoon or merely a decorator. We have become more refined, more subtle. Primitive men had to differentiate themselves by the use of various colours, modern man needs his clothes as a mask. His individuality is so strong that he cannot

express it any longer by his clothing. The lack of ornament is a sign of intellectual power. Modern man . . . concentrates his own power of invention on other things.[30]

These 'other things' concern less the display of rank or reputation than the defensive cultivation of an inner authenticity. Here we are in Simmel's mental landscape of the metropolis. For modern man, in contrast to Rousseauian man, the battle as Simmel sees it is to 'preserve the autonomy and individuality of his existence in the face of overwhelming social forces', to resist 'being levelled down and worn out by a social-technological mechanism.'[31]

The result of this conflict, suggests Simmel, was a hyper-inflation of individualism. Modern man dedicates his power of invention to hiding his sense of an interior, intimate self from the world. The Roman mask of identity and distinction has long disappeared. Now a mask of anonymity conceals difference and so guards a sense of identity.[32] For Simmel and Loos and other modernist men about town, a commonplace exterior is an aesthetic tactic which deflects the force of all the imposed technologies and narratives of the self.

> The commonplace is good form in society. . . . It is bad taste to make oneself conspicuous through some individual, singular expression. . . . Obedience to the standards of the general public in all externals [is] the conscious and desired means of reserving their personal feelings and their taste.[33]

'How should one dress?' asks Loos. 'Modern,' he answers. And that means creating an unreadable surface. 'One is modernly dressed when one stands out the least.' Loos takes Nietzsche's view that it is the 'remarkable antithesis between an interior which fails to correspond to any exterior and an exterior which fails to correspond to any interior' which makes modern man modern. The masks of public life are no longer either mimetic or indexical. 'No one dares to appear as he is, but masks himself as a cultivated man, as a scholar, as a politician. . . . Individuality has withdrawn within: from without it has become invisible.'[34]

Loos followed this logic of interiority through to his architecture. Houses should be like men about town. Their outsides should present an inconspicuous face to the world, as standardised as dinner jackets. 'The house does not have to tell anything to the exterior,' he insisted; 'instead, all its richness must be manifest in the interior.'[35] Inside, all the lines of sight were directed into the house, not out onto the city. His windows were often opaque or curtained. Sofas stood with their backs resolutely to windows.

This turning away from the world, or turning inward to the domestic interior, Simmel again explained in terms of the essential defensiveness of style. Surrounding yourself with the fashionable accessories of the *Jugendstil*, because it was at once personal and shared with a wider taste community, provided 'a counterbalance and a cloak' for 'the exaggerated subjectivism of the times.' The obsessive stylisation of the domestic interior was less a means of self-expression that a symptom of self-protection.

> What impels people so strongly toward style is the unburdening and masking of the personality that is the essence of style. Subjectivism and individuality have accelerated almost to breaking point and in the stylised creations of form

Adolf Loos, Moller
house, Vienna
(Graphische
Sammlung Albertina,
Vienna)

Adolf Loos, House
for the Vienna
Werkbundsiedlung,
1930–32 (Graphische
Sammelung
Albertina, Vienna)

. . . there lies a tempering and toning down of this extreme individuality into something general and more universal.[36]

Modern man exercises his power of invention less in a dandyism than in the cultivation of an interior world. This is not just a *private* world, but one that carries a newly charged sense of *intimacy*. It is evident not only in the style of your room, but above all in the world of the psyche.

In his essay on 'Fashion', Simmel uses an image that echoes Loos's dictum that 'all the richness must be manifest in the interior.' 'Over an old Flemish house,' he remarks, 'there stands the mystical inscription: There is more within me.'[37] The implication is that behind the mask of masculine anonymity, just as behind the facade of the house, there lies complexity, depth, and plenitude. The mask, like the obsession with domestic style, represents a phobic reaction against the hyperactivity and overstimulation of the modern metropolis. Take it off and you will find the real man. But, of course, this is where we came in – with O. Henry's joke that there's no there behind the image. Ego is always and only imaginary, formed in the play of display and reflection in public life.

A cynic might therefore see modern man's clothes as a not-so-subtle piece of advertising. Even if gorgeous excess has given way to the surrealist insouciance of Magritte's suit and bowler hat or the demotic semiotics of Gap, that ordinary sartorial exterior is now presented as the promise of extraordinary richness within. In that sense, men's clothing remains a display of authority. This is the double bluff of modern masculinity: the assertion of authority through its manifest disavowal. We need no badges of office or pompous uniforms, we protest disdainfully. The only authority we claim is the authenticity of who we really are. But that authority, however ironic, however austere, is an imposture nonetheless. The phallus is still a fraud. 'If the penis was the phallus, men would have no need of feathers or ties or medals,' comments the Lacanian analyst Eugénie Lemoine-Luccioni. She may be wrong about the style, but her inference is valid. 'Display [*parade*], just like the [feminine] masquerade, thus betrays a flaw: no one has the phallus.'[38]

Is the argument that the modern man about town gets his new clothes from the same tailor as the Emperor? Not quite, because that would again suggest that when you strip away the clothes you find the real man, however puny he may be. On this I agree with Lacan. The ego is nothing but 'the superimposition of various coats borrowed from the bric-a-brac of its props department.'[39] Beneath the man about town's clothes is *nothing*. But, despite that, this masculinity is not quite a confidence trick. This nothing is once again the necessary nothing we keep coming up against, the abstraction that is the subject, the empty space that makes appearance, conduct, and consciousness possible. Being a citizen, being a man about town, being a person – these are not identities, they are performances.

Now, of course, such performances are fundamentally implicated in logics of sexual differentiation. That is why the metaphor of masquerade has been used primarily in recent years to theorise the experience of being a woman in a man's town. Writers from Lacan onwards have taken up Joan Riviere's assertion in the late nineteen twenties that womanliness and the masquerade 'whether radical or superficial . . . are the same thing' in order to explain the excessive or fetishistic or parodic nature of feminine self-presentation. Masquerade, they suggest, embraces the dislocation between subjectivity and role, and the performativity of the gendered ego.[40] The comparative latitude of ego as performance, and so the possibilities of cross-dressing

August Sander,
Cologne, 1927
(Rheinisches
Bildarchiv, Museen
der Start Köln)

Walker Evans,
Havana, 1932
(Walker Evans
Archive,
Metropolitan
Museum of Art, New
York)

and other subversive tactics, have been seized on as ways to undermine the tendency to essentialism in the notion of identity.

What might this perspective mean for the notion of the woman about town, and also for both women and men as citizens?

THE CITIZEN AND THE WOMAN ABOUT TOWN

Many solutions have by now been offered to the intriguing Case of the Elusive *Flâneuse*. There was no such person, say some who have tried to find her. There was such a person, say others, but previous investigators like Kracauer and Benjamin either did not notice her or chose not to talk about her. Or, there was such a person, but her identity was mistaken and she was looked for in the wrong place. The modern woman about town appeared less often as a cross-dressing *flâneur* than as a shopper, an artist, a philanthropist, a suffragist, or (during a craze of the eighteen nineties) as a bicyclist. She was to be found in the department stores, the great exhibitions, the art galleries and public libraries, the parks and promenades, and in the tea-rooms, restaurants and hotels which defined a new type of public space. And, it has been suggested, we should have been looking here in the first place. These liminal spaces constituted a new public arena, one less clearly distinguished from the private or the domestic, but one which may well have been more important in the formation of modernity than the romanticised street of the narcissistically heroic *flâneur*.[41]

Maybe the problem is different. Could it be that we are mistaking the genre? What if this is not a mystery at all, but a ghost story? Perhaps it really does not matter very much whether or not there *was* such a person, whether or not there *might* have been such a person, or even whether or not there was *supposed* to be such a person. The really perplexing question, for me, is this: why does the spectral presence of the *flâneuse* haunt the discussion? What, in any case, is at stake in this story?

First, there is a question of desire and identification. To put it bluntly, why on earth should any woman *want* to be a *flâneur*? Usually, the answer is that, quite reasonably, women (specific women, not the category woman) want to be able to walk the streets without being physically or verbally hassled, without being given the eye in an aggressive, intrusive, or demeaning way, and without it being assumed that they are a prostitute. The young Russian artist Marie Bashkirtseff is often quoted as a woman who did walk the streets of Paris in the eighteen seventies and eighties. But even she commented on the irritation of not simply being able to wander about or to make sketches without a carriage or a companion to protect her from other people in the street.

> What I long for is to be able to go out alone! To come and go; to sit down on a bench in the Garden of the Tuileries, or, better still, of the Luxembourg; to stand looking into the artistically arranged shop windows; to visit the churches and museums; to stroll through the old streets of the city in the evening.[42]

Bashkirtseff says nothing here about wanting to take on the identity of a *flâneur*, to be seen as a *flâneuse*. Women in public have (I assume) always had their own purposes and itineraries and have simply wanted to be allowed to get on with them. That wish, so far as I can see, need not entail taking on *any* imaginary identity, and certainly not that of the *flâneur*. It *does* entail at least an implicit claim to a right,

Germaine Krull,
Paris, ca. 1925 (The
J. Paul Getty
Museum, Los
Angeles)

though: the right to act in a self-chosen way, the right to be an agent, the right to walk the city streets unmolested and unchallenged.

That raises a different issue. The geographer Gillian Rose has criticised the masculinism of the geographical imagination which has, for her and many other women, turned 'the innocent transparency of the empty street' into 'an aggressive plastic lens pushing on me'.[43] Without denying the validity of that experience, what strikes me is the Rousseauian premise underlying the way it is described. In what sense could 'the street' ever be empty, or innocent, or transparent? Because it is an imaginary and visual domain, the street is always already textured with meaning. Joan Copjec spells out the theoretical rationale for turning to semiotics rather than optics in understanding such a space.

> Because it alone is capable of lending things sense, the signifier alone makes vision possible. There is and can be no brute vision, no vision totally independent of language.... And because signifiers are material, that is, because they are opaque rather than translucent, refer to other signifiers rather than directly to a signified, the field of vision is neither clear nor easily traversable. It is instead ambiguous and treacherous, full of traps.[44]

Although Copjec is here talking about the space of art rather than the space of the city, her comments clarify why a meaning-less transparency is unthinkable. City space has never been, and can never be, culturally unmarked or neutral. It is a force field charged and polarised by an avaricious and eroticised gaze which is predominantly gendered male and which is one of the less attractive things metaphorically condensed in the figure of the *flâneur*. Even if acting the man about town is itself an instance of masquerade, that does not mean that, on the streets, there are no differences between the performance of masculinity by men and the performance of femininity by women, or any creative or subversive permutation of these roles. The point is that exercising that right in an eroticised public space brings the formal equality of citizens ('*regardless of . . .*') into conflict with the imaginary reality of the mediated city. The Berlin-based critic Ulrike Scholvin encapsulates the difference for women: 'The cities into which we carry our projections in order to lose ourselves in them are blocked with images that our wishes have not produced.'[45]

From this point of view, masquerade may be seen as an imaginative performance – a performance in the register of the imaginary – which is an attempt to solve, or at least manage, a problem or an anxiety generated by the symbolic. So, what seems to be at stake in the feminist debate about *flânerie* is not only whether women have the right to walk the street, but also the fact that different women have had the imagination to walk it differently.[46] Ulrike Scholvin does not ask for the street and the city to be de-eroticised or rendered innocently transparent. On the contrary, it is the suffocation of the desire she brings to the city by a crass and bathetic sexualisation of its space and imagery that offends her. Urban eroticism also figures as a central argument in Iris Marion Young's *political* defence of the city. City life, she says, 'instantiates difference as the erotic' and offers 'the pleasure and excitement of being drawn out of one's secure routine to encounter the novel, strange, and surprising.'[47] The argument is not that that urban space be cleansed of the imaginary, nor rendered entirely risk-free. It is that risk and danger should be matters of choice and negotiation, not of careless oppression nor the penny-pinching inadequacy of street lighting or public transport.

La Notte (dir.
Michelangelo
Antonioni), 1963

What then might be the implications of this line of thought for an understanding of citizenship and of personhood? Some initial questions and possibilities present themselves. For a start, thinking back to my earlier arguments and examples, it is not hard to see that Rousseau's image of the natural self being deformed as it is forced to choose to acquiesce to the General Will of society, Schiller's image of the wound imposed by civilisation, and Freud's image of symbolic castration are all variations on a single theme. They share a model of the self being formed as alienated because subject to the authority of the symbolic, the Other – the Law Giver for Rousseau, Culture for Schiller, the Name-of-the-Father for Freud. It is this model that explains the recognition of oneself as not whole, and so the desire for identification articulated in terms of a master-signifier, and so the possibility and need for masquerade as a strategy.

Given this modern (post-Enlightenment) structure of subjectivity, we might ask what sort of masquerade citizenship is. We can also worry about how we parade the streets, or get angry that only some of us are allowed to. But I want to take a step back. I want to ask again how the empty, lacking subject of democracy enters onto the stage of the theatre which is civil society. With an intense commitment to political participation and a passionate belief in the life-and-death importance of citizenship, is often the answer from communitarians. Here is a random example of that attitude, expressed in this case by David Marquand:

> . . . the central message of civic republicanism is that the Self can develop its full potential and learn how to discharge its obligations to other selves only through action in the public realm of a free city – that politics is both a civilised and a civilising activity; that it is, indeed, the most civilised and civilising activity in which human beings can take part.[48]

Implicit in this romantic-republican ethic,[49] and sustaining its masquerade, is a fantasy scenario in which the fulfilment of the self is linked to the longed for development of society as a rational and non-conflictual community. To say that this scenario is a fantasy is not to trivialise it. But to recognise that it *is* a fantasy (understood here as the *mise-en-scène* of desire) should make it possible to examine how different ways of performing politics have been authorised for men and women, in the same way that the symbolic space of the city allows or prohibits different modes of appearing in public.

Renata Salecl takes a more radical step. She sees in the sexually differentiated masquerade of citizenship further evidence that citizenship denotes an empty place. Rather as the phantom of the *flâneuse* marks the impossibility of the *flâneur* as an identity, Salecl shows that men cannot *be* the symbolic place of citizenship any more than women can. Rather, masculine and feminine enactments of citizenship embody different ways of experiencing the impossibility of identity.

> 'Masculine' and 'feminine' are . . . the two modes of the subject's *failure* to achieve the full identity of Man. 'Man' and 'Woman' together do not form a whole, since *each of them is already in itself a failed whole.*[50]

Salecl then goes on to distinguish two logics of citizenship. The first, 'male' logic is a logic of universality. That is: 'all people have rights, with the exception of those who are excluded from this universality (for example, women, children, foreigners, etc.).' This is the logic that I described earlier, in which substantial universal rights are seen as desirable in principle, but unachievable in our fallen world – and therefore, for some, either a confidence trick or not worth bothering with. In contrast, in Salecl's 'feminine' logic, 'there is no one who does not have rights; i.e. everybody taken individually possesses rights, but precisely because of this we cannot say that people as such have rights.' These are rights without guarantees, in other words, rights that always have to be declared in the making of political community. From my perspective, this logic underlines the importance of not confusing the position of the subject with the identity of the citizen. The claim that no one should remain without rights 'means that no one can universally possess them'.[51]

That again calls into question the terms of the debate about gender and *flânerie*. At the same time it makes me wonder whether a politics of identity, understood as a claim to recognition (and support) for a self-defined group by the state, would fall within Salecl's male or feminine logic. Insofar as the assertion of collective identity as the warrant for citizenship rights is still premised on the Rousseauian logic of politics as the bridge back to this primordial identity, then I suspect the logic is male.

So how would it then be possible to imagine an emancipatory politics outside the logic of lucid self-knowledge and authentic identity? What would it mean to live without the comforting myth of self as ultimate truth?

For a start, it would mean saying yes to the inevitably fictional nature of identity and the otherness of the self. Strip away all the masks of social performance, and what will you find? Nothing unique, nothing natural, suggests Lévi-Strauss in his introduction to Mauss's work, but nonetheless a potential for action.

> Going down into the givens of the unconscious, the extension of our understanding, if I may put it thus, is not a movement towards ourselves; we reach a level which seems strange to us, not because it harbours our most secret self, but (much more normally) because, without requiring us to move outside ourselves, it enables us to coincide with forms of activity which are both at once *ours* and *other* . . .[52]

In this light, emancipation would be not the recovery or liberation of the true self, but an uncanny sense of the self as contingent. This is the experience of freedom which Gianni Vattimo aptly defines as 'a continual oscillation between belonging and disorientation'. It embraces the historicity and finiteness of subjectivity. And yet it is, genuinely, freedom. Vattimo quotes Nietzsche. It is the freedom of 'continuing to dream knowing one is dreaming.'[53]

THE CITIZEN AND THE MONSTER

What is the relationship between the citizen and the man about town? Distant kinship linked by a bond of affection, it might appear, if the opening of Robert Louis Stevenson's *Strange Case of Dr Jekyll and Mr Hyde* (1886) is anything to go by.[54] Every Sunday, that exemplary citizen, 'Mr Utterson the lawyer', and 'Mr Richard Enfield, his distant kinsman, the well-known man about town' take a stroll around London together. For both men, these largely silent walks are 'the chief jewel of each week.'

It is Enfield who gives Utterson the first account of Hyde, having witnessed him trampling over a little girl at three o'clock one morning. The memory is prompted when they notice a sinister door. Through this Enfield had seen Hyde disappear, although he fails to recognise it as the rear entrance to the home of Dr Jekyll. He knows that Hyde has some claim on Jekyll, but he cannot imagine what it is.

The man about town sees the terrible things that can happen in the city at night. But eventually it is the man of law who discovers their significance. To Utterson are entrusted the documents that allow the story to be told, and it is eventually he who breaks down the door to Jekyll's laboratory to confirm the dreadful truth. That secret is, of course, Jekyll's non-identity.

This doubling of the self suggests a less sanguine perspective on the relationship between the citizen and the man about town. The split is not between the good Jekyll and an evil Hyde. Hyde is wholly evil, it is true, but for Jekyll he embodies the wish to act the man about town more than a respectable doctor can allow himself to do. The worst of Jekyll's youthful faults had been 'a certain impatient gaiety of disposition, such as has made the happiness of many, but such as I found it hard to reconcile with my imperious desire to carry my head high, and wear a more than commonly grave countenance before the public.' Hence repression, or at least masquerade: 'I concealed my pleasures.' And hence the split already latent in Jekyll, his 'profound duplicity of life.'

Normally, such anxieties might have been displaced or projected onto the Other, onto woman.[55] In this *Strange Case*, however, there are no significant women characters. The founding anxiety of masculine sexuality is turned back on itself, and produces Hyde as the embodiment of perversion, as abjection, as the ruin of 'the very fortress of identity'. The tension between the citizen and the man about town is revealed as constitutive of modern male sexuality. Its magnetic poles are the demands of civic virtue and the hedonism of the city at night.

Twenty years or so after *Jekyll and Hyde*, in the same year that Loos commented on the defensive masquerade of modern man's clothes and Simmel wrote his essay on fashion, Freud published ' "Civilised" Sexual Morality and Modern Nervous Illness' (1908):

> Experience teaches us that for most people there is a limit beyond which their constitution cannot comply with the demands of civilisation. All who wish to be more noble-minded than their constitution allows fall victims to neurosis; they would have been more healthy if it could have been possible for them to be less good.[56]

This might prompt us to temper David Marquand's civic enthusiasm. It is also a reminder, if one were needed, that for all their historicity and contingency, structures of personality have real somatic effects. Their history is also the history of erotic compulsion and emotional disorder.

Yet it would miss the point to reduce Jekyll and Hyde to a case of 'mental illness'. Hyde *is* monstrous, and he is a thoroughly modern monster. To suggest where the Enlightenment project went wrong, Slavoj Zizek uses the analogy of the baby and the bath water. Philosophers like Rousseau wanted to get rid of all the gunk of corrupt civilisation in order to recover the healthy, unspoiled and natural infant of the ego. Not only did they manage to throw out that baby in the process. In its place, they found themselves left with a monstrous residue: all those monsters from Frankenstein's creation to George Romero's shopping mall zombies which register the 'specific dimension of the uncanny that emerges with modernity.'[57] The pure 'subject of the Enlightenment', concludes Zizek, 'is a monster which gives body to the surplus that escapes the vicious circle of the mirror relationship.'[58]

Here lies the danger of trying to fill in the empty place of subjectivity, rather than learning to live with an ego whose fugitive identities are conjured up in the inescapable play of images and reflections. The search for lucid self-knowledge or absolute self-fulfilment may unleash Hyde, what should have remained hidden. The monsters of the Enlightenment remind us why, by the same token, we should learn to respect the opacity of others. Communitarians tell us that every nook and cranny of the social body should be 'cracked open to politics' (Roberto Unger) or that the opacity of participants in social life should be dissolved (Michael Sandel).[59] Would that produce the mutual harmony and clear-sighted rationality of a Rousseauian utopia? Or are such injunctions no more than the elevation of narcissism to a political principle? The fantasy of transparency may produce monsters as much as the sleep of reason. The good citizens and zealous republicans should leave us flawed men and women about town some space.

Mariane Breslauer,
Paris, 1929
(Berlinische Galerie)

chapter 5

Fat Lady in the Cab

Imagining urban space

To imagine is to make present to my mind's eye what is absent. As I write, enervated by summer diesel smog and distracted by the noise of drilling from across the road, *imagining* the city may seem, on the face of it, a perverse and redundant activity. The city is hardly *not there*. Why do I need to imagine it?

It is because, however insistent this traffic, these buildings, and those inconsiderate bastards may be, my sense of this combination of information and effects as uniquely *urban* is mediated through the sociological, cultural and political associations discussed in previous chapters. It is these connotations that are condensed in the imaginary space of *the city*. You know what I mean about being in the city, not only because your lungs and ears have been assaulted like mine, but because you too operate with the city as a category of thought and experience. The city has come to indicate – and may actually have produced – a unique way of seeing and being. Unable to contain the unbounded spread of London, Paris, Berlin, or New York in an all-encompassing image, we recall the city through metonymic images and fleeting events. These include the stereotypes of the Eiffel Tower or the Manhattan skyline. But often we share the pragmatic urban aesthetic shown by the heroine of Virginia Woolf's *Mrs Dalloway*: 'what she loved was this, here, now, in front of her; the fat lady in the cab.'

In looking at some examples of how that urban aesthetic works, I also want to develop a further stage in my argument that 'the city' stands for, or demands, a certain style of politics which has to take account of that experiential, imaginative dimension. Here I take my motto from that most down-to-earth and iconoclastic of urban critics, Jane Jacobs: 'Designing a dream city is easy; rebuilding a living one takes imagination.'[1] Those who fantasise about turning the city into an efficient machine misrecognise not just the social relations, but the very *space* of the city. They see it as a territory to be bounded, mapped, occupied and exploited, a population to be managed and perfected. They want to render the city transparent, to get the city right, and so to produce the right citizens. This is a dream which, in disavowing them, is doomed to reproduce and repeat the anxieties, repressions, and censorships that provoke the dream. It wishes away the aggression and anxiety that are also part of urban experience. As I have already argued in previous chapters, the city is not a problem that can be solved. That is why rebuilding a living city – a city characterised by the jumbling together of multiple and conflicting differences – demands (to borrow Richard Kearney's phrase) a poetics of political imagination.[2]

How would that poetic imagining differ from the conventions of modernist planning? First, it would show a different understanding of *space*, seeing it as something other and more than a field of mathematical calculation and political instrumentalism. This imagination would be sensitive to the history of modes of mapping and representing space – the cone of vision, perspective, the plane of representation, the conventions of cartography, the simultaneism of cubism, cinematic montage, and so forth – which themselves entail different modes of subjective experience of space. It would therefore take account of what Victor Burgin, following Freud and Lacan, calls 'the history of psychical, or interior space', space as projection and introjection.[3] This is the *living* space of the city.

Where and how might this living space exist? In Doris Lessing's novel *The Four-Gated City* (1969), the protagonist, Martha Quest, is a Marxist intellectual recently arrived in the London of the 1950s from what was then Rhodesia. Martha Quest is no Le Corbusier, but she tends to see London in the conventional political and aesthetic terms of the time, as socially deprived and ugly. For Iris, however, a local woman with whom Martha is staying, the neighbourhood is a palimpsest, textured and animated by layers of history and memory.

> Iris, Joe's mother . . . knew everything about this area, half a dozen streets for about half a mile or a mile of their length; and she knew it all in such detail that when with her, Martha walked in a double vision, as if she were two people: herself and Iris, one eye stating, denying, warding off the total hideousness of the whole area, the other, with Iris, knowing it in love. With Iris, one moved here, in a state of love, if love is the delicate but total acknowledgement of what is. . . . Iris, Joe's mother, had lived in this street since she was born. Put her brain, together with the other million brains, women's brains, that recorded in such tiny loving anxious detail the histories of windowsills, skins of paint, replaced curtains and salvaged baulks of timber, there would be a recording instrument, a sort of six-dimensional map which included the histories and lives and loves of people, London – a section map in depth. This is where London exists.

This should not be read as a sentimental celebration of secure feminine identity grounded in working-class community. Nor is the London cityscape simply there to connect *The Four-Gated City* to a specific geographical location at a specific historical time, the cultural setting within which the novel's action can take place.[4] In describing Iris's mundane spatial projection and introjection of desire and anxiety, Lessing hints at something uncanny in urban space. J Hillis Miller calls this the atopical.

> This is a place that is everywhere and nowhere, a place you cannot get to from here. Sooner or later, . . . the effort of mapping is interrupted by an encounter with the unmappable. The topography and the toponymy . . . hide an unplaceable place. It was the locus of an event that never 'took place' as a phenomenal happening located in some identifiable spot and therefore open to knowledge. This strange event that took place without taking place cannot be the object of a cognition because it was a unique performative event. This

strange locus is another name for the ground of things, the preoriginal ground
of the ground, something other to any activity of mapping.[5]

This is a difficult argument, but Miller's phenomenology of space offers some
clues that I shall pursue in my attempt to understand how we imagine the city.
Almost paradoxically, he suggests that we cannot imagine space as such. What we
imagine, he suggests, is always an event or events taking place. Our imagination is
inherently narrative. Space is less the already existing setting for such stories, than
the constitution of space through that *taking place*, through the act of narration. What,
then, is the nature of these space-producing events? Do they simply map spaces or
represent events? Not really, suggests Miller. Rather, they project events onto space.
To gloss Lefebvre's concept of representational space, they generate a narrational
space.[6]

Narratives about cities imagine events taking place in an urban topography. They
conjure up the space of the city through the projection of these narrative images:
Woolf's fat lady in the cab, for example. It is in this sense that the real to which they
refer is atopical. The events narrated did not take place, or not like that, although
their effect is real enough. (Think of Toon Town in *Who Framed Roger Rabbit?*) Such
narratives are therefore best thought of as 'potent speech acts'. Imagined cityscapes,
suggests Miller, 'have to do with doing rather than knowing.'[7] This pedagogy of the
symbolised city is at work as much in films, novels, and poetry as it is in architectural
plans and political programmes. Equally, though, the atopical – the strange event
which never took place and yet which generates representation – is to be found at
the heart of the most rationalistic urban utopia.

Hillis Miller links the atopical to the non-transparency of social relations and the
obscurity of the self to the self. This opacity is also bound up – this is the second
point of difference from planners' dreaming – with a particular imagining of *time*.
Planners and urban sociologists tend to operate with a pretty straightforward view of
time. Recollections of past cities either define the problem that is to be solved (if you
are Le Corbusier) or offer a nostalgic route to salvation (if you are Prince Charles).
Whether you are Le Corbusier or Prince Charles, the present is presented as pretty
awful, as a failure of the will to change and/or as a fall from grace. Plans for the future
represent not only a programme for action, or a prediction of what tomorrow's city
will look like, but another potent speech act designed to bring that perfect future
into being. Put like that, it is clear that we are not dealing with a past of memory, a
present of description, and a future of imagination and planning. The past exists as
the projection backwards of present concerns. The desire for a good city in the
future already exists in the imagination of the past. The future tense of urbanist
discourse turns out to be less predictive than optative, although expressed in the
present tense of the architectural drawing. Jane Jacobs's description of this staging of
urban fantasies as dreaming chimes with Freud's comment that, in the dreamwork,
and especially in daydreams, 'a thought expressed in the optative has been replaced
by a representation in the present tense.'[8]

Expressed in the future perfect, urban reformism often disavows the viscous complexity of the present by representing a desired state as already having been
achieved. The event that is yet to occur, and so unknowable, is represented not only
as knowable, but as already past.[9] Politically, this naming the unknowable – giving
an identity or substance to the people, community, or citizenship – is incompatible
with a radical democratic imagination that acknowledges historicity and contingency,

and can live in a present which turns out to be a loop within the chain of signifiers, 'the cross-over point between an untrustworthy past and a promised future that has already begun to decay.'[10] The past is a projection as well as a determinant of the present; the future is less a playground for unconstrained speculation, than a summons to 'inventiveness within an inextirpable framework of constraints.'[11] It is this temporal tangle that defines the 'now' that we inhabit.

For Foucault, freedom consists in the critical reflection on this present: quite a different politics from the normative projection of universal principles in dream cities. The imagination necessary to rebuild a living city works with a different temporality.

> Our history is such that we cannot choose from past possibilities as from a catalogue (we in fact always start somewhere), and such that we cannot project ahead an ideal to resolve in advance all problems that will confront us (there in fact exists no such ideal).[12]

This is less a politics of the right answer than a suspicious ethical reflection on the structures and styles of urban thought that produce this fantasy of the architect as spiritual policeman. It is not a turn away from politics, but a turning round on politics to question its traditions and codes. It entails fewer moral certainties and no dream cities. It looks instead at the political, institutional, and symbolic grammar of how we see, what we can imagine, how we act. This politics offers not the comforts of familiar rhetorics and conventional ways of solving problems. It is a poetics of imagination in that it makes those codes strange in order to liberate new ways of thinking. If it is the business of imagination to make politics distrust itself, and to remind it that its principles are not literal facts but constructs of imagination, argues Richard Kearney, 'it is also its business to encourage politics to remake itself by remaking its images of the good life.'[13]

The task of this chapter, then, is to understand what sort of *act* is involved in three different modes of imagining metropolitan life which constitute a loose and no doubt tangled temporality of past, present, and future. The first, in the past tense, is autobiographical remembering. The second is the projected present of novelistic description. The third, future oriented mode is architecture.

REMEMBERING A CITY

What sort of act is it to remember a city, to make the past city present? I discovered while researching this chapter that Virginia Woolf grew up in the same London street as me, in Hyde Park Gate – 'that little irregular cul-de-sac which lies next to Queen's Gate and opposite to Kensington Gardens', as Woolf described it. She was there sixty years before me, from the early eighteen nineties through the turn of the century, and hers was a much grander experience than mine. Woolf's family, the Stephens and the Duckworths, were self-conscious social insiders in late Victorian London. But there is a shared sense that living in that street was formative, not because of the topography of the place necessarily but because both Woolf and I remember it as the precursor of later biographical developments and intellectual priorities. 'Though Hyde Park Gate seems now so distant from Bloomsbury, its shadow falls across it,' Woolf recalled. '46 Gordon Square could never have meant what it did had not 22 Hyde Park Gate preceded it.'[14] But there is, in Woolf's memoir, also an indication of memory as performative act. She becomes the spectator of her own formation.

> I felt as a tramp or a gypsy must feel who stands at the flap of a tent and sees the circus going on inside. Victorian society was in full swing; George [Duckworth] was the acrobat who jumped through hoops, and Vanessa and I beheld the spectacle. We had good seats at the show, but we were not allowed to take part in it. We applauded, we obeyed – that was all.[15]

Woolf glosses this almost voyeuristic relationship to her past, and her marginalisation to the position of spectator, in terms of 'the laws of patriarchal society.' For me, it provokes other associations, in their own way equally theatrical in their structure. I recall that 8B, our rented flat, was at the top of a building on the corner of Hyde Park Gate, looking over Kensington Gardens in the front, and down the cul-de-sac at the back. This gave us a view over a rich cast of characters, although at the time the drama seemed generally quite unremarkable. Down the street lived, at number 20, Winston Churchill, then in the dog days of his final term of office as Prime Minister and later in resentful retirement. Opposite him, at number 18, lived the sculptor Jacob Epstein, who represented a face of modernism that was acceptable to the English at least to the degree that he had been the butt of endless philistine humour. An interesting conjuncture, now I come to think of it, and one that Woolf herself might have appreciated: the representative of a patriarchal myth of Empire over the road from a cosmopolitan and bohemian artist.

The point of this digression into autobiographical recollection is simply to show the relevance of Hillis Miller's notion of atopicality to the imaginative recreation of the past. Looking at a photograph of Hyde Park gate which I took in the late nineteen fifties, the period details of cars and clothes do not bestow authenticity on the image. On the contrary, they heighten the foreign-ness of my past. Recollection involves above all feelings and effects, condensed into fragmentary narratives. Memory is not just the bringing to mind of past facts. Notoriously, the vivid events recalled from childhood may or may not have taken place, and yet the reworking of the past plays a crucial role in our sense of who we are. These imagined events are a working through of current desires and anxieties, a way of managing them by staging them as a narrative. In my case, the new knowledge that Virginia Woolf lived in Hyde Park Gate too becomes part of my loving narrativisation of the place – a building demolished in the nineteen seventies, a street I have not visited for twenty years or more, but still a place that is central to my imagining of the city and to my experience of myself as formed in and by London. Equally, my rewriting of Hyde Park Gate in terms of a juxtaposition between a politics of national identity and a modernist aesthetics is no doubt a symptom of my present intellectual interests, not how I experienced the place at the time. The future is always already written into the recollected past. There is an uncanny edge to recollections of our past cities, which is symptomatic not only of the atopicality of narrative but also of the temporal disjunctures of memory and imagination. 'The individual is debarred from any benign sensation of temporal flow,' notes Lacan: 'past, present, and future will always stand outside each other, unsettle each other, and refuse to cohere.'[16]

James Donald, Hyde
Park Gate, London,
late 1950s

DESCRIBING A CITY

In order to imagine the unrepresentable space, life, and languages of the city, to make them liveable, we translate them into narratives. We remember or misremember events and imagine them taking place against a symbolic topography. This is true not just of individual memory. It is evident in the intimate connection between the modern metropolis and the development of aesthetic genres and technologies of communication. I have already discussed the relationship between the city and the cinema. Here I return to a question briefly raised in chapter one: what can we learn about an urban imagination from the cities described and narrated in novels? What sort of act are these accounts? These are not questions about the aesthetic function of the cityscape. Rather, again, they concern the social function of imagined cities.

I have argued that the way the city is narrated in novels – the structure and form of the genre – has disseminated certain perspectives, certain ways of seeing, and so certain structures of imagination. Among the more familiar are the opposition between rural utopia and urban nightmare; the *Bildungsroman* narrative of heroic self-creation in the great city; the Dickensian search for the subterranean networks of community beneath the unreadable and irrational surface of the class-divided city; and the social complexity of the city recorded through its demotic idioms and slang by French novelists from Balzac to Zola.

The nineteenth century novel-city, characterised by frenetic activity and social illegibility, exists as a cast of mind, and is peopled by a type of personality that is recognisably and pedagogically urban. On the one hand, the novel's structural openness to the city's multiple points of view and to the Babel of linguistic diversity gives the genre a semblance of democratic inclusiveness, an urban tolerance of difference. On the other hand, the formal organisation of this plenitude often appears to embody a powerful will to domination, a desire to subjugate urban heterogeneity to the design of an omnipotent, panoptic narrator. This mix of tolerance and paranoia produced a repertoire of responses to the city, from popular melodramas about master criminals and secret conspiracies to the *flâneur*'s contemplative, aestheticising gaze.[17]

The relation between novel and city is not merely one of representation. The text is actively constitutive of the city. Writing does not only record or reflect the fact of the city. It plays a role in producing the city for a reading public. The period of the rise of the novel saw the emergence of other genres for recording, for instituting, the truth of the city. As we have seen, population surveys, police records, sanitary reports, statistics, muck-raking journalism, and photography all rendered the city an object of knowledge, and so an object of government. The boundary between these documentary records and fictional narratives is more permeable than one might suppose. There is a free migration of images and narratives between archive and library. Their circulation provides the symbolic currency through which we recall, describe, and so negotiate the city. It provokes and channels the projection of desire and anxiety onto the city.

At their best, novels imagine the sort of *living* city that Jane Jacobs says is so difficult to rebuild; difficult because the city exists in that complex living, not just in their architecture or design. Novels are speech acts in that they help to construct that living symbolic city. Take two examples, very briefly: *Mrs Dalloway* (1925) by my anachronistic neighbour Virginia Woolf, and *Berlin Alexanderplatz* (1929) by Alfred Döblin.[18] My argument is that their narration of London and Berlin in the nineteen twenties encounters the sort of unmappable – or un-narratable – place that Hillis Miller talks about: the 'place that is everywhere and nowhere, a place you cannot get to from here.'

Neither novel tells of a provincial heroine or hero arriving with high hopes in the capital city only to discover a social and spiritual wasteland (although there is a spectral residue of that plot structure in the character of the shell-shocked ex-soldier Septimus Smith in *Mrs Dalloway*). By the nineteen twenties, after the trauma of total war and with new forms of transport and new media of communication transforming urban life, the discontinuity and complexity of the metropolis had become so intense as to defy narration in that conventional form. These two novels attempt to reproduce the inner speech of the metropolis, the mental life stimulated by its size, speed, and semiotic overload. In their different ways, each of them is modernist both in the way it *sees* the metropolis and in the way it narrates the *experience* of the metropolis. I would argue, for a start, that both see the city through a cinematic structure of visibility.

In his review of *Berlin Alexanderplatz* in 1930, Walter Benjamin placed the novel in the epic tradition of modernism which he helped to articulate in his collaboration with Brecht. This epic style was one feature of the new realism that emerged as an alternative to expressionism in post-War Germany. The *Neue Sachlichkeit* rejected illusionism in favour of the objectivity of historical facts, it celebrated the possibilities opened up by technological reproduction, and it championed the pedagogic power of gesture rather than characterisation. For Benjamin, Döblin's adaptation of cinematic montage techniques represented an attempt to recreate an epic relationship between artist and public. 'The material of the montage is, after all, by no means random,' he commented. 'Genuine montage is based on documents.' Montage thus represents something more than a way of reproducing the multifaceted, disjunctural experience of time and space, the shocks that characterise metropolitan life. Its documentary basis makes a claim to both authenticity and authority by anchoring the work in the life of the people. As a mode of narration, montage promises a more provocative selection and juxtaposition of images, and so – according to its own lights, at least – a more interactive, less consumerist and less manipulative experience of reading.[19]

In a review of James Joyce's *Ulysses*, written while working on *Berlin Alexanderplatz*, Döblin acknowledged that 'the movies have invaded the territory of literature,' and it is probable that for his experiments in montage Döblin took Ruttmann's *Berlin: Symphony of a Great City* as his primary model.[20] Just as the film opens with shots from a train entering the city, for example, so there is a quasi-cinematic manipulation of time and space in the first chapter of Book 2, 'Franz Biberkopf Enters Berlin'.[21] Ruttmann's structure of the passage of a day interspersed with little human dramas is echoed here as the bustle of the day on the Rosenthaler Platz gives way to increasingly intimate encounters and conversations in the late afternoon and then in the evening. The rhythm and use of diagonal motion in Ruttmann's editing find literary equivalents in Döblin's focus on the activities in and around Rosenthaler Platz in the East End of Berlin. The stops along the route of the 68 trolley as it runs from north to east are listed, with Rosenthaler Platz in the middle and Herzberge Insane Asylum at the end. The documentation of different aspects of metropolitan activity is linked to the four streets which radiate from the square: the AEG factory, the railway station, commerce, construction, and so forth.

Using montage as a principle of narration enables Döblin to play with shifting and

Raoul Hausmann,
Berlin, 1931 (Centre
Georges Pompidou)

multi-faceted points of view, and to mimic the epic factography of film. Daringly, the chapter opens with a sequence of graphics. The bear of Berlin is followed by small stereotypes depicting 'Trade and Commerce', 'Street Cleaning and Transport', 'Health Department' through to 'Finance and Tax Office'. This is followed by a montage of public notices and announcements: 'The scheme for the addition of an ornamental rosette to the street wall of No. 10 An der Spandauer Brücke . . . is hereby published'; '– I have granted to Herr Bottich, hunting lessee, with the consent of the Police President, authority, liable to cancellation at any time, for the shooting of wild rabbits and other vermin . . .'; '– Albert Pangel, master furrier, who may look back upon an activity of almost thirty years as an honorary local official, has resigned his honorary office . . .' (46/7). Then for the first time the presence of the narrator as *metteur-en-scène* is indicated. 'The Rosenthaler Platz is busily active,' he announces. The nature of its diverse activities is documented, initially in long shot but then with a cut to a near accident as 'a man with two yellow packages jumps off from the 41' and other vignettes of the messiness of everyday life. These include a double suicide ('In a little hotel over there in that dark street two lovers shot themselves early yesterday morning, a waiter from Dresden and a married woman, both of whom, however, had registered under false names'), and an account of a 14-year-old boy with a stutter who gets on the No. 4 tram. The latter story incorporates a flash forward to the boy's future life as a tin-smith and his death at the age of 55.

The final section of the chapter closes in on two passages of dramatic dialogue, with explicit narration restricted to stage directions. In the first, a morphine-addicted ex-high school teacher consoles a young man who has been sacked with a mixture of cynical street wisdom and his love of metropolitan life: 'I enjoy the Rosenthaler Platz, I enjoy the cop at the Elsasser corner, I like my game of billiards, I'd like anyone to come and tell me that his life is better than mine.' (53) The second dialogue conveys the sexualisation of space in the city. At 8 p.m. a young girl and an elderly man meet for an assignation in Brunnenstrasse.

> Upstairs they smile at each other. She stands in the corner. He has taken off his coat and hat, she lets him take her hat and music-case. Then she runs to the door, switches off the light: 'But not long today. I have so little time, I must get home, I won't undress, you are not going to hurt me?' (55)

After this fade to black, these characters disappear from the narrative. The epic sweep of *Berlin Alexanderplatz* embraces many such anonymous stories. There are five million stories in the city, as the prologue to *The Naked City* almost used to say, and the story of the ex-prisoner Franz Biberkopf is just one. To some extent, he can be seen as Everyman, or perhaps better as Anyone in the city. Certainly, there is no attempt at detailed psychological analysis.

Virginia Woolf also had aspirations to inclusiveness in *Mrs Dalloway*. 'I want to give life and death, sanity and insanity,' she wrote in a diary entry. 'I want to criticise the social system, and to show it at work, at its most intense.' What is striking about the novel, however, especially in comparison with *Berlin Alexanderplatz*, is its introversion, the experience of London as psychic space. It names places and streets with the same detailed precision as Dickens, but here the references to locations and events are always mediated through the subjective thoughts of the main characters. Psychological states are not so much caused by the cityscape, as projected onto it.

Erich Comeriner,
Berlin,
Friedrichstraße, ca.
1930 (Bauhaus-

The boundary between inner and outer is shown early on to be blurred and uncertain:

> For having lived in Westminster – how many years now? over twenty, – one feels even in the midst of the traffic, or waking at night, Clarissa was positive, a particular hush, or solemnity; an indescribable pause; a suspense (but that might be her heart, affected, they said, by influenza) before Big Ben strikes. (4)

Whereas Döblin renders the city in terms of a modernist epic, Woolf offers a modernist impressionism. Like Döblin, Woolf was self-consciously trying to write about the experience of the modern city after Joyce. Notoriously, though, she had a mixed and rivalrous response to reading *Ulysses*. In her diaries, although she was able to recognise its liberating and critical novelty, she admitted feeling 'puzzled, bored, irritated, & disillusioned as by a queasy undergraduate scratching his pimples.'[22] Leaving aside such reservations, the more considered comments in the essay 'Modern Fiction' stress Woolf's endorsement of Joyce's rejection of the tyranny of Edwardian narration. He, modern like her, was able to recognise the empirical reality of 'an ordinary mind on an ordinary day' – a mental reality similar also to that diagnosed by Georg Simmel. For Woolf:

> The mind receives a myriad impressions – trivial, fantastic, evanescent, or engraved with the sharpness of steel. From all sides they come, an incessant shower of innumerable atoms . . .[23]

This bombardment of images and events defines the task of the modern novelist:

> Let us record the atoms as they fall upon the mind in the order in which they fall, let us trace the pattern, however disconnected and incoherent in appearance, which each sight or incident scores upon the consciousness.[24]

What would be the paradigm for a modernist literary aesthetic capable of rendering this pattern in literary form? How might it be possible, Woolf asked elsewhere, to capture in the novel 'the power of music, the stimulus of sight, the effect on us of the shape of trees or the play of colour, the emotions bred in us by crowds, the obscure terrors and hatreds which come so irrationally in certain places or from certain people, the delight of movement . . .'?[25]

However different the outcome, Woolf, like Döblin, turned to the cinema for an analogy, if not inspiration. For her, it was not the explosive epistemological power of montage that was the attraction. Rather, it was the ontological precision of the camera that opened up new ways of recording and dramatising London. Laura Marcus has shown how Woolf used her 1926 essay 'The Cinema' 'to explore the roles of space, movement and rhythm in narrative film and fiction.'[26] Despite Woolf's predictable reservations about the stupidity and vulgarity of the medium (and especially of literary adaptations), she saw cinema as potentially the most appropriate form for expressing the complex experience of modernity and the shock effects of the city.

> The most fantastic contrasts could be flashed before us with a speed which the writer can only toil after in vain; the dream architecture of arches and

battlements, of cascades falling and fountains rising, which sometimes visits us in sleep or shapes itself in half-darkened rooms, could be realised before our waking eyes. No fantasy could be too far-fetched or insubstantial. . . . How all this is to be attempted, much less achieved, no one at the moment can tell us. We get intimations only in the chaos of the streets, perhaps, when some momentary assembly of colour, sound, movement, suggests that here is a scene waiting a new art to be transfixed.[27]

The camera, as a recording instrument capable of charting the drama and impressionistic chaos of the city, finds its literary equivalent in the narrative eye of *Mrs Dalloway*.

In people's eyes, in the swing, tramp, and trudge; in the bellow and the uproar; the carriages, motor cars, omnibuses, vans, sandwich men shuffling and swinging; brass bands; barrel organs; in the triumph and the jingle and the strange high singing of some aeroplane overhead was what she loved; life; London; this moment of June. (4/5)

But this love of London is not the love of Iris, Joe's mother. It is not the knowing, forgiving love of familiarity, the sense of a self rooted and recorded in place. Rather, the eye of *Mrs Dalloway*, its *recording movement*, mimics the tracking, panning, and analytical camera of cinema by harking back to the distanciating vision of *flânerie*.

So Peter Walsh, the flawed and disappointed colonial administrator, cuts a swathe (he fancies) through the often kitsch memorials of imperial, post-War London and even has an encounter (he fantasises) with a classic Baudelairean *passante*.[28] The society hostess and MP's wife Clarissa Dalloway moves observing but, as far as she can tell, invisible through the crowds of Bond Street. However frivolous, limited and selfish she may be, Clarissa is the woman of the crowd in the sense that only there, in others, does she exist.

. . . what she loved was this, here, now, in front of her; the fat lady in the cab. Did it matter, then, she asked herself, walking towards Bond Street, did it matter that she must inevitably cease completely; all this must go on without her; did she resent it; or did it not become consoling to believe that death ended absolutely? but that somehow in the streets of London, on the ebb and flow of things, here, there, she survived, Peter survived, lived in each other, she being part, she was positive, of the trees at home; of the house there, ugly, rambling all to bits and pieces as it was; part of people she had never met; being laid out like a mist between the people she knew best, who lifted her on their branches as she had seen the trees lift the mist, but it spread ever so far, her life, herself. (10/11)

Her walk through London conjures up a place that she cannot get to, which is herself, her 'precious and reassuring' past (12), but above all her precarious present and future. Clarissa's past – childhood, the country – is not preserved in the 'this, here, now' of the city. On the contrary, her past has become atopical, the irrecoverable locus of identities that might have been, of choices not made, of paths not taken. This past is disquieting as soon as she recalls it here and now: Peter's return

Alfred G. Buckham,
London, ca. 1925
(The Royal
Photographic Society
Collection, Bath,
England)

puts her decision to reject him for Richard again in question, and also reminds her of Sally Seton and their kiss, with all that promised and threatened. Her walk through London provokes not thoughts of the continuity of identity, but disquiet at the lack of subjective fixity.

> She had the oddest sense of being herself invisible; unseen; unknown; there being no more marrying, no more having of children now, but only this astonishing and rather solemn progress with the rest of them, up Bond Street, this being Mrs Dalloway; not even Clarissa any more; this being Mrs Richard Dalloway. (13)

This narration is not only a record of images, but a projection of multiple selves – past, future, imaginable selves – onto the cityscape being recorded. Clarissa's flashback to her childhood is both nostalgic and anxious, the recall of a lost self and a sense of multiplying possible selves. In contrast, the bus journey of Elizabeth Dalloway, Clarissa's competent daughter, prompts a flash forward: the busy-ness of Chancery Lane inspires not introspection and retrospection, but fantasies of the great works she will do. Woolf's section map in depth here captures the complex temporality of London in 'this moment in June'; a present which, as in Simmel's Berlin, is regulated by the imposed chronology of the clock. Elizabeth's daydream of the future comes to an end as she remembers: 'She must go home. She must dress for dinner. But what was the time? – where was a clock?' (179)

The simultaneity of past, present, and future in the life of the city tests the limits of novelistic narrative. Döblin's solution is epistemological montage, Woolf's the passage of ontological perception. This tangled temporality also suggests why the experience of the modern city has so often produced hallucination, new types of mental illness, and, in the case of Septimus Smith, suicide. Whereas Peter Walsh fancies himself as a figure in the drama of London, and Clarissa fears that, unless hailed by a member of her social set like Scrope Purvis, she is merely an invisible part of the scenery, in Septimus Smith's paranoid perception of Bond Street he is both out of place and in the way.

> Everything had come to a standstill. The throb of the motor engines sounded like a pulse irregularly drumming through an entire body. The sun became extraordinarily hot because the motor car had stopped outside Mulberry's shop window . . . And there the motor car stood, with drawn blinds, and upon them a curious pattern like a tree, Septimus thought, and this gradual drawing together of everything to one centre before his eyes, as if some horror had come almost to the surface and was about to burst into flames, terrified him. The world wavered and quivered and threatened to burst into flames. It is I who am blocking the way, he thought. Was he not being looked at and pointed at; was he not weighted there, rooted to the pavement, for a purpose? But for what purpose? (18/19)

At the beginning of *Berlin Alexanderplatz*, Franz Biberkopf too hallucinates as he readjusts to what seems the chaos of Berlin in comparison with the ordered confinement and routine of prison. The crowd in the streets seem lifeless, like the wax mannequins in a shop window: 'Outside everything was moving, but – back of it – there was nothing! It – did not – live!' (12) Inanimate objects like trams seem terrifyingly alive, and Biberkopf has the first attack of his recurring vertiginous fear that the roofs will slide off the houses. Like the hysterical Septimus Smith and Clarissa Dalloway with her 'panic fear' in the metropolis, Biberkopf cannot draw a line between inner and outer states.

Septimus Smith is very much the type described by Simmel in 'The Metropolis and Mental Life'. Unlike Baudelaire's detached *flâneur*, he is the provincial new-comer to the city, subjected to '*the intensification of nervous stimulation* which results from the swift and uninterrupted change of outer and inner stimuli.' With every crossing of the street, the metropolis 'sets up a deep contrast with small town and rural life with reference to the sensory foundations of psychic life.' Elsewhere, 'the rhythm of life and sensory mental imagery flows more slowly, more habitually, and more evenly.'[29] Although traumatised by the War – *Mrs Dalloway* is set only five years after its end – Septimus Smith's mental instability is exacerbated by the unbearable normality of the city.

> London has swallowed up millions of young men called Smith; thought nothing of fantastic Christian names like Septimus with which their parents have thought to distinguish them. Lodging off the Euston Road, there were experiences, again experiences, such as change a face in two years from a pink innocent oval to a face lean, contracted, hostile. (110)

Both *Mrs Dalloway* and *Berlin Alexanderplatz* follow Simmel in linking the *experience* of the metropolis to what might be called the psychic and spatial diseases of modernity: Smith's hysteria, Biberkopf's agoraphobia, Clarissa's neurasthenia. Many such diseases appeared towards the end of the nineteenth century, as an emerging psychological discourse displaced the primarily medical paradigm for describing the dangers of Great Cities used by reformers like Chadwick and Kay-Shuttleworth. All these diseases were linked not only to degeneracy but also to the perceived femi-nisation of metropolitan life and modern culture. (In fact, most of the people treated for them were probably men.)[30] In the city dweller's psychic space of projection and introjection, the danger was that the boundaries between self and environment, like those between past and present, or male and female, become uncertain and unreliable. Such disorientation produces a retreat into an interiority, either mental or physical, or both, and a disabling inability to admit feelings. Life in the city becomes un-narratable, and so, in a more acute sense, un-imaginable. These transient diseases – 'neurasthenia' was dropped as clinically meaningless in the nineteen thirties – were themselves attempts to name, and so manage, the mental life of the metropolis.

The aesthetic architecture of *Mrs Dalloway* and *Berlin Alexanderplatz* enacts these modern spatial phobias. Once such phobias were recognised and acknowledged as a feature of modern experience and its modernist representation, argues Anthony Vidler, 'neurasthenia found its role as a veritable stimulus for aesthetic experiment.' The forms it took were those of 'stream of consciousness, of entrapment, of intoler-able closure, of space without exit, of, finally, breakdown and often suicide.'[31]

This neurotic motivation behind modernism seems to indicate an aesthetic of despair. Franz Biberkopf is incarcerated in Herzberge Insane Asylum; Septimus Smith's suicide is announced at Clarissa's party by the blundering and quackish nerve doctor, Sir William Bradshaw. But another, perhaps surprising, feature common to the two novels is an unanticipated note of hope, however constrained and uncertain, on which they both end. In the asylum Biberkopf confronts death and is, however implausibly, redeemed and reborn, both subjectively and politically. He is thus, as Benjamin ironically observed, granted 'access into the heaven of literary characters' and – against all the odds and all the evidence – the narratability of the city is re-asserted.[32] Clarissa Dalloway's partial redemption is bought at the price of Smith's suicide. He becomes her surrogate:

> A young man had killed himself. And they talked of it at her party – the Bradshaws, talked of death. He had killed himself – but how? Always her body went through it first, when she was told suddenly, of an accident; her dress flamed, her body burnt.... They went on living (she would have to go back; the rooms were still crowded; people kept on coming).... Death was defiance. Death was an attempt to communicate, people feeling the impossibility of reaching the centre which, mystically, evaded them... (241/42)

Having confronted the atopicality of being – 'the centre which, mystically, evaded them' – the novel ends with a re-affirmation of Clarissa's being, even if that being is contingent on the specular gaze of another. That is about as grounded as subjective existence gets in modernity.

> 'I will come,' said Peter, but he sat on for a moment. What is this terror? what is this ecstasy? he thought to himself. What is it that fills me with extraordinary excitement?
> It is Clarissa, he said.
> For there she was. (255)

REBUILDING A CITY

What sort of speech acts are *Mrs Dalloway* and *Berlin Alexanderplatz*? They enact a way of seeing which can be linked to the perceptual technology of cinema, and a subjective experience of the city that is manifested elsewhere as phobic spatial diseases. How, then, do the novels help us to respond to Jane Jacobs's slogan: 'Designing a dream city is easy; rebuilding a living one takes imagination'?

First, they reinforce my view that the type of planning associated above all with Le Corbusier has to be set in the context of aesthetic modernism if it is to make any sense. As a contemporary of Döblin and Woolf, Le Corbusier too knew that urban space had been transformed through the imaginary of the mass media, and he incorporated this perception into his aesthetic.[33] In his more sweeping and fanciful plans for redeeming the modern city, he also seemed to raise their perception of its psychological dangers into a political, even almost religious, principle. His therapeutic modernism was driven by an atopical terror, by the desire for a space cleansed of all uncanny mental disturbances, or even, it seems, of events.[34] The radiance, air and transparency that make up his image of the good city in the perfect future are symptoms of a phobic reaction against the narrative reality of the street, the disgust at the possibility of being touched by strangers diagnosed by Simmel.

> The street is full of people: one must take care where one goes ... every aspect of human life pullulates throughout their length ... a sea of lusts and faces.... Heaven preserve us from the Balzacian mentality of [those] who

would be content to leave our streets as they are because these murky canyons offer them the fascinating spectacle of human physiognomy![35]

It is this phobic disgust – is it claustrophobia, a paradoxical agoraphobia, or simply a phobia against people *en masse*? – which drove his obsession to reduce the messiness of people in cities to the abstraction of mathematical order: 'the Great City, which should be a phenomenon of power and energy, is today a menacing disaster, since it is no longer governed by the principles of geometry.' His response, madder by far than anything in *Mrs Dalloway* or *Berlin Alexanderplatz*, was to dream up his City of Tomorrow in which geometric order displaces narrative: 'Little by little, and basing each point on cause and effect, I built up an ordered system of the grouping of such cells as would replace with advantage the present chaos to which we are subject.'[36]

The second lesson I would take from a reading of Döblin and Woolf is about the *living* nature of the city Jane Jacobs talks about. The city exists in lives as complex, as opaque, and as painful as those the novels depict. But is that not a lesson already well learned? In today's anti-modernist backlash, discussion starts with the existing cultures and communities of cities, and asks how they might be regenerated. Postmodern traditionalists share Prince Charles's dream of urban design which would be able 'to nurture human life and to give dignity, imbuing people with a sense of belonging and a sense of community.' Culturally savvy architects like Richard Rogers and policy minded urbanists like Franco Bianchini and Ken Worpole argue for a re-vitalised and re-enchanted city, one that people can imagine or narrate to themselves, one that is designed to encourage civilised encounters with strangers: 'a potential place for commonality, where some form of common identity could be constructed and where different ages, classes, ethnic groups and lifestyles could meet in unplanned, informal ways.'[37] These enthusiasts paint a seductive picture of an urbane and cosmopolitan life – a vision of Habermas's public sphere in which the strenuous republican disciplines of public participation often seem less important than a good meal and a decent bottle of wine in a pavement café.

Sadly, I agree with Kevin Robins that in both the traditionalists and the cosmopolitans, 'there is an imaginative deficit in the claimed "re-imagination" of urban culture.'[38] What is missing, Robins suggests, is any real sense of the city not only as the space of community or pleasurable encounters or self-creation, but also as the site of aggression, violence, and paranoia. That is why I have insisted that imagining the city in ways that can encompass such forces should be prior to any attempts to re-build actually existing cities. To reject traditional modes of planning is not to give up hope, even though the hope that I detected in *Berlin Alexanderplatz* and *Mrs Dalloway* may now look like reckless optimism in comparison with the representational urban space to be found either in more recent novels, or in academic urban studies. Think of Salman Rushdie's *Satanic Verses*, or the London saturated by poisonous histories in Iain Sinclair's *Downriver*. Think of the demented and impenetrable semiotic networks of urban California described by Thomas Pynchon in *The Crying of Lot 49*, or of Mike Davis's *film noir* political economy of Los Angeles. Or think even of the sci-fi cyber-city of capital flows, information flows, and power flows conjured up by writers like Manuel Castells, William Gibson, and Saskia Sassen.[39]

Faced with this often paranoid, sometimes scatological and yet in some ways sublime poetics of the city, how is it still possible to imagine intentional urban change? For a start, however often it is quoted, it is worth recalling Doreen Massey's gentle rebuke against getting over-excited by all the dystopian metaphors and science fiction stuff.

> For amid the Ridley Scott images of world cities, the writing about skyscraper fortresses, the Baudrillard visions of hyperspeace . . . most people actually still live in places like Harlesden or West Brom. Much of life for most people, even in the heart of the first world, still consists of waiting in a bus-shelter with your shopping for a bus that never comes.[40]

It is certainly true that there is an uneven development in ways of seeing and experiencing the city, and most of us operate with 'residual' modes most of the time. Perhaps that is why Kevin Robins argues less for change in the city than for a change in the way we live in the city. He imagines a post-feminist heroism which forgoes the illusion of wholeness, coherence, or narratability in favour of a tolerant, melancholic acknowledgement of, and engagement with, complexity – a post-modern version of Iris, Joe's mother, perhaps, and her loving intimacy with the city. Robins quotes Elizabeth Wilson:

> The heroism – for both sexes – is in surviving the disorientating space, both labyrinthine and agoraphobic, of the metropolis. It lies in the ability to discern among the massed ranks of anonymity the outline of forms of beauty and individuality appropriate to urban life.[41]

But isn't this heroic attitude still trapped within the narcissistic and domesticating aestheticism of *flânerie*? Doesn't it avoid the stubborn reality of difference and the opacity of others? The problem (to which I shall return) is not just how to live in the city, but how to live together.

Is it then possible to imagine change that acknowledges difference without falling into phobic utopianism, communitarian nostalgia, or the disavowal of urban paranoia? To begin at the other end, how might it be possible to imagine the spatial manifestation of a radical democracy? For a start, one would have to acknowledge, as I have tried to do here, the historicity and contingency of the spatial representations and projections which allow and constrain such imagining. Second, therefore, the imagining would take the form not of a dream city, but a re-thinking of the processes and technologies of change. It is the impossibility of representing the social relations of the city in a single normative image or an all-encompassing narrative that lends this style of imagination its sublime edge and, Ernesto Laclau might agree, places it within a radical democratic imaginary. His account of society as 'mere event' perhaps goes too far in the opposite direction from Le Corbusier's dream of the city as pure space.[42] But read Laclau with Hillis Miller's account of space as constituted by event (and so inherently temporal) in mind, and then he does offer a political imagination couched in terms of narrative rather than *topos*, of pragmatics rather than representation, of living cities rather than dream cities.

> Society, then, is ultimately unrepresentable: any representation – and thus any space – is an attempt to constitute society, not to state what it is. But the antagonistic moment of collision between the various representations cannot be reduced to space, and is itself unrepresentable. It is therefore mere event, mere temporality. . . . [T]his final incompletion of the social is the main

source of our political hope in the contemporary world: only it can assure the conditions for a radical democracy.[43]

This approach to space as event would have to acknowledge, and in a quiet way might even celebrate, the fictional element in all architecture, its necessary attempt to imagine social relations taking place. Architecture to that degree is also a critical commentary, a making strange of what is. The important point is to avow this proper degree of fantasy in the architectural imagination, and not to make the mistake of assuming any particular piece of design or planning will have social consequences that are wholly predictable. Such an architecture would therefore have two aspects: a critical power of remembering in grasping urban space as historically and temporally layered; and an imagination that combines aesthetics and ethics in formulating possible changes to the fabric of the city. The question, then, is how a poetics of political imagination might be effectively allied to a pragmatics of architecture and design.

One architect in whose writings at least I have found something of this style is Bernard Tschumi – in the nineteen sixties an architectural activist influenced by the Situationists who more recently has collaborated with Jacques Derrida. Tschumi's starting point is that, in contemporary urban society, 'any cause-and-effect relationship between form, use, function, and socio-economic structure has become both impossible and obsolete.' If that is true, how can you improve people's experience of the social by changing the urban environment? No longer can you assume that people's experience of space will be determined by your plan for that space; that buildings and the uses of buildings are the same thing; or that there is a transparent relationship between space and the movement of bodies within space. Instead, Tschumi calls for an architectural imagination that starts from 'the pleasurable and sometimes violent confrontation of spaces and activities.' It is the *disjunction* between use, form, and social values which gives architecture its subversive and creative power. The space in and on which architects work is neither coherent nor homogeneous nor marked by clear boundaries:

> . . . we inhabit a fractured space, made of accidents, where figures are disintegrated, *dis*-integrated. From a sensibility developed during centuries around the 'appearance of a stable image' ('balance', 'equilibrium', 'harmony'), today we favor a sensibility of the disappearance of unstable images: first movies (twenty-four images per second), then television, then computer-generated images, and recently (among a few architects) disjunctions, dislocations, deconstructions.[44]

When offered the chance to transform the Parc de la Villette in Paris, this was the spatial imagination Tschumi brought to bear. He wished neither to create a conventional architectural masterpiece, nor to fill in the gaps in what existed, scribbling in the margins of the architectural text. This left him two options. Either:

> Deconstruct what exists by critically analysing the historical layers that preceded it, even adding other layers derived from elsewhere – from other cities, other parks (a palimpsest)

Or:

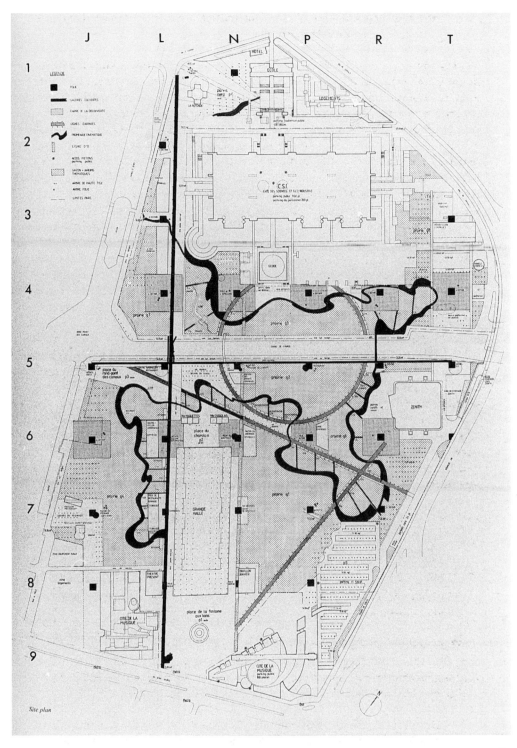

Bernard Tschumi,
Plan for La Villette,
Paris (© Bernard
Tschumi)

> Search for an intermediary – an abstract system to mediate between the site
> (as well as all given constraints) and some other concept, beyond city or
> program (a mediation).[45]

Tschumi had explored the possibilities of the palimpsest model in earlier projects, but here he felt that 'its inevitably figurative or representational components' were incompatible with the programmatic, technical, and political constraints on the project. He went for the strategy of *mediation* which would, he hoped, allow 'a strong conceptual framework while simultaneously suggesting multiple combinations and substitutions.'

Where did Tschumi turn for his mediating system and concept at La Villette? His answer is both familiar and surprising. His first mediation involved a grid of large red cubes around the park which he calls *Folies*: a reference not just to eighteenth century architectural follies, but to a spatial understanding of madness and the psychoanalytic relation of transference. This was the deconstructive or critical aspect of the project. The other mediating principle was one of construction or assemblage, a means of exploring 'the set of combinations and permutations that is possible among different categories of analysis (space, movement, event, technique, symbol, etc.), as opposed to the more traditional play between function or use and form or style.' His first analogy for this style of imaginative construction is the type of *montage* to be found 'in Dziga Vertov's or Sergei Eisenstein's work in the cinema.'[46] As far as I can see, Tschumi was making no great polemical point about madness as urban experience nor about cinema as urban perception. Nevertheless, he did take the theme of madness and the techniques of cinema which I detected in *Berlin Alexanderplatz* and *Mrs Dalloway* and translate them into an apparently arbitrary principle of construction.

What appeals to me about Tschumi is his acute awareness that architectural imagination is contingent on technologies of vision and perception as well as the codes and traditions of architecture as a discipline – and, of course, the political and economic realities that will determine, often in the first instance, how urban space gets changed. Tschumi's is an architecture that works through dis-juncture, dislocation, and dis-integration. What he was aiming for in his schemes for La Villette was a plan, certainly, but not a *telos*; a strategy for rebuilding a living city park, rather than a dream park or a theme park. Aware of the city as temporal palimpsest, he remembered the past and acknowledged that we in the present cannot legislate the future. His plan therefore attempted to *build in* flexibility, tolerance, difference, restlessness, and change. Rather than trying to determine the future, he thinks on behalf of an imaginable but indeterminate future.

> One part could replace another, or a building's program be revised, changing
> (to use an actual example) from restaurant to gardening center to arts work-
> shop. In this manner, the park's identity could be maintained, while the cir-
> cumstantial logics of state or institutional politics could pursue their own
> independent scenarios. Moreover, our objective was also to act upon a strategy
> of differences: if other designers were to intervene, their projects' difference
> from the *Folies* or divergence from the continuity of the cinematic promenade
> would become the condition of their contributions.[47]

'An organizing structure that could exist independent of use, a structure without center or hierarchy': this seems to be what deconstructionist architects are after. They see architecture less as functionalist than as performative, in the same way Hillis Miller describes literary topographies as 'potent speech acts'. Although they do not imagine that the physical structure of their buildings will be without consequences, they have no wish to determine those consequences, and they know that they could not do so even if they wanted to.

It is in that sense that they see the future city in which their buildings will stand as a theatre for the experiences and tactics of future citizens. I suggested earlier that the tragic flaw in Le Corbusier's work may have been his inability to create a passage between his search for the timeless values of architectural form and his political conviction that these values could be imposed on a recalcitrant humanity by exploiting the resources of modern technology and modern capitalism. What emerges from the dialogue which architects like Tschumi and Peter Eisenman have developed with Jacques Derrida is a concern with just that elusive space between form and building, and so a poetics of architectural imagination.

This Derrida designates *chora*, the mythological bridge which for Plato linked the intelligible and the sensible, mind and body. It is a term that not only signifies space and location, but which also has specifically feminine connotations of maternity, nurturance, and containment.[48] It is within this generative *space between* that the architecture of architecture, its sustaining logic, might be disturbed. This is where Derrida and the architects in dialogue with him dissent most vividly from the tradition of modernist planning. The ambition is not to use architecture to engineer certain social outcomes, but to do architecture differently. Hence the questions posed about architecture by Derrida:

> How is it possible . . . to develop a new inventive faculty that would allow the architect to use the possibilities of the new technology without aspiring to uniformity, without developing models for the whole world? An inventive faculty of the architectural difference which would bring out a new type of diversity with different limitations, other heterogeneities than the existing ones and which would not be reduced to the technique of planning?[49]

In response, Derrida proposes not blueprints but a way of proceeding: a community of architects and philosophers responding to 'the desire for a new location, new arcades, new corridors, new ways of living and thinking.' As against Le Corbusier's desire for a city built to obliterate and reconfigure the desires of its population, Derrida asks, more modestly, for: 'Places where desire can recognise itself, where it can live.'[50]

It goes without saying, but I shall say it again, that no building can guarantee such recognition. The virtue of architecture in this key is that at least it accepts the fact. It knows that architecture cannot exist outside tradition, that signs of aesthetics and functionality cannot be (and should not be) wholly effaced, that the very fact of *building* a building constrains the radicalism of its conception. Peter Eisenman acknowledges the difficulty of architectural attempts 'to dislocate that which it locates.'

> This is the paradox of architecture. Because of the imperative of presence, the importance of the architectural object to the experience of the here and now, architecture faces this paradox as does no other discipline.[51]

I am not going to make any claims about the success or failure of the buildings created by Tschumi and Eisenman in living up to this programme. My concern is different. Going back to idea of the imagination needed to rebuild a living city, my question is whether there is any reason why their style of architectural imagining, aesthetically daring and yet scrupulously ethical, should stop anyone from working in an intentional way to change the fabric of the city.

In a polemical short review of contemporary architectural practices and theories, Mary McLeod suggests that there may well be. However impressive or exhilarating the architecture, she asserts, aesthetic daring always risks falling back into a puerile avant-gardism – a term that seems to her to be often 'a more polite label for angry young men, sometimes greying young men.'[52] Such jibes aside, McLeod argues more seriously that the residual modernism of architects labelled deconstructionist or postmodern, and their perception of themselves *as* an avant-garde, have diverted their attention away from the everyday experience of space as it has been theorised by Lefebvre and de Certeau. In contrast, Elizabeth Grosz remains unyieldingly theoretical in her emphasis on philosophical premises rather than architectural outcomes. She feels that it is worth the 'considerable negotiation' required to make Derrida's engagement with architects and architecture 'relevant to feminism'. She goes about this by reading Derrida with Irigaray; or rather, by proposing to re-read Derrida on Plato's *chora* after reading Irigaray against Derrida. What emerges are not architectural prescriptions, but a dauntingly ambitious set of social, psychic and spiritual changes necessary if the epistemological grounds of architecture are to be transformed. On one point, however, Grosz is quite clear. It is this:

> unless men can invent other ways to occupy space; unless space (as territory which is mappable, explorable) gives way to place (occupation, dwelling, being lived in); until space is conceived in terms other than according to the logic of penetration, colonisation, and domination; unless they can accord women their own space, and negotiate the occupation of shared spaces; unless they no longer regard space as the provenance of their own self-expression and self-creation; unless they respect spaces and places which are not theirs, entering only when invited, and accepting this as a gift, can they share in the contributions that women may have to offer in reconceiving space and place.[53]

These changes will not be achieved simply by creating more convivial city spaces where a woman about town might feel more at ease, desirable as that is. But this wish-list is a reminder of what is at stake in imagining urban space, and, especially, why the way architects think about space is so important.

Despite Mary McLeod's exasperated scepticism, I would still argue that the deconstructionists, although by no means only they, have been trying to think their way towards a less determinist, more open-minded and more tolerant – or more *tolerating* – conception of space and a more negotiative approach to architecture. There is no reason to suppose that this way of thinking and acting is incompatible with purposeful changes to spaces in cities. But an emphasis on performativity rather than predictable outcomes should make planners think differently about what they are doing, and why they are doing it. You are not going to produce total social transformation. You are not going to make the city into a home, at least not in the sense of expunging all traces of the uncanny from it, nor filling out its atopicality, nor domesticating all traces of alterity and difference. So how might it be possible to conceptualise the possibilities *and limits* of change? The point of examining the imaginary cities constituted by novels and films is that it is often artists rather than urbanists who have found the language and images to teach us not only the joyous potential of cities, but also that, as Anthony Vidler reminds us, 'no amount of space or structure can make a home where no home can exist.'[54]

What should citizens demand from architects and planners? What can we hope for from cities? What, in particular, can we hope for from imagining the city differently? All of us long for a place that is bounded and secure, where the noise stops, and where we are sustained by the love of those we love, or – more desperately – by infantile fantasies of plenitude and security. This urgent desire for home is real enough, and should not be dismissed as hopeless nostalgia. Equally, though, we have to admit that, in the end, no such place exists this side of the grave. That is why Le Corbusier's Radiant City has the chill of the Necropolis about it, and why the urbane life of café and square can transmogrify so easily into an Expressionist Dance of Death. City life as a normative ideal acknowledges not only the necessary desire for the security of home, but also the inevitability of migration, change, and conflict, and so too the ethical need for an openness to unassimilated otherness.[55] The city becomes the symbolic space in which we act out our more or less imaginative answers to the question which defines our *ethos*: 'how to be 'at home' in a world where our identity is not given, our being-together in question, our destiny contingent or uncertain: the world of the violence of our own self-constitution.'[56]

The drillers have packed up and gone home now, and the rush hour traffic has reduced to an occasional bus or car. There is a scent of rosemary from my tiny town garden. From the pub over the road drifts the sound of the juke box and the whoop of an over-excited drinker. Here, now, in front of me, a moment of peace this summer evening in the city. Tomorrow, I imagine, the aggravation starts again.

David Vestal, View
from the Automat,
East 59th Street,
New York, 1950
(© David Vestal
1998)

chapter 6

Noisy Neighbours

On urban ethics

I want to pick up and address the question of John Rajchman's which I left resonating at the end of the previous chapter. Our problem (and who *we* are is of course already the problem) is this: 'how to be "at home" in a world where our identity is not given, our being-together in question, our destiny contingent or uncertain: the world of the violence of our own self-constitution.'[1] When I wonder how that question gets answered in the real-imagined city, it presents itself in more demotic terms. How can we stroppy strangers live together without doing each other too much violence?

In looking for answers, my first feeling is one of scepticism towards two obvious responses. One, which I think of as the cultural studies answer, says that what makes living together possible is *community*. That may sound hopelessly old fashioned, like Richard Hoggart or early Raymond Williams, not the cultural studies of difference, hybridisation, multiculturalism and antagonism. Maybe. I still suspect that many of these current concerns are premised on a sense of community as lost, complicated, impossible, under erasure, yet to be formed, or whatever – but certainly not irrelevant. That is why it is still important to remind ourselves just how central community was in Raymond Williams's work, and in what form.

> The only landscape I ever see, in dreams, is the Black Mountains village in
> which I was born. When I go back to that country, I feel a recovery of a
> particular way of life, which appears, at times, as an inescapable identity, a
> more positive connection than I have known elsewhere. Many other men feel
> this, of their own native places, and the strength of the idea of settlement, old
> and new, is then positive and unquestioned.[2]

Community here is a fact, 'positive and unquestioned'. Leaving home can only be traumatic. What motivated Williams, and inaugurated cultural studies, was the impulse to create a democratic common culture capable of restoring that loss, and so healing or at least ameliorating the psychic wounds of modernity.

It could be argued that Williams's identification of community with settlement and settlement with place is simply anachronistic. It might be read as a belated replay of the conflict in which, as usual, the settled organic consolations of

Gemeinschaft win out emotionally and politically over the mechanical alienation of *Gesellschaft*. That might be Doreen Massey's view:

> On the one hand, communities can exist without being in the same place –
> from networks of friends with like interests, to major religious, ethnic or polit-
> ical communities. On the other hand, the instances of places housing single
> 'communities' in the sense of coherent social groups are probably – and, I
> would add, have for long been – quite rare.[3]

Rare they may be, but Williams remained fiercely wedded to their enduring value. The comments in one of his last books, *Towards 2000*, published in 1983, about the 'angry confusions and prejudices' provoked in British working-class communities when 'the most recent immigrations of more visibly different peoples' 'intersect with more selective forms of identity' have become notorious.[4] Whatever the political implications, the *conceptual* damage was done by Williams's regression into a binary opposition between real community and spurious citizenship – *Gemeinschaft* and *Gesellschaft* again, in surprisingly unmediated form.

> For unevenly and at time precariously, but always through long experience
> substantially, an effective awareness of social identity depends on actual and
> sustained social relationships. To reduce social identity to formal legal def-
> initions, at the level of the state, is to collude with the alienated superficialities
> of 'the nation' which are nothing but the limited functional terms of the
> modern ruling class.[5]

Here, though, I want to stress just how wedded to place Williams's notion of community was, and by implication to *a place in the country*. 'A socialist position on social identities', he wrote, should support 'lived and formed identities either of a settled kind, *if available*, or of a possible kind, where dislocation and relocation require new formation.'[6] Again he looks back to the Welsh home of his childhood as a sign of hope.

> It is by working together and living together, with *some real place* and common
> interest to identify with, and as free as may be from external ideological
> definitions, whether divisive or universalist, that *real* social identities are
> formed.[7]

Williams's desperate investment in the authenticity of place bursts out in his angry disdain for what he ambiguously calls 'minority liberals and socialists' who raise an eyebrow at such claims. 'By the nature of their work or formation,' complains Williams, they are 'themselves nationally and internationally mobile [and so] have little experience of those rooted settlements from which, though now under exceptionally severe complications and pressures, most people still derive their communal identities.'[8]

What is the issue in this version of community? There is something disturbing and *odd* going on here. It is how this oddity is linked to the idea of the city that I want to understand. A clue to the reason that Williams's anxieties come out in racial terms in *Towards 2000* may be found if we go back ten years to look at his earlier, and more sympathetic, book *The Country and the City*. One of its themes is the history of differences between 'country' community and 'city' society. Rereading the book, it is noticeable how there too Williams starts with an encomium to the rural settlement of his childhood. He gives the city its due, but the effort shows. He has felt the pulse of the city, he claims, its 'identifiable and moving quality', its 'dynamic movement'.

> H.G. Wells once said, coming out of a political meeting where they had been discussing social change, that this great towering city was a measure of the obstacle, of how much must be moved if there was to be any change. I have known this feeling, looking up at great buildings that are the centres of power, but I find I do not say 'There is your city, your great bourgeois monument, your towering structure of this still precarious civilization' *or I do not say only that*; I say also 'This is what men have built, so often magnificently, and is not everything then possible?'[9]

Although it is more brutally expressed in *Towards 2000*, the passion that drives *The Country and the City* already seems to have been an animus against metropolitan and especially cosmopolitan cultures. This reaction was deep and long-standing. Williams felt that he came to the metropolis as a stranger – 'so much so', he admits in the 'Culture is Ordinary' essay in 1958, 'that for years I had violent headaches whenever I passed through London and saw underground advertisements and evening newspapers'.[10] If you want to *hear* how grudging was Williams's admiration for the city, then compare his elegiac and earnest invocations of authentic rural community with the rhetorical fireworks of a writer who revels in a worldly, if slightly melancholy, cosmopolitanism. Here is Salman Rushdie defending *The Satanic Verses* as a hymn to migration and dislocation.

> If *The Satanic Verses* is anything, it is a migrant's eye-view of the world. It is written from the very experience of uprooting, disjuncture and meta-morphosis (slow or rapid, painful or pleasurable) that is the migrant condition, and from which, I believe, can be derived a metaphor for all humanity. . . . Those who oppose the novel most vociferously today are of the opinion that intermingling with a different culture will inevitably weaken and ruin their own. I am of the opposite opinion. *The Satanic Verses* celebrates hybridity, impurity, intermingling, the transformation that comes of new and unexpected combinations of human beings, cultures, ideas, politics, movies, songs. It rejoices in mongrelisation and fears the absolutism of the Pure. *Mélange*, hotchpotch, a bit of this and a bit of that is how newness enters the world. It is the great possibility that mass migration gives the world, and I have tried to embrace it. *The Satanic Verses* is for change-by-fusion, change-by-conjoining. It is a love-song to our mongrel selves.[11]

So, we might ignore Raymond Williams's tenacious commitment to an idealized village community as an anachronism, or dismiss it – no doubt on aesthetic grounds as much as for any theoretical or political reasons – as a dour and puritanical alternative to the gusto of Rushdie's celebration of newness and movement. But I still do not think we would have got to the heart of the matter. The oddity of his indiscretions in *Towards 2000* has less to do with what his nostalgia attaches itself to, than with the nostalgia itself.

Here, Lyotard may offer a clue to what is going on. In an essay which is both a jeremiad against the megalopolis and a warning against any nostalgia for the *domus* and all its *unheimlich* baggage, Lyotard identifies the link between that nostalgia and political writing.

> It is impossible to think or write without some facade of a house at least rising up, a phantom, to receive and to make a work of our peregrinations. Lost behind our thoughts, the *domus* is also a mirage in front, the impossible dwelling. Prodigal sons, we engender its patriarchal frugality.

For Williams, the issue seems to have been an obviously profoundly felt ambivalence about the fact that he *did* leave the Black Mountains. This theme was worked through most intensely in his series of novels about his relationship to his Welsh past. What comes across from them is something of the migrant's unease about living, temporally, emotionally and socially rather than geographically, in *border country*. In his more theoretical and programmatic writings, too, Williams's projected socialist vision, his home in the future perfect – Lyotard's *mirage in front* – remained always mediated through a projection of that remembered, spectral community.

> Thus things past are remembered ahead. The beginning, the awakening, offers itself only at the end as its inscription, by the writing of the remembrance, in its working-out. Always to be reread, redone. And the dwelling of the work is built only from this passage from awakening to the inscription of the awakening. And this passage itself does not cease to pass. And there is no roof where, at the end, the awakening will be over, where we will be awake, and the inscription will have ceased to inscribe. There is no *domus* as the rhyme of time, that is so. But nostalgia for the lost *domus* is what awakens, and our domain nowadays is the inscription of this awakening.

Here Lyotard's argument suggests a degree of convergence between Williams's excessive investment in community and Rushdie's possibly equally excessive celebration of migration. Each is an experiential and political strategy for dealing with the (more or less conscious) loss of the *possibility* of home with which we live. Rushdie's is an almost Nietzschean yes-saying, Williams's is a disavowal – 'I know very well that home is a mirage, *but even so . . .*'

> So only transit, transfer, translation and difference. It is not the house passing away, like a mobile home or the shepherd's hut, it is in passing that we dwell.[12]

This is the home/un-home which Rushdie and Williams share – and the home, incidentally, that echoes in a more existential register the *mobile privatisation* which Williams saw as the major social consequence of television.[13] Although Lyotard may take a gloomier view of contemporary urbanity than Rushdie, he rules Williams's alternative out of court. In doing so, however, he makes it possible to understand why it continued to haunt Williams's writing.

> I wanted to say only this, it seems. Not that the *domus* is the figure of community that can provide an alternative to the megalopolis. Domesticity is over, and probably it never existed, except as a dream of the old child awakening

and destroying it on awakening. Of the child whose awakening displaces it to the future horizon of his thoughts and writing, to a coming which will always have to be deferred. . . . Thought today makes no appeal, cannot appeal, to the memory which is tradition, to bucolic *physis* to rhyming time, to perfect beauty. In going back to these phantoms, it is sure to get it wrong – what I mean is, it will make a fortune out of the retro distributed by the megalopolis just as well (it might come in useful). Thought cannot want its house. But the house haunts it.[14]

The way that Williams *gets community wrong*, I suspect, has something to do with a confusion between the intractable *singularity* of home for him (or for you or me) as opposed to the *idea* of community. He translates a sense of loss, our routine sense of being not quite at home, into a cultural-political programme for restoring the conditions of a plenitude which can only ever exist as memory. This then presupposes that community, the question of how we live together, must take the form of collective affiliation, though not necessarily a common identity.

To say that Williams *gets it wrong* is not to say that (for example) Rushdie's post-colonial cosmopolitanism gets it right. The question of community is not one that has a right answer. It cannot be got right because community is always a question in the present, here and now, and so requires open-ended, provisional and changeable answers – answers on the run. Phantoms of the past projected onto utopias in the future may appear to offer some refuge or security, but only at the cost of disavowing the evanescent, unhomely reality of living in the present.

Rereading Williams through Lyotard suggests how the question of community constitutes shared ground between cultural studies and some contemporary European philosophy. If we start from the question of living in the present with strangers, we could then go on to ask other questions: In what might that commonality consist? How is it socially sustainable? Such questions are, in fact, close to what Raymond Williams seems to have intended by his elusive concept of a common culture. This implied neither a common identity nor a set of traditions or attributes held in common. Rather, he envisaged broad social participation in the never completed process of making meanings and creating values. This version of an always emerging, nego-tiated common culture reveals the affinity between Williams and Habermas. It also leads directly to the second of the two obvious answers to Rajchman's question that I mentioned at the beginning of the chapter. This is the political theory answer, which similarly stresses not community as identity but the productive process of social interaction. What makes living together possible is *rational deliberation*. Some of the axioms underlying the argument are unexceptionable. It seems pretty self-evident that if we strangers are to live together in at least reasonably peaceful coexistence, then we need to talk about matters of mutual interest, and it seems sensible to seek non-violent ways of negotiating conflicts. If you have been formed within cultural studies, however, what is extraordinary about most discussions of deliberative dem-ocracy is how *thin* they are in their descriptions of the cultural, semiotic and psycho-logical aspects of such negotiations. I am still enough of a Gramscian to insist that if democracy is to have any substantial reality, then it needs to be rooted in the soil of culture, and not just in constitutional arrangements or in the etiquette of citizenship. And as Raymond Williams among others showed, if you are interested in the forma-tion of a democratic culture, then you have to understand and take seriously the texture and rhythms of living together: its spatial manifestations, its disjunctural temporalities, its ordinariness and its social complexity, as well as its political consequences.

As I think about the city and its communities, or rather, as I try to think community *through* and *with* the city, I find myself confronting again the founding questions of both political theory and cultural studies: the question of living together; and the question of talking to each other. I also find myself interrupted by the way these questions are addressed in an odd couple of movies made forty years apart. The possibility, the humour and the difficulty of urban community are the topic of both the post-War Ealing comedy *Passport to Pimlico*, directed by Henry Cornelius in 1949, and Spike Lee's 1989 film, *Do the Right Thing*.

THE LIMITS OF COMMUNITY

In many ways, on the surface, the two films could hardly be more different. *Passport to Pimlico* is an allegory about the need for national unity and individual self-discipline during a period of economic austerity. The residents of a London street near Victoria Station discover that they are part of an estate ceded to a Duke of Burgundy centuries before, and not part of England. They revel, briefly, in their new found freedom from food and clothes rationing, from licensing hours, and from other petty restrictions imposed by a bureaucratic state. They soon find their freedom a mixed blessing, though. Spivs move in, the law moves out. They are bullied and then isolated by the State. Finally a political compromise is reached Pimloco returns to the national family.

Spike Lee's *Do the Right Thing*, although more recent, has itself begun to look like a period piece, an historical slice of specifically late nineteen eighties New York life. In part, it is an almost anthropological study of the way that what Freud called 'the narcissism of minor differences' between ethnic, racial and national groups is invested in icons, objects, and anthems. Most notorious are the photographs of Italian Americans on the wall of Sal's Famous Pizzeria which so offend Buggin' Out, but there are also the T-shirts, trainers and ghetto blasters, and the rap music which drives Sal wild.[15] As the title suggests, though, *Do the Right Thing* is above all a lesson in ethics. The film provoked controversy on its release. It was accused of advocating violence, especially in the way it presented the action of Mookie (the character played by Spike Lee) in throwing a garbage can through the window of the Pizzeria after Radio Raheem has been killed by white policemen. This might be more accurately described as an ambiguity in directing the spectator's judgement of black violence against white property, rather than all the other acts of violence which punctuate the film.[16] But even that may be too partial a reading. The question posed by Mookie's action and reiterated, with no decisive answer, by the two quotations which close the film – one from Martin Luther King, the other from Malcom X – is rather different. It is about the disparate and competing ethical discourses that are always in play in any urban community, and so about responsibility and ambivalence. (The possibility of community, the necessary horizon of communication, is gestured to in the film by the framing patter of the local radio DJ, Señor Love Daddy.)

I hope these brief summaries help to explain why I sometimes think of *Do the Right Thing* as a displaced, critical remake of *Passport to Pimlico*. Both films are about small urban communities under pressure, having to confront the question of whether, and in what sense, they *are* communities. Both (like *The Satanic Verses*) use a

Henri Cartier-
Bresson/Magnum
Photos, Berlin, 1962

heat wave as their metaphor. As the temperature rises, the rules and routines of coexistence begin to break down. Tempers fray. People ask, are you one of *us*, or not? If not, what are you doing in this part of town? And so, explicitly in Lee's film and through a comic disavowal in *Passport to Pimlico*, they both reveal the violence of the constitution of any community based on the principle of a common essence.

The two films dramatise what is at stake in the idea of community as the expression of identity. The problem is that if you assume a defining essence – this is what and who we are – then inevitably the question of community translates itself into the drawing of boundaries – this is where we belong, and beyond here are those who don't belong. The image of the Burgundian enclave on the Thames, a community of fate surrounded by barbed wire and causing a headache for the bumbling mandarins of Whitehall, feels less cozy since the break-up of the former Yugoslavia. The boundaries *within* Bed-Stuy may be more symbolic than spatial, but if anything they are even more volatile.

Teased by Mookie about his heroes – Magic Johnson, Eddie Murphy, Prince – Sal's son Vito says, 'Magic, Eddie, Prince. They're not niggers. They're not really black. They're more than black.' At the heart of the film is a rondo of racial invective addressed to camera by different characters: Mookie against Italians, Sal's racist son Pino against 'the blacks', a Puerto Rican against Koreans, the white policeman who later kills Radio Raheem against Puerto Ricans, the Korean grocer against Mayor Koch and the Jews. One of the three bludgers who sit like a street-corner chorus commenting on the action says this about the Koreans:

> Look at those Korean motherfuckers across the street. I bet you they haven't been off the boat a year before they open up their own place. . . . A motherfuckin' year off the motherfuckin' boat and they already got a business in *our* neighbourhood. A good business. Occupying a building that had been boarded up for longer than I care to remember.

When the violence erupts after Radio Raheem's killing, it is these men who turn from Sal's to the grocery store. They are only deflected when the Korean repeatedly protests, 'I'm black.' 'An effective awareness of social identity depends on actual and sustained social relationships,' insisted Raymond Williams. I dread to think what he would make of the grocer's semiotically arbitrary but politically expedient act of self-naming!

Nevertheless, the Korean grocer may be doing the right thing. His pragmatic response to the question of community cannot easily be squared with Williams's image of community as a home lost and to be regained in the common culture of the future. It is, however, more in line with the premise of Jean-Luc Nancy's *The Inoperative Community*, 'that the political is receptive to what is at stake in community'.[17]

> . . . I start out from the idea that such a thinking – the thinking of community as essence – is in effect the closure of the political. Such a thinking constitutes closure because it assigns to community a *common being*, whereas community is a matter of something quite different, namely, of existence inasmuch as it is *in* common, but without letting itself be absorbed into a common substance. Being *in* common has nothing to do with communion, with fusion into a body, into a unique and ultimate identity that would no longer be exposed. Being *in*

common means, to the contrary, *no longer having, in any form, in any empirical or ideal place, such a substantial identity, and sharing this* (narcissistic) *'lack of identity.'* This is what philosophy calls finitude . . .[18]

Nancy then follows Aristotle in linking politics and the city. When Aristotle said that man is by nature an animal intended to live in the *polis*, he meant that, even if the space of the city has to be shared with others, citizenship as an aspect of the *good life* is an ethical status achievable only through active and responsible participation in its public deliberations. These deliberations at the same time embody the good life and take as their topic the question of what constitutes that life, and how citizens should best order their common affairs to achieve it. In the *polis*, then, community is never given. It is always in question. To 'live well' means not necessarily to live in comfort, or in wealth, or even in peace. It means to be part of the community which is contingent on the question of community; which exists by virtue of addressing Rajchman's question of being ' "at home" in a world where our identity is not given, our being-together in question.' That is the specific sense in which city life is inescapably political. Despite the consoling return home at the end of *Passport to Pimlico* or the cultural protectionism of *Do the Right Thing*, the question of urban community cannot be resolved through recovered identity, social consensus, or perpetual peace without boundaries. Iris Marion Young suggests that the city offers a normative ideal for politics because it entails, quite practically, an openness to unassimilable difference.[19] She is right to the extent that we do not need to share peremptory cultural traditions with our neighbours in order to live alongside them. We *do* need to be able to talk to them, while at the same time accepting that they are, and will remain, strangers. Or rather, we have to talk to them, while remembering that *we* are, and remain, strangers.

STRANGERS

I am using strangers in a particular sense, to insist that even those with whom we are told we share an 'identity' remain largely, and ultimately, opaque to us. I am not talking only, or even primarily, about migrants, foreigners, or aliens as strangers. I am thinking about 'us'. Even so, let's pause to reflect on the term. The concept of *the stranger* may offer clues to the possibility, as well as the difficulty, of urban community.

In his essay on 'The Stranger', Simmel attempts to define the figure's unique social importance.

> . . . the union of closeness and remoteness involved in every human relationship is patterned in a way that may be succinctly formulated as follows: the distance within this relation indicates that one who is close is remote, but his strangeness indicates that one who is remote is near.[20]

The stranger is insider and outsider, intimate and alien. 'Despite his being inorganically appended to it, the stranger is still an organic member of the group.' How? It is not clear to members of the group.

> For a stranger to the country, the city, the race, and so on, what is stressed is again nothing individual, but alien origin, a quality which he has, or could

have, in common with many other strangers. For this reason, strangers are not really perceived as individuals, but as strangers of a certain type. Their remoteness is no less general than their nearness.[21]

But, Simmel admits, he does not really know how to characterise the stranger's uneasy status. All we can say is that 'it is put together of certain amounts of nearness and of remoteness'. Which is where he started.

How might we take this further? We could switch perspective from 'group' to 'stranger', as Homi Bhabha did when he championed Rushdie's *Satanic Verses* as a celebration of 'the hybrid hotchpotch of the mongrel postmodern novel with 'black, brown and white leaking into each other' in tropicalised *Ellowen Deeowen* (L-o-n-d-o-n) or *Mumbai* (bastardised Bombay)'. Bhabha insisted that migration has become the key optic through which to make sense of today's great cities. 'The historical and cultural experience of the western metropolis *cannot* now be fictionalised without the marginal, oblique gaze of its postcolonial, migrant populations cutting across the imaginative metropolitan geography of territory and community, tradition and culture.'[22] But is it just a question of the migrant view *cutting across* the imagined community? Doesn't the enigmatic nature of the stranger that perplexed Simmel, the simultaneous nearness and remoteness, suggest also a move in the opposite direction: not just outwards towards empathy for the migrant, but inwards towards a recognition of our strangeness to ourselves?

Je est un autre, said Rimbaud. Or, as the jolly policeman exclaims in *Passport to Pimlico*, 'Blimey, I'm a foreigner!' That *Blimey* marks him as London (in terms of Williams's 'actual and sustained social relationships') just as he enunciates his 'formal legal definition' as a Burgundian citizen. But the joke bites because, whatever Williams says, what we actually learn 'through long experience substantially' is *not* 'an effective awareness of social identity.' It is quite a different lesson, at least according to Julia Kristeva: 'we know that we are foreigners to ourselves, and it is with the help of that sole support that we can attempt to live with others.'[23]

Both claims – effective identity versus innate foreignness – may be equally assertions, and both are probably equally utopian. By acknowledging that the desire for identity is a neurotic symptom, though, Kristeva grasps that Simmel's dynamic of strangeness, of the near and the remote, operates as a fact of psychic life just as much as of social life. The logic of the stranger is the logic of the uncanny disseminated into the social. Strangeness both informs our relationships with others, and opens up possible new forms of community, a new politics:

> The foreigner is within me, hence we are all foreigners. If I am a foreigner, there are no foreigners. . . . The ethics of psychoanalysis implies a politics: it would involve a cosmopolitanism of a new sort that, cutting across governments, economies and markets, might work for a mankind whose solidarity is founded on the consciousness of its unconscious – desiring, destructive, fearful, empty, impossible. Here we are far removed from a call to brotherhood. . . . On the basis of an erotic, death-bearing unconscious, the uncanny strangeness . . . sets the difference within us in its most bewildering shape and presents it as the ultimate condition of our being *with* others.[24]

In his book *On Toleration*, Michael Walzer objects that 'if everyone is a stranger, then no one is': 'unless we experience sameness in some strong form, we cannot even recognize otherness'. If you accept Kristeva's internalizing of the logic of strangeness, he worries, then 'the politics of difference, the ongoing negotiation of group relations and individual rights, would [be] abolished.'[25] But Walzer's argument in turn only makes sense if you assume that the politics of community is a negotiation between groups with what Nancy would call 'a common being', a given identity. Walzer cannot contemplate giving up on the substantial reality of the 'experience of sameness'. To lose *that* notion of affiliation would be, as far as he is concerned, to give up on politics. No, says Nancy.

> What the community has 'lost' – the immanence and the intimacy of a communion – is lost only in the sense that such a 'loss' is constitutive of 'community' itself.
>
> It is not a loss: on the contrary, immanence, if it were to come about, would instantly suppress community, or communication, as such.[26]

This is a key point. Many of the more or less communitarian approaches to the question of how we can live together with which I have most sympathy – Charles Taylor on the politics of recognition, Will Kymlicka on minority rights, even Iris Marion Young on communicative democracy – founder for me on this rock.[27] They may criticise the normative ideal of community, but when it comes to describing the actual negotiations of communal politics, the group actors (so far as I can see) bear identities just as normative, and derived from the same logic of belonging and exclusion. They seldom quite capture the wiliness, the aggression, and the everyday paranoia which are inescapable features of sharing urban turf.

TALKING TO EACH OTHER

It is tempting to turn again to literature and to contemporary cinema for imaginative lessons in that reality (*Falling Down*, for example, or *La Haine*). Here, though, I shall try to get its measure by considering two tales about community as communication told by two gurus from different wings of cultural studies.

The first parable comes from the marxist geographer David Harvey, in gloomy mood. In an article on 'Social Justice, Postmodernism and the City' published in 1992, he describes a vivid but explosive social mix that was to be found in Tompkins Square Park in New York's Lower East Side in the late nineteen eighties. In August 1988, there had been a 'police riot' in the park. Despite that, by the following year some three hundred homeless people were sharing the space with skateboarders, basketball players, mothers and toddlers, chess players, dog walkers, members of various sub-cultures, and the occupants of the gentrifying real estate around the park. At night, the contrasts became even more dramatic. Harvey quotes an article from the *International Herald Tribune* in August 1989.

> The Newcomers Motorcycle Club was having its annual block party at its clubhouse at 12th Street and Avenue B and the street was lined with chromed Harley Davidsons with raised 'ape-hanger' handlebars and beefy men and hefty women in black leather. A block north a rock concert had spilled out of a 'squat' – an abandoned city-owned building taken over by outlaw renovators, mostly young artists – and the street was filled with young people whose purple hair stood straight up in spikes. At the World Club just off Houston

Bruno Barbey/
Magnum Photos,
Rue Gay-Lussac,
Paris, 11 May 1968

Street near Avenue C, black youths pulled up in the Jeep-type vehicle favoured by cash-heavy teen-age crack moguls, high powered speakers blaring. At the corner of Avenue B and Third, considered one of the worst heroin blocks in New York, another concert was going on at an artists' space called The Garage, set in a former gas station walled off by plastic bottles and other found objects. The wall formed an enclosed garden looking up at burned-out, abandoned buildings: there was an eerie resemblance to Beirut. The crowd was white and fashionably dressed, and a police sergeant sent to check on the noise shook his head, bemused: 'It's all yuppies.'[28]

On a good day, says Harvey, Tompkins Square Park may have appeared to represent the image of city life as disparate groups talking to each other which is idealised by writers like Iain Chambers ('*all those sounds, images, and diverse histories that are daily mixed, recycled and "scratched" together on that giant screen that is the contemporary city*'), Iris Marion Young ('*a politics that takes account of and provides voice for the different groups that dwell together in the city without forming a community*') or, from an earlier generation, Jane Jacobs (with her call on city designers to respect '*spontaneous self-diversification among urban populations*' and to be more enthusiastic about '*the aesthetic problems of expressing it*').[29]

On a bad day – shades of *Do the Right Thing* – difference simply degenerated into violence. In 1991 the authorities evicted everyone from the park, and closed it entirely 'for rehabilitation' while mounting a permanent guard of at least twenty police officers. This presents Harvey with his problem.

> And what should the policy-maker and planner do in the face of these conditions? Give up planning and join one of the burgeoning cultural studies programmes which revel in chaotic scenes of the Tompkins Square sort while simultaneously disengaging from any commitment to do something about them? Deploy all the critical powers of deconstruction and semiotics to seek new and engaging interpretations of graffiti which say 'Die, Yuppie Scum'? Should we join revolutionary and anarchist groups and fight for the rights of the poor and culturally marginalised to express their rights and if necessary make a home for themselves in the park? Or should we throw away that dog-eared copy of Jane Jacobs and join with the forces of law and order and help impose some authoritarian solution on the problem?[30]

Initially this tugs at the conscience, as it is meant to. On closer inspection, though, the alternatives on offer turn out to be as bogus as they are manipulative. Harvey starts by setting up an opposition between *the policy-maker and planner* grappling with the reality of the streets and the disconnected irresponsibility of *cultural studies*, *deconstruction*, and *semiotics*. Notice how he then slides into a collusive *we* which presumably excludes those bad objects but embraces the politically *engagé* Harvey, the horny-handed sons of planning, and the recruitable reader.

As Harvey was Professor of Geography at the University of Oxford at the time, there is a touch of bathos in this self-image of gritty and embattled solidarity. Perhaps a short course in cultural studies would have done him no harm. *Lesson one*: don't take everything you read in the *International Herald Tribune* at face value, however deliciously prurient the story and however conveniently it fits your argument. *Lesson two*: don't forget that educational institutions (even Oxford) are part of the fabric of urban experience, and not an escape from it. *Lesson three*: be sceptical of academics flaunting a rhetoric of 'the streets' to lend a spurious authority to their theoretical positions or their political prejudices. *Lesson four*: don't censor out of the account the way that cultural studies and deconstruction *have* engaged with policy making processes that have shaped urban policies and architecture.

Rather than lecture Harvey, I would prefer to explore the possibility of a conversation. For a start, we find a measure of common ground in a shared scepticism about any idea that 'community is going to save us all.' In a more recent article, Harvey writes:

> Community, endowed with salving powers, is perceived as capable of redeem-
> ing the mess which we are creating in our cities. This mode of thinking goes
> all the way from prince Charles and the construction of urban villages through
> to communitarian philosophies that, it is believed, will save us from crass
> materialism.[31]

No disagreement there. I could also go along with Harvey's warning against treating community as a thing instead of *process*, even though we might differ about what that means. I see it as a warning against reducing the singularity of each and every working out of the process of living together to no more than a manifestation of a unifying idea of community. Harvey is interested primarily in rescuing 'community activism' from the fetishisation of community and reinserting it into what I would see as an overly unified process of 'more general mobilisation.'[32] Hence my suspicion. As Doreen Massey has shown in her comments on *The Condition of Postmodernity*, David Harvey's *generality* means in practice a trivialisation of all differences other than class. Again, recruitment rather than understanding seems to be the aim. Massey quotes this passage as an example of Harvey's desire for 'a unity enforced through the tutelage of one group over others.'[33]

> The importance of recuperating such aspects of social organisation as race,
> gender, religion, within the overall frame of historical materialist enquiry
> (with its emphasis upon the power of money and capital circulation) and class
> politics (with its emphasis upon the unity of the emancipatory struggle) can-
> not be overestimated.[34]

Yes it can, all too easily, I would say. And Harvey seems to have conceded a little ground on that. There are, he admits in the more recent *Justice, Nature and the Geography of Difference*, 'many circumstances in which the intertwining of, say, racial, gender, geographical, and class issues creates all sorts of complexities that make it imperative for several sets of oppressions to be addressed.' Sadly, the concession is just setting us up for the sucker punch.

> But the converse complaint must also be registered: those who reject Marx's
> political commitment and the notion of class agency that necessarily attaches
> to it in effect turn their backs on his depiction of the human destitution,
> degradation and denial that lie at capitalism's door and become complicitous
> as historical agents with the reproduction of the particular set of permanences
> that capitalism has tightly fashioned out of otherwise open, fluid, and dynamic
> social processes.[35]

I'm bad people. End of conversation.

Or almost. I still feel that the scepticism towards communitarianism (though from different perspectives) and the anti-anti-urbanism which I share with Harvey should make some dialogue possible. I agree with his sense that publicness is more important than community, and that dialogue is more important than identity. He even acknowledges the need for a new poetics of the city in the final paragraph of *Justice, Nature and the Geography of Difference*. But for all that, and for all his impressive marshalling of facts and figures, and for all his telling anecdotes, what comes through his writing is above all a desire to make the refractory, opaque reality of the anthropological city conform more closely to *his* vision of an equitable society – his concept city, if you like.

In his judgement on the drama in Tompkins Square, he does not pause to ask whether a way of living in common was being brokered through the actual and symbolic violence in its shared, contested space – and, if so, what sort of community it was – nor, if it failed, why it failed. Harvey is not interested in that. He already knows the answer to the question of community: it is the ability of Marxism 'to synthesize diverse struggles with divergent and multiple aims into a more universal anti-capitalist movement with a global aim through a theoretical understanding of its potentialities.'[36] Paradoxically, I would respond, this militant confidence forecloses the question of the political. For Nancy, in sharp contrast to Harvey, the political is about 'not the organisation of society but the disposition of community as such.' *Political* means, for me, strangers working out how to live together. It denotes, says Nancy, 'a community consciously undergoing the experience of its sharing.'[37]

If you want to hear a differently experienced, but equally vibrant account of what sharing urban space feels like, this time from the inside, then listen – as my second example – to Dick Hebdige before he left Stoke Newington in north London for the comparative tranquillity of California.

> Lying in bed at 4 a.m. on one occasion unable to sleep because of the racket emanating from the squatters' house I decided to 'have it out' with them 'once and for all'. I got dressed and walked into the night air which was filled with the whine and screech of feedback and guitar. Having failed to rouse them by knocking on the door and shouting through the letter-box, I picked up an empty beer can and threw it at the first-floor window. The noise died off suddenly as the window was thrown open and a line of faces appeared. In the course of the ensuing argument I yelled (and I could hear the old man in my voice): 'Can't you turn the amplifiers down?' This seemed to strike a note of discord. There was a brief hiatus (was 'amplifier' an obsolete term? Didn't musicians use amplifiers any more?) and then the response came loud and clear: 'You don't understand.' Opting like an irate father for a well-worn strategy – one that had been used on myself by 'authority figures' many times in the past – I shouted back 'I don't *care* whether I understand or not! Just keep the ——— noise down! There are families with young babies in this street.' The absurdity (and the irony) of this exchange between the members of 'an anarchic youth subculture' and a 'former expert on subcultural resistance' was lost on me at the time but walking back towards my house five minutes later, I felt strangely elated, lighter on my feet: I was turning my back not only on a quieter scene, but also on an earlier incarnation. Released from the obligation

> to 'understand', I was free to sleep – at last! – the dreamless sleep of the senex
> or the fool.[38]

This is the everyday reality of how people in cities negotiate their – our – common existence. If we do, this is how we communicate with our neighbours. Hebdige's anecdote offers a number of insights into the way that communication works (or fails to work).

First, this is obviously not an example of Habermas's ideal of communication free from coercion, nor of Aristotelian deliberation about what constitutes the good life. Dick Hebdige wants his neighbours to shut up, and if that means chucking beer cans and confronting them with a bit of verbal aggression, then fine. 'It is not a question of establishing rules for communication,' says Nancy in a more theoretical register, 'it is a question of understanding before all else that in "communication" what takes place is an *exposition*: finite existence exposed to finite existence, co-appearing before it and with it.'[39]

Notice then, secondly, the anxious quotation marks which mark out Dick Hebdige's strangeness to himself. These are not *my* words, murmurs the self on his shoulder even as an overtone, even as he utters them. The words are part of a script for the event which he did not write, but which he cannot disown. His identity, or individuality, is here not an essence, but a performance. This performance is for an audience of others, the stroppy squatters.

Hence, thirdly, it is also an illustration of the way that self is formed in sociation. This is not an identity given by any shared being supposedly immanent to an idea of community. It is an instance of Nancy's 'exposition': the fact that ' "my" face [is] always exposed to others, always turned toward an other and faced by him or her, never facing myself.'[40]

Fourthly, the process of negotiating conflict through exposition does not require or entail mutual transparency, and, for Hebdige in this case at least, it apparently has little to do with an obligation to understand the other. In its own profane way, though, it is nonetheless ethical. Even if it fails as communication or deliberation, the row can be read as a compromised demonstration of the two cardinal virtues of urban co-existence: *tolerance* and *responsibility*. Deprived of sleep, Hebdige understandably reaches the limits of his tolerance. But is this the same thing as being intolerant or acting irresponsibly?

It is a key question, for it determines whether the negotiation of living in common can continue or breaks down. As a counterpoint, here is another anecdote which illustrates roughly how and where the boundaries might be drawn. It concerns an incident, this time featuring nosey neighbours – or violently intrusive fellow citizens – in Berlin in the nineteen seventies. It is recounted in Verena Stefan's novel *Shedding*.

> On the way home I pass a tavern. Two men and two women are sitting at a table right next to the sidewalk. Noticing me, one of the men is taken aback. He remarks to the others. They turn to stare at me.
>
> I am wearing a long skirt and a sleeveless teeshirt. In one hand I carry a shopping bag which holds three bottles of wine. The man leans over the railing and stares fixedly at me as I approach. Something about this situation alarms me more than usual. The man's expression is not lustful or lewd, but instead quite righteously indignant. As I pass him he says, incensed: Hey baby, what happened to your boobs?

Gilles Peress/
Magnum Photos,
Sarajevo, March–
September 1993

> My spine stiffens. The man is twice my size and half drunk besides. The others laugh in agreement. Two steps later I hear the shrill catcall whistling past my ears. From the corner of my eye I see the men's legs and hear, after the whistle: Jesus, what knockers!
>
> I crouch, ready to pounce. And then what? I ready myself to lash out. How to attack? Only five more steps until I can push open the heavy door to the building, rest the shopping bag next to the mailbox, take out the mail, go through the inner courtyard to the side entrance, climb the two flights of stairs, unlock the apartment door, enter the kitchen, open the refrigerator, carefully place the three bottles of wine on the shelf, let the door close and look about the kitchen, arms hanging down at my sides. My breasts hang against my ribcage, warm, sun-filled gourds. Under them, tiny rivulets of sweat had gathered and now dissolve, one drop at a time.[41]

Put to one side the fact that this is taken from a novel, and also that we should really hear from the other parties involved in both cases: the musicians and the drinkers, whose truth would no doubt be a bit different. Let's just assume for the moment that both Dick Hebdige and Verena Stefan are telling the truth. The first question is then whether Dick Hebdige was right to shout at his neighbours and whether Verena Stefan's character had a right not to be shouted at. If the answer to both is *yes*, the next question will be how to reconcile the two answers.

What is at issue in both cases are the unspoken *rules* or *grammar* of urban living. These are important in part because whether or not they are followed is what makes life bearable or unbearable. For Nancy, the sharing of a *logos* is what, in a classical sense, defines the life of the *polis* as a good life.

> *Logos* means many things. But one of its meanings is this: something (that one can at times determine as 'language', at times as 'reason', and in many other ways as well) whose only worth lies in being exposed (among other ways, as when a face lights up, opening), that is, in being shared.[42]

Here I am concerned primarily with whether and how tolerance and responsibility were being enacted in these confrontations. In *On Toleration*, Michael Walzer is less interested in the nitty-gritty of neighbours dealing with each other than in the social toleration of cultural, religious and way-of-life differences 'when the others are not fellow participants and when there is no common game and no intrinsic need for the differences they cultivate and enact.'[43] Even so, the five attitudes or modes of toleration he distinguishes provide a useful starting point. At the soft end of the scale, there is 'a resigned acceptance of difference for the sake of peace.' This may shade into a passive, relaxed and benign indifference – 'It takes all kinds to make a world.' For many philosophers, according to Walzer, the only acceptable definition of toleration is 'a kind of moral stoicism: a principled recognition that the 'others' have rights even if they exercise those rights in unattractive ways.' What is missing from that definition is the active endorsement of difference which characterises Walzer's most positive forms of toleration. One appears most forcefully as *curiosity*, a respect for otherness, 'a willingness to listen and learn', and the sort of openness to differences that characterises Iris Marion Young's work. The other is an *enthusiasm* for difference: 'an aesthetic endorsement, if difference is taken to represent in cultural form the largeness and diversity of God's creation or of the natural world; or a functional endorsement, if difference is viewed, as in the liberal multiculturalist argument, as a necessary condition of human flourishing, one that offers to individual men and women the choices that make their autonomy meaningful.'[44]

What strikes Hebdige as absurd – the lack of sympathy or communication between 'a "former expert on subcultural resistance"' and 'the members of "an anarchic youth subculture"' – seems quite logical when plotted against this typology. According to Walzer's reasoning, the apparent dissonance between Hebdige's enthusiastic aesthetic endorsement of (sub)cultural difference and his inability to be stoically accepting when faced by its noisy reality in the early hours should come as no surprise. Again, Walzer is concerned with different differences, but the principle is the same:

> ... in any pluralist society there will always be people, however well entrenched their own commitment to pluralism, for whom some particular difference – perhaps a form of worship, family arrangement, dietary rule, sexual practice, or dress code – is very hard to live with. Though they support the idea of difference, they tolerate the instantiated differences.[45]

Or not, in these cases. In the experience narrated by Stefan, the harassment is an act of pure intolerance. It is a denial of her right to walk the street, even to walk home. It is a refusal to tolerate even the most minor of differences in shared space – her offence is presumably the transgression of some imagined dress code. It sees only threat or challenge in any display of autonomous female eroticism. It substitutes the violence of humiliation for conversation or pleasure or just leaving in peace. Hebdige's case is different. Although he refuses to tolerate an instantiated difference – thinking that playing loud music at four is the morning is all right – does that mean that he was acting in an intolerant way?

Perhaps the key to the episode is to be found in the punch-line. 'Released from the obligation to 'understand', I was free to sleep – at last! – the dreamless sleep of the senex or the fool.' Why does Hebdige qualify his sleep in the way he does? He worries that this was not just the sleep that is possible without the noise – justification enough, you might think – but the sleep of irresponsibility. Is his anxiety that he has turned into an old man, and so become authoritarian, intolerant, and devoid of empathy? Is his ability to sleep a symptomatic failure to perform what the novelist Milan Kundera calls 'the imaginative act of tolerance'?[46] As if in answer, Richard Kearney talks about the 'irreducibly ethical scruple' of *answerability* as a last line of defence against 'the limitless circularity of mirrors, the looking-glass play of blank parody, the echo-chamber of *imagos*' in postmodernity.

> The other will not leave imagination be. It insists that our images remain insomniac, that the forgotten be recalled, that the pastiche of mirror reflections be penetrated until we reach the other side, the other's side. Imagination is summoned to invigilate the dark night of the post-modern soul until the other comes, even if only and always in the come-back of a trace. After imagination there is still the trace of its passage, its wake – the impossibility of sleeping and forgetting. At the end of the day, imagination cannot take leave of the other.[47]

Having, in his own view, played the authoritarian fool, Hebdige can sleep the sleep of the irresponsible fool. But, neither fool nor authoritarian nor irresponsible, he does not forget. He discharges his ethical debt to the noisy others by telling us about them. What he perhaps tells us about himself in the process is that his performance was in significant measure a masquerade: a piece of play acting which enabled him to shut them up without unleashing the full, murderous force of his enmity. In *Politics of Friendship*, Derrida quotes Nietzsche:

> *The wise man pretending to be a fool.* The wise man's philanthropy (*die Menschen-freundlichkeit*) sometimes leads him to *pose* as excited, angry, delighted, so that the coldness and reflectiveness of his *true* nature . . . shall not harm those around him.[48]

This leads Derrida to speculate on a new political wisdom 'inspired by this lie's wisdom, by this manner of knowing how to lie, dissimulate or divert wicked lucidity.'

> What if it demanded that we know, and know how to dissimulate, the principles and forces of social unbinding, all the menacing disjunctions? To dissimulate them in order to preserve the social bond and the *Menschenfreund-lichkeit*? A new political wisdom – human, humanistic, anthropological, of course? A new *Menschenfreundlichkeit*: pessimistic, sceptical, hopeless, incredulous?[49]

So is Dick Hebdige's unwilled buffoonery what the practice of toleration would look like in the sort of community-always-in-question envisaged by Nancy?

It suggests in any case a vanishing point between the virtues of toleration and *responsibility*. Hebdige was not wrong to respond to the action of his neighbours. He worries that he does not respond, as it were, 'in his own name', as Hebdige-the-expert-on-subcultures rather than a parodic, dissimulating 'voice of authority'. That seems less important, though, than his demand that *they* respond to his complaints, to respond as neighbours. That is, he insists that they respond before the question of community, as people having to find a way of living in common. This is the fundamental difference between his refusal to tolerate irresponsibility and the intolerance of the drinkers harassing Verena Stefan's heroine. Hebdige insists (to use another phrase that might have slipped out along with the invocation of families with babies) that the musicians show some *respect* – which is exactly what her tormentors deny to her.

Derrida again comments on the links between *respect* and *responsibility*, terms 'which come together and provoke each other relentlessly.' In languages of the Latin family, he observes, respect refers 'to distance, to space, to the gaze' and responsibility refers 'to time, to the voice and to listening'

> There is no respect, as its name connotes, without the vision and distance of a *spacing*. No responsibility without response, without what speaking and hearing *invisibly* say to the ear, and which takes *time*.[50]

Derrida's concern is the 'respectful separation' inherent in the 'co-implication of responsibility and respect' which, he suggests, 'seems to distinguish friendship from love.' Or, we might add, which distinguishes being in common (neighbourliness) from common being (community): a neighbourliness which means allowing fellow citizens space, and listening when their neighbours demand that space.

This is the pragmatic urbanity which can make the violence of living together manageable.

URBAN ETHICS

What does it mean to be a citizen? Aren't citizens simply people who live in cities? Not the way republicans, communitarians and most political theorists tell it, they're not. At least as far back as the Greeks, as we have already seen, citizenship has involved duty and performance and identity. From Aristotle through Rousseau to Hannah Arendt and today's champions of deliberative democracy, the republican *polis* has entailed a conceptual geography of citizenship centred on the agora, the forum, or the secular piazza, rather than the home, the street, or the neighbourhood. This geography gives a spatial dimension to communitarian philosophy. Michael Walzer extols its virtues:

> The square or piazza is the epitome of open-mindedness. Here public space is surrounded by a mix of public and private buildings: government offices, museums, lecture and concert hall, churches, shops, cafés, residences. . . . In the square itself, people meet, walk, talk, buy and sell, argue about politics, eat lunch, sit over coffee, wait for something to happen. . . . They are different people, with different purposes, educated by the space they share to a civil deportment.[51]

It is also, says Richard Rogers, the philosophy embodied in a public conception of architecture.

> The paradigm of public space is the city square or piazza: without it the city scarcely exists. City squares are special because their public function almost eclipses any other use they might have – people come to them principally to talk, demonstrate, celebrate, all essentially public activities. . . . I admit that, to me, scarcely any pleasure compares with that offered by a city square.[52]

It is a seductive picture, but one that needs to be complemented (at least) by the unsettling vignettes of urban confrontation painted by David Harvey, Dick Hebdige and Verena Stefan. The arts of living in the city are more demanding, more diverse, and more ingenious than Walzer and Rogers suggest. They require a variety of skills: reading the signs in the street; adapting to different ways of life right on your door-step; learning tolerance and responsibility – or at least, as Simmel taught us, indifference – towards others and otherness; showing respect, or self-preservation, in not intruding on other people's space; exploiting the etiquette of the street; picking up new rules when you migrate to a foreign city. It is through this rougher urbanity, rather than the nice disciplines of 'civil deportment', that the modern urban self is routinely formed.

Start from this more profane *logos* of city life, though, and where does that leave politics? Although I have suggested that Dick Hebdige's run-in with his neighbours fits Nancy's definition of the political (*le politique*) to the extent that it was 'receptive to what is at stake in community' that does not mean that what they were doing was *politics – la politique*, or the play of forces and interests engaged in a conflict over the representation and governance of social existence.[53] Neither the protocols of the row (the assertion of conflicting rights), nor the social space in which the scene was played out (home owner versus squatters), nor even the reason for the row (the competing claims of sleep and loud music as elements of the good life, and the resources necessary to achieve them) were unconnected to politics. Nevertheless, even when a degree of social co-operation was achieved and acknowledged on both sides as more or less fair, that still was not politics.

The lesson is that not everything is political, that not even everything personal or communal is political. Remember that John Rajchman defined his question about 'how to be 'at home' in a world where our identity is not given, our being-together in question, our destiny contingent or uncertain' as constituting an *ethos*. If ethics is then a better description than politics of what was going on that night in Stoke Newington, does that confine the negotiations of the street to a private, or at least a non-public, space? What is the relationship between the sort of community being worked out here and membership of a political community?

In trying to show how social relations are constituted by the constantly shifting boundary between 'the social' and 'the political,' Ernesto Laclau describes the constitution of the social in terms quite close to Rajchman's. Where Rajchman talks about 'the violence of our own self-constitution', Laclau talks about the institution of the social.

> The moment of original institution of the social is the point at which its contingency is *revealed*, since that institution . . . is only possible through the repression of options that were equally open. To reveal the original meaning of an act, then, is to reveal the moment of its radical contingency . . . by showing the terrain of the original violence, of the power relation through which that instituting act took place.[54]

We experience our social world as simply the way things are, as objective presence, because that contingency is systematically forgotten. Nor can we hope to return to that original moment of institution. Nevertheless, argues Laclau, it is possible to rediscover the contingent nature of this apparently objective world when new antagonisms emerge, and so (we can add) when new communities form. This is where the social borders the political.

> The sedimented forms of 'objectivity' make up the field of what we will call the 'social'. The moment of antagonism where the undecidable nature of the alternatives and their resolution through power relations becomes fully visible constitutes the field of the 'political'.[55]

If Dick Hebdige and the squatters were to join forces and lobby their local council for spaces where musicians can play extremely loudly without frightening the babies or waking the academics, then that presumably would be a political action. If, whether out of self-interest or political-aesthetic conviction, they all found themselves campaigning against the criminalisation of rave culture in England by the Criminal Justice Act,[56] then that too would be political. But what exactly – or inexactly – would mark the transition from the social to the political? It would be the moment of decision, and especially the decision to act together, which for Laclau (if I understand him right) would be a hegemonic moment, the formation of a new point of political agency.

This helps to explain why, *contra* David Harvey, I am reluctant to regard negoti-ations about sharing urban space in everyday life as pre-political in any sense of being either undercooked politics or simply a recruiting ground for 'real' politics. Equally, however, it suggests why it remains important to insist nonetheless that there is a boundary between the social and the political, however mobile and however fuzzy it may be.

That boundary shifts because it is always in question. It is negotiated as we talk to each other in the city. That is why we need both a theorised concept of community and thick descriptions of how strangers talk to each other. It is in that spirit, I think, that Iris Marion Young, a political theorist unusually open and sensitive to cultural concerns and insights, has recently proposed a *communicative* model of democracy to replace the conventional *deliberative* model. What worries her about most accounts of deliberative democracy is their tendency to equate democracy with rational deliber-ation, and then to equate rational deliberation with critical argument. This produces a cultural bias which 'tends to silence or devalue some people or groups.'[57] Young therefore wants to open up the discussion in two ways. First, who should get to speak in a communicative democracy? 'Differences of culture, social perspective, or particularist commitment' should be seen not as a problem, but as 'resources to draw on for reaching understanding'.[58] Individual understandings and preferences, she asserts, will be most effectively transformed by the communicative encounter with differences of meaning, culture, social position, or need. Second, how should those who speak be allowed to speak? Not just in the form of critical argument, insists Young. Allowing the more textured and seductive forms of 'greeting, rhetoric, and storytelling' would acknowledge and enhance the locatedness and depth of the discussion, both in terms of the address to a specific audience and also by opening up a wider range of cultural repertoires.

Given my argument in this chapter, I am naturally sympathetic to Young's expan-sive view of communication. It seems to be opening up politics to the ethical and cultural concerns which I have been exploring in borderline public spaces. So why am I not wholly convinced? I think it is to do with the way she draws the boundary between the political and the cultural (or social). For a start, Iris Young remains notably more committed to consensus and agreement as the outcome of communica-tion even than someone like Habermas. Her concern, as I understand her, is to dismantle barriers preventing effective access to the public sphere as the forum of political discussion, rather than to question whether such discussion *is* what consti-tutes both politics and the political. That is why, in the end, I am not persuaded by Young's appeal to the city as a normative ideal *for politics*. Her city is a wonderful image of how we should understand and approach the always unpredictable, some-times painful, and often intensely pleasurable give and take of everyday dealings with neighbours: what the down-the-line deliberationist Seyla Benhabib calls 'the informally structured process of everyday communication among individuals who share a cultural and historical life world.'[59] But, from a different perspective, I agree with Benhabib that this is not politics.

As I suggested in chapter four, when making the case for an extremely formalist understanding of citizenship as a symbolic order, the problem is not to make *Gesellschaft* feel more like *Gemeinschaft*. Nor is it to expand the definition of politics to soak up ethics. Nor is it to collapse either into the other. Iris Young calls for 'a broader conception of communicative democracy' in order to open up prefer-ences and understandings to challenge and change. Her justification for wanting to

legitimise greeting, rhetoric and storytelling, however, are 'female accounts of dia-
logical reason' and 'male Afro-American and Latino articulations of cultural biases in
dominant conceptions of deliberation'.[60] In other words, even though opinion is to
be put in question by the act of communication, these supposedly primordial gender
and ethnic identities are apparently to be accepted as sufficiently stable grounds for
that critique. Such identities are apparently not to be exposed as themselves contingent on the event of talking to each other; as enacted rather than given, as self-
constituted. Compare this with Nancy's account of communication, here quoted at
greater length.

> How can we be receptive to the *meaning* of our multiple, dispersed, mortally
> fragmented existences, which nonetheless only make sense by existing in
> common? In other words, perhaps: how do we communicate? But this ques-
> tion can be asked seriously only if we dismiss all 'theories of communication',
> which begin by positing the necessity or the desire for a consensus, a continu-
> ity and a transfer of messages. It is not a question of establishing rules for
> communication, it is a question of understanding before all else that in "com-
> munication" what takes place is an *exposition*: finite existence exposed to finite
> existence, co-appearing before it and with it.[61]

Here again we confront the simultaneous constitution of community and individual, of the individual in community, and the possibility of political community.
Whatever his scepticism about the concept of space, or perhaps more because of his
sense of space being constituted through the temporality of the event, Ernesto
Laclau identifies the base on which 'a radical democratic alternative' might be constructed as 'the multiplication of 'public spaces' and their constituencies beyond
those accepted by classical liberalism.'[62] This multiplication of singular public spaces
seems closer to the mark than Young's encompassing city and respectful communication. Such spaces, or such moments of publicness,[63] might *happen* in the piazzas so
admired by Rogers and Walzer, in the streets and suburbs of London, in the parks
and pizza parlours of New York, or even in Welsh border villages. What would make
them public would be that communication of finite existences, those moments of
community, of our self-constitution as *our*-selves.

In this chapter, I have been arguing that more is lost than gained by colonising all
the everyday negotiations of urban life for either 'community' or 'politics'. To do so
simply diverts attention from the complexity and difficulty and singularity of the
social, and thus undermines the possibility of imagining what a democratic *culture*
might look like or feel like. My guess, hardly surprisingly, is that it would look pretty
much like living in a city, though somehow, slightly, utopianly different. Where does
this leave the question of urban (or any other) community? Gone is any idea of
transcendent identity. Gone too is an ideal of virtuous citizenship. In the offing may
be a thicker description of the openness to unassimilable difference, and so also a
concern with the mundane, pragmatic but sometimes life-or-death arts of living in
the city. These skills shade into and out of the virtues made possible by the great
adventure of the city: politeness as well as politics, civility as well as citizenship, the
stoicism of urbanity, the creative openness of cosmopolitanism.

In short: the question of community, and so the question of *polis* as both city life
and the political, demands a response in terms of ethics as well as politics. It is less a
question of identity than of toleration, responsibility, justice, and space. Thinking

about that in an urban register, it is tempting to conclude that the greatest of these virtues is space. For Jean-Luc Nancy, community in its modern forms is experienced not as 'a work to be produced, nor a lost communion, but rather as space itself, and the spacing of the experience of the outside, of the outside-of-self.'[64] This I would say (of course I would) is still the space, the reality, of the city.

Richard Kalvar/
Magnum Photos,
Tokyo

chapter 7

Postcards

A postcard, typically, is mailed home from a foreign city. Place is condensed in an image, the image is authenticated by your scribbled account of being there, and this impression of another real-imagined city is stamped and posted to a distant part of the world. That is why, for Derrida, the postcard is an instance of telecommunication.[1]

POSTCARD FROM SINGAPORE

Well, here I am, in postcard mode, writing on the forty third floor of, it says in the lift, the world's tallest hotel, the Westin Stamford in Singapore. I can believe it. From the bar on the seventieth floor, especially at night, the Singapore cityscape is spectacular yet somehow predictable. It is a bit like New York, of course, which remains the template. With its giant neon signs and video screens, the comparison with the cinematic future cities in *Blade Runner* or *Akira* is hard to avoid. What comes first to my mind, however, perhaps because I have been reading through my manuscript here, is Paul Citroën's collage *Metropolis*. The view has the same dominant tone of orange, but above all it shares that in-your-face massiveness which, in 1923, Citroën saw latent in the modernist city. That virtual city, invisible but even then imaginable, has now been realised, and not just here.

The view from the seventieth floor, or even the forty-third, offers a familiar temptation. Like de Certeau's *dieu voyeur* without the expertise, the whitefeller tourist is all too prone to look down from his tower and blather on to his laptop about the postmodern, postcolonial, posthistorical world implicit in the nocturnal cityscape of Asia. Even with Singapore spread before me, though, I feel no inclination to foretell the future wonders and horrors of life in the wired city. I am acutely aware that, even as I want to understand Singapore's disconcerting *newness*, still I look at this city, here and now, through a prism of European references and with a modernist eye. When I think about the future, I cannot help recalling the past.

Does that sound too elegiac and utopian? As I write the words, I hear implicit in their tone a certain way of seeing the world; one that is, I cannot deny, irredeemably European and masculine. That is, to be sure, a limitation. But to acknowledge the limits of one's thought may have its own advantages. Might not my perspective – a critique of the present and an attempt to imagine the future through the detour of the past – also allow the possibility of *working through* that past? This way of thinking, for all its constraints and collusions, at least avoids the disavowals and repressions so obvious in many gung-ho predictions about future cities. I hope it might be an instance of what Deleuze is getting at as he elaborates on what Foucault meant by a critical reflection on living in the present.

> To think means to be embedded in the present-time stratum that serves as a limit: what can I see and what can I say today? But this involves thinking of the past as it is condensed in the inside, in the relation to oneself (there is a Greek in me, or a Christian, and so on). We will then think the past against the present and resist the latter, not in favour of a return but 'in favour, I hope, of a time to come' (Nietzsche), that is, by making the past active and present to the outside so that something new will finally come about, so that thinking, always, may reach thought.[2]

In a more intuitive way, reacting to the presence of this cityscape, I find myself thinking Singapore and London together. That does not mean I assume that the present reality of Singapore and the other great cities of the new Asia embodies *the future*. Nor would I accept that my recollections of London and the imagined (and implicitly European) modern city I have been writing about are no more than the rags and remnants of *the past*. Therein lies the teleological trap its critics are right to say is inherent in the concept of modernity. Rather, the resonances between this perceived Singapore and my imagined London, especially the changing London of the nineteen eighties that set me off on this adventure, now shape the way I think about the city in future; or in favour, I hope, of a city to come. The poetics of the modern city involve not just the porous and unstable boundaries between reality and imagination, but these disjunctural, asynchronous temporalities, these signifying time-lags.[3]

Singapore in the Asian economic hangover of the late nineties may be just the place from which to reflect on the story of Mrs Thatcher's London. The links between the two cities go a long way further back, of course. At least from the nineteenth century on, they have both been shaped by the mutual dependencies between the trading and political control centres in metropolitan Europe, and the many 'peripheral' world cities formed and transformed by an imperialist world economy.[4] Here is *The Communist Manifesto* on that phase of globalisation.

> All old established national industries . . . are dislodged by new industries, whose introduction becomes a life and death question for all civilized nations, by industries that no longer work up indigenous raw material, but raw material drawn from the remotest zones; industries whose products are consumed, not only at home, but in every quarter of the globe. In place of the old wants, satisfied by the production of the country, we find new wants, requiring for their satisfaction the products of distant lands and climes. In place of the old local and national seclusion and self-sufficiency, we have intercourse in every direction, universal interdependence of nations.[5]

So there is nothing new about the idea that Singapore and London are part of the same story, whether the story is capitalism, colonialism, modernity, or globalisation. In a sense, though, that is the danger of such concepts. They all tend to reduce the singularity of events (and cities), whenever and wherever, to being manifestations of one underlying cause.

Acknowledging that *theoretical* objection to globalisation does not mean we cannot ascribe much of what has happened to both Singapore and London over the past few decades to the *pas de deux* between labour and place (to use Richard Sennett's typically elegant phrase).[6] There have been attempts to reinvent both cities as nodal points in a global market place and a network of planetary telecommunications, as switches in a circuit through which can flow information, people, resources, freight, airline traffic and, above all, capital. Especially in the eighties, both Singapore and London seemed to confirm that Manuel Castells was right to believe that 'the meaning of the space of places' was being superseded by the 'space of flows'.[7]

What were the differences and local variations, though? Singapore is a small city-state of three million people, with no rural hinterland, limited natural resources, and inadequate supplies of water.[8] Since independence in 1965, despite those constraints, it has developed into the world's second busiest port after Rotterdam, it has become a major oil refining centre, it has established a major electronic components industry and it has achieved a leading role in shipbuilding and repairing. It is one of the few countries where the number of tourists per year is greater than its resident population.

The unsentimental pragmatism with which Singapore has been rebuilt recall Le Corbusier at his most ruthlessly visionary. The attitude of Singapore's leadership towards the urban landscape, says the architect David Turnbull, has been 'abstract, aggressive, utilitarian, and exploitative.'[9] Turnbull's audit of the achievements recalls the litanies of Haussmannisation.

> In a twenty-year period the number of housing units has increased fourfold, and shops, offices, and hotels tenfold. The slum and squatter population has been reduced from 783,000 in 1970 to 28,000 in 1990. The number of new housing units built over the same period increased from 189,600 to 735,900. Over 2,000 kilometers of roads, highways, and expressways have been constructed; ten percent of the land area (6,000 hectares) has been reclaimed from the sea. . . . Over five million trees and shrubs have been planted and nearly 1,800 hectares of parks, gardens and recreation spaces have been created, forming a garden city.[10]

Singapore, Turnbull concludes, 'is a global city, strategically, economically, and culturally.'[11] That is what London wanted to be, too; or, rather, what some people wanted London to become. It emerged as one of the key metropolitan centres sustaining the information-based global economy, along with New York and Tokyo, and second-tier cities like Paris, Hong Kong and Singapore, when its financial markets were reorganised and deregulated in the Big Bang of October 1986.

The particular local consequences were again affected by the space and the histories of London. Despite earlier predictions, the new flows of power did not hollow out its centre. Although manufacturing industry and many middle class residents continued to drift away, the logic of processing information required both telecommunications technologies and personnel to be consolidated in offices that themselves became, so to speak, part of the central computer. London's strategic role as the primary centre for processing international capital made it a magnet.[12] Elite workers arrived from the world's richest nations, along with rich investors from poorer countries. There was a boom in office and residential property, followed by the inevitable glut of office space, and the slump of 1987.

Even if 'power rules through flows', even Castells acknowledged that people still 'live in places.' To evoke the singularity of London, imagine a re-born Dickens standing on Tower Bridge in the late eighties, or perhaps taking an elevator to the top of Cesar Pelli's Canary Wharf tower. How might he have read the spatial and social networks of London at the century's end? What would he have seen in its cityscapes and riverscapes?

Looking towards the City, at first glance Dickens would see a landscape dominated by new skyscrapers similar to those to be found in any other business district in any other major city, in Manhattan or Singapore. This skyline was the monument to another frenzy of speculative building, both in the City itself and in the Docklands Redevelopment Project to its east. Part of Dickens's story might then be a juicy melodrama of hubris and greed brought low. He could tell of ministers enticing overseas developers with massive subsidies and sweeteners, of the speculators' failure to galvanise Docklands into any sort of social life, of desperate but doomed rescue packages as the hangover hit after the Thatcher binge, and finally of how Olympia & York, proud owners of the Canary Wharf complex, went spectacularly bust. Dickens might also draw moral lessons from the Disneyfied physical fabric of Docklands. Glitzy facades, the intrusive surveillance of closed circuit television and a few works by fine architects like Richard Rogers and Aldo Rossi could not hide the lack of any social or aesthetic vision, an inadequate infrastructure and often jerry-built private residences.[13]

I can almost hear Le Corbusier telling us that he told us so. But Dickens, I suspect, would have homed in on the social consequences. Flush young City workers moved into the upper-income residential enclaves of Docklands. The working-class population of the Isle of Dogs, which had grown up around the now defunct docks industry, moved out. Despite the promises, the investment in the riverside schemes failed to 'trickle down' to other parts of the East End, like Tower Hamlets and Newham. Over the decades since the War, these boroughs had been a first English home for settlers from the low-income Commonwealth countries – the West Indies, India, Pakistan, and, particularly in these cases, Bangladesh – and their British-born children. By the early nineties, most of the old cargo-handling and dock related jobs in the area had disappeared.[14] Unemployment in the Docklands hinterland was thirty percent and rising. A quarter of homes were overcrowded, six thousand people were living in emergency accommodation. Both old and new inhabitants were trapped by limited employment opportunities, poor education, and declining welfare provision.

'Remember Manchester?' Engels might mutter to Dickens. 'Remember Haussmannisation?'

Docklands is a story that begs to be told in Victorian terms, whether as a sentimental novel, as the sort of report produced by Chadwick and Kay-Shuttleworth, or as a journalistic exposé in the tradition of Engels and Mayhew. One of the most passionate and despairing chroniclers of the social fall-out of Docklands was a Tower Hamlets doctor who combined Kay-Shuttleworth's social conscience with Engels's political commitment. David Widgery describes the sick people he met in his surgery, records the squalid living conditions which often contributed to their illnesses, and juxtaposes both against a bigger economic and political picture.[15] For Widgery, the eighties in London was the decade when 'one became hardened to the sight of hunched and dishevelled human bundles in doorways, disused buildings, even skips. Some enterprise, some culture.' The attempt to 'outflank the City of London to its east' with 'an identikit North American financial district' during the recession of the late eighties merely tightened the screw of deprivation and suffering. Widgery found the optimism that inspired him to become a doctor in the East End being ground down into 'a kind of grudging weariness punctuated with bouts of petty fury.'

'I'm watching something die and I wish I wasn't,' he wrote. 'Perhaps the best thing that can be done is to record the process.' But what died? In what terms should its passing be imagined and described? And what was being born in its place?

In one telling, it was community that died, a way of life. That is how Widgery saw it. That is how the local campaign against the Docklands development presented it, too, as the last stand of 'the real isle of Dogs'. The trouble was, this time things really *had* changed, and that campaign failed largely because it remained trapped within a desperate, backward-looking vision of community and identity.[16] Repackaged and sentimentalised, this same vision of London community resurfaced at this very moment in the phenomenally successful television soap opera *EastEnders*. The historian Bill Schwarz notes the irony.

> . . . just as in 1960 *Coronation Street* brought to a national public the culture of a particular working-class formation – two-up-two-downs, football and the dogs, the corner pub and so on – at the very moment when it had all but disappeared as a dominant form, so perhaps in the 1980s the media construction of *EastEnders* cultivates a curiously anachronistic idea of a collective identity, in which Albert Square casts a magical spell of cohesion on all its otherwise diverse inhabitants.[17]

These images of 'the community that died' or the soap opera community were symptoms of the weakening of the links between community, place, and identity. The *EastEnders* vision of London was, as it were, a defensive reaction, and it was part of the same pathology that produced the racialisation of urban discourse in the nineteen eighties. When Prince Charles visited Spitalfields in East London in July 1987, according to the *Guardian*, he encountered a place that was less like 'home' than 'like a third world country.'[18] 'Do you really think this is your city any longer?' the racist mayor of New York imagines asking his complacent white constituents in *The Bonfire of the Vanities*, Tom Wolfe's 1988 novel about Manhattan and Manhattanisation. 'It's the Third World down there!' This is the racialised rhetoric prefigured, and to some extent explained, in the study of 'mugging' and urban politics published in 1978 by Stuart Hall and his colleagues in *Policing the Crisis*.[19] They took *crime* as the key mediating metaphor of urban life. They looked at the stereotypes of black youth disseminated through the mass media and the judiciary, and at the political movement to what they called a law-and-order state. Presaging both the social logic of Thatcherism and the uprisings in Brixton, Handsworth, Liverpool and Bristol in the nineteen eighties, *Policing the Crisis* showed how all the perceived failings of modern urban planning and the welfare state, as well as the vulnerability of urban populations to crime, were condensed into the demonic symbol of the black mugger and later the black rioter.[20]

Learning from the approach taken by *Policing the Crisis*, a less Victorian telling of nineteen eighties London might focus less on the death of community, than on a transformation in ways of perceiving urban problems and imagining community. In 1994, Nikolas Rose called this *the death of the social*. By that, he meant the displacement of that object of knowledge and government whose emergence in the reformist rationalities of the nineteenth century, and flowering in the therapeutic modernism of twentieth century architecture, I described in chapter two.[21] 'The social', in this sense, is both an urban imaginary and a largely taken for granted principle of political thought, manifest in the technologies of social work, social insurance, social citizenship, and planning. By the nineteen eighties, suggested Rose, it was being replaced by a different rationality, that of advanced liberal government.

> Advanced liberal strategies of government seek to govern through acting upon the educated and managed choices of individuals and families, through instrumentalising individual desires for self-promotion and self-protection, through enhancing desires for maximisation of quality of life. Rather than seeking to bind experts into centrally administered bureaucratic apparatuses of social government, they seek to re-draw the boundaries of the political, and to govern through a range of intermediate, semi-autonomous regulatory bodies, authorities and forms of expertise, imagined according to new logics of competition.[22]

Just before the British election of 1997, the shadow minister then responsible for social services made a highly publicised visit to Singapore and the other Asian tiger economies to learn how a new Labour government might move beyond the old paradigm of the welfare provision. At first glance, this confirms Rose's hypothesis. It also seems to give credence to a claim made by the Singaporean architect Tay Keng Soon in 1995, while the economic times were still good.

> I think what people are starting to realize is that this is the most advanced city-state in human civilization, this is the twenty-first century city and if they don't like what they see then they'd better do something about it fast: because this is the future of urban living and a host of countries are lining up to learn how to copy what they've done here.[23]

Even so, it would be misleading to say too baldly that advanced liberalism or the Singaporean model was *replacing* the social as a principle of government. Rose's subtle and imaginative diagnosis does not imply a linear temporality from social welfare/London/ the past to advanced liberalism/Singapore/the future.

Just as the physical city is a palimpsest, a complex layering of architectural imaginings that are given a physical reality, destroyed, and built over, so we might think of the layering of social visions in which the past remains a force in the present, and also in our present attempts to think the future. 'Social' ways of thinking are not simply going to disappear. They will be reworked and displaced in new ways of perceiving and imagining and representing the city.

As I think about eighties London from nineties Singapore, then, what I take from Rose's obituary is that what died along with the social is a certain modernist conception of the city, a certain ideology of planning. Yesterday's mashed potatoes, I'll be scolded; Jane Jacobs was driving the stake through Le Corbusier's heart forty years ago! True enough. But what was her alternative, and what new and different ways of thinking have planners and architects come up with since?

In 1961, Jacobs ended *The Death and Life of Great American Cities* with a witty and debunking attempt to rethink 'the kind of problem a city is'. How, she asked, does the problem, or the complex set of problems, that we call the city get thought about? Today, there are articulate voices arguing that planning in the key of *the social* has, for sure, had its day, but that there are new songs to be sung about community, difference, and publicness which are more attuned to our times.[24] But when these are translated into plans, it still often seems to me that they too fail to get out of the bind in which Jacobs found herself. I mean this: isn't thinking about the city *as a problem* itself part of the problem? By continuing to take it for granted that the city is *some* kind of a problem, however complex, does that not presuppose that the city-problem is susceptible to some kind of solution, however politically modest and ingeniously postmodern? Didn't Jane Jacobs, and don't most of today's planners, in the end stay within the logic of the social (however disaggregated) that produced many of the things she so disliked in modern city planning?

Take just one post-social thematic: the revival of publicness as a political ideal, and so the attempt to reanimate public space in cities. I have already talked about Michael Walzer's understandable love affair with the urban piazza. For him, the virtue of public space, which he prefers to call *open-minded* space, is that it is 'designed for a variety of uses, including unforeseen and unforeseeable uses, and used by citizens who do different things and are prepared to tolerate, even take an interest in, things they don't do.'[25] The same vision drives Richard Rogers's schemes for recreating the centre of London. An image comes to mind. In the lead-up to the British general election in 1992, Rogers and the Labour Party's shadow arts spokesman took part in a television programme in which (a bit like the Spice Girls in their movie five years later) they toured the capital in an open-topped double decker bus.[26] This perspective allowed Rogers to diagnose the capital's ills without appearing to indulge in too much modernist *hauteur* (no towers for him), and to express again his plans for reinvigorating London's public and civic life by putting motor traffic in its place and giving precedence to public space. Why do I sympathise, but not quite believe? One reason is that Rogers seems still to believe that you can build publicness. The point is not to switch from Le Corbusier's vision of the social to Rogers's vision of the public (or to visions of community or difference or whatever), but to get away from the idea that you can build any of them into being. I go along with Rem Koolhaas in his answer to a tricky question from a student:

> I think we are still stuck with this idea of the street and the plaza as a public domain, but the public domain is radically changing. I don't want to respond in clichés, but with television and the media and a whole series of other inventions, you could say that the public domain is lost. But you could also say it's now so pervasive it does not need physical articulation any more. I think the truth is somewhere between. But we as architects still look at it in terms of a nostalgic model, and in an incredibly moralistic sense, refuse signs of its being reinvented in other more populist or more commercial terms.[27]

The premise that Koolhaas shares, at least implicitly, with other architectural thinkers like Bernard Tschumi and Bernard Caché (for all their differences) is that the city is *not* a problem for architecture. That is not to say that there are not lots of real problems to be solved in cities. Of course there are. To say that the city is not a problem (ontologically) is simply to acknowledge the limits of architecture.

Architecture – that is, shaping and framing the physical spaces in which we live – cannot solve the problems we have created for ourselves by living the way we do, and should not be expected to do so. It is unreasonable to ask planning and architecture to do the work of government, just as it is a mistake to assume that government is the same thing as politics. Government addresses the question of how to manage populations and resources. The political addresses the question of how to manage the violence inherent in living together. Neither singly nor in combination are these questions susceptible to an aesthetic solution: the planned city, the city in the future perfect.

That is why, when asked what role a critical architecture should have in shaping future cities, Rem Koolhaas replies, 'none'. A post-architectural style of intervention will be governmental rather than aesthetic, addressing the infrastructural determinants of realisable cities rather than picturing the ideal qualities of dream cities.[28]

POSTCARD FROM THE PLANE

On the plane from Singapore back to Western Australia, now, and so subject to another temptation: what I think of as Marc Augé's temptation. In many ways, his *Non-Places* is an engaging and persuasive book. It conjures up a topography of motorways, supermarkets, airport lounges, and multi-storey car parks: all those spaces that crystallise around the banal and functional flows of transport, circulation, commerce, and leisure. What worries me is Augé's prologue about the jet-setting exploits of the mythical executive 'Pierre Dupont'. The temptation is again that of a seductive perspective: not the planner or tourist up a tower this time, but the airborne, rootless man about the globe. I remind myself once more of that iconic touchstone of contemporary reality, Doreen Massey's bus shelter in Harlesden – which, incidentally, conveys the experience of *non-place* with an exquisitely mundane precision that even Augé never quite manages – and also recall her salutary comments on the male blinkers on much of this type of writing.

Perhaps my resistance to the non-place perspective helps to explain my contrasting reactions to the two books I have brought on the flight. One is a report on empirical research undertaken by a group of sociologists at the Roehampton Institute.[29] Their topic is the impact of globalisation on a cross-section of people living in the south London borough of Wandsworth, and especially in Tooting, in the nineteen nineties. As it happens, Wandsworth is where my mother's family lived, and where she grew up between the nineteen twenties and the nineteen forties. Thirty years later, in the nineteen seventies, I spent five years working there as a secondary school teacher. So, oddly enough, as I fly over the Indian Ocean, I find myself thinking back to that largely unremarkable but, in memory, likeable place, Tooting.

In their interviews, the Roehampton sociologists are struck above all by the varied ways in which different people respond to what they call microglobalisation. They also recognise that people's everyday reality is no longer (if it ever was) limited to the place where they live. People have learned to live both *here* and *there* at the same time.[30] Just as I think about London from Singapore, people in Tooting hark back to Singapore, India, Sweden, or wherever. They, like me, translate this ultramontane sense of home from nostalgia into conversation by means of the wonders of e-mail and (let's not forget) cheaper rates on the equally mysterious but by now taken for granted telephone.

Martin Albrow observes the consequence of this liquid sense of identity and social belonging. It is:

> ... the possibility that individuals with very different lifestyles and social networks can live in close proximity without untoward interference with each other. There is an old community for some, for others there is a new site for a community which draws its culture from India. For some Tooting is a setting for peer group leisure activity, for others it provides a place to sleep and access to London. It can be a spectacle for some. For others the anticipation of a better, more multicultural community.[31]

People, in short, actively 'construct locality'. They do so *imaginatively*, making use equally of trans-cultural symbolic resources (kinship and friendship networks, tradition and memory, media images and myths) as well as the latest communication technologies. Albrow's conclusion about how people live in the city today has a familiar ring to it.

> What they experience is not, therefore, in general anything like the traditional concept of community based on a shared local culture. Rather they engage in something like a cavalcade where passing actors find minimal levels of tolerable co-existence with varying intimations of other people's lives.[32]

This suggests rather a different reality from Augé's assertion that 'place becomes a refuge for the habitué of non-places.'[33] The evidence points to the individually managed flow of global cultural resources in a place – even Tooting. What especially strikes me in Albrow's account, though, is the way that it echoes both Simmel's impressions of the mental life of the metropolis, and also the creative montage of here and there to be found both in the aesthetic of cinema and in the modernist fiction of Joyce and Dorothy Richardson.

That is not to say that nothing has changed between the modernist twenties and the globalised nineties. Rather, again, it seems that a poetics of the modern city has been reworked and transformed, not negated. This is what I take Deleuze to be getting at in his idea of the past being 'condensed in the inside, in the relation to oneself'. My applause for his insistence on 'making the past active and present to the outside so that something new will finally come about' may then help to explain the irritation I feel with my other book for the journey, William J. Mitchell's *City of Bits*.[34]

My dislike (I admit it) of the genre of cyber-futurology is provoked by the way that, so often, it recoups the future for the present, rather than embracing the *limit* of the present as a precondition for thinking in favour of a time to come. That is not to diminish the importance of the new information and communication technologies. Nor is it to deny that they will have effects on the architecture of future cities – just as, for example, the telephone, along with elevators, made skyscrapers a sensible form of building.

What I resent in *City of Bits* is the kitsch way Mitchell appropriates and sanitizes the imagery of urbanity and publicness. On the one hand, he wants the Internet to be entirely new, and so utterly different from the modern city: 'the worldwide electronic network – the electronic agora – subverts, displaces, and radically redefines our notions of gathering place, community, and urban life.'[35] And that's not the half of it. The Net will supposedly do away with the institutional fabric of modern urban life. No more libraries, no more museums, no more theatres, schools, or hospitals. Just Net sites. On the other hand, unable (inevitably) to imagine a *really* different future, Mitchell tarts up his pedestrian daydreams with the glamour of the city and the virtues of urbanity. Surfing the Internet is 'like Baudelaire strolling through the buzzing complexity of nineteenth-century Paris.'[36] 'Click, click through cyberspace; this is the new architectural promenade.'[37] 'The online environment of the future will increasingly resemble traditional cities in their variety of distinct places, in the extent and complexity of their 'street networks' and 'transportation systems' linking these places, in their capacity to engage our senses, and in their social and cultural richness.'[38] 'James Joyce surely would have been impressed; city as text and text as city. Every journey constructs a narrative.'[39] 'I am an electronic *flâneur*. I hang out on the network. The keyboard is my café.'[40] (This silliness reminds me of a childhood joke. 'What's the difference between a postbox and an elephant?' 'I don't know.' 'I won't ask you to post my letters, then.')

Logged on, Mitchell believes he lives in the immediacy, the real time, of the virtual world city. He appears to give little thought to the new colonials living in the deferred time of the crowded megalopolis.[41] He would no doubt dismiss me as a 'materiality chauvinist',[42] a throw-back stuck in the modern city – which, nonetheless, is the ideal to which he aspires. What he fails to spot is that the position of the *flâneur* derives its epistemological power from being that little bit anachronistic. Similarly, he makes the mistake of believing that any technology, even one as clever and useful as the Internet, guarantees free rein to the imagination. The power of imagination, I have argued, lies in its ability to shimmy across and around the boundary between the real and the imaginary, and to explore the ethical possibilities of the 'as if'. That is how imagination is linked to publicness. Publicness happens occasionally, fleetingly, and unpredictably. You cannot build publicness, let alone institutionalise it, either in the city or on the Net.

That is why I remain sceptical about the power of the Internet to deliver, at last, participatory democracy. My doubts reflect my understanding of the public and of politics rather than Luddite prejudices. Mitchell is not one of the more extreme cyber-communitarians. Nevertheless, he makes grand claims. The Net, he assures us, 'will play as crucial a role in twenty-first-century urbanity as the centrally located, spatially bounded, architecturally celebrated agora did (according to Aristotle's *Politics*) in the life of the Greek polis.'[43] Rather than pursue the idea of politics as the *question* of political community, he assumes that it is a design brief for architecture. With one eye as ever on the rear-view mirror, he contrasts the creation of cyber-communities with the spatial formation of political community in ancient Rome.

> The new sort of site is not some suitable patch of earth but a computer to which members may connect from wherever they happen to be. The foundation ritual is not one of marking boundaries and making obeisance to the gods, but of allocating disk space and going online. And the new urban design task is not one of configuring buildings, streets, and public spaces to meet the needs and aspirations of the *civitas*, but one of writing computer code and deploying software objects to create virtual places and electronic interconnections between them.[44]

Compare this brash recipe for recreating a public sphere with Rem Koolhaas's hesitation and uncertainty in his comments, which I quoted above. The public domain, for Koolhaas, is *lost*: as dead as community, as dead as the social. And yet at the same time the supposedly passed away public domain has become so *pervasive* that it *does not need physical articulation*. When I say you can no more build publicness on the Net than in the city, I am simply repeating Koolhaas's perception. And if his logic seems familiar, that is because we have indeed encountered it before. This, again, is the language of a spectre that haunts the city. The public domain is always, inherently, a *phantom* sphere.[45] Publicness means not a rebuilt Trafalgar Square with stylish cafés and the hum of civilised conversation in place of traffic jams, desirable as that is. Nor is publicness an idealised sphere of intersubjective transparency and communication free from domination or constraint. Nor is it a news group on the Net. It is, to repeat, the question – the virtuality, if you prefer – of community. As Rosalyn Deutsche puts it, with an echo of Simmel and a feminist twist: 'In the phantom public sphere, man is deprived of the objectified, distanced, knowable world on whose existence he depends and is presented instead with unknowability, the proximity of otherness, and, consequently, uncertainty in the self.'[46] What space for *that* urbanity is there in Mitchell's nostalgic and moralistic future?

Forget Mitchell. The negative lesson of his lack of imagination, and also the positive lesson of those creative citizens in Tooting, is that the worst way to think about the future is to predict it, or to see it as the logical conclusion of what is new now. Thinking *in favour of* the future has to involve an excavation of the palimpsest of the present; a present made actual, for me, by thinking the city.

POSTCARD FROM EAST FREMANTLE

Home now, at least back in the inescapably contingent home of the migrant. When I arrive, my two young daughters are watching Disney's *Peter Pan*, with its (of course) sentimentalised but still magical panorama of London, and its own version of virtual community in Never-Never Land. (It is surprising how often an angel's eye view of London turns up in Disney. It is there too in *101 Dalmatians* and *Mary Poppins*, for instance.) Deal with the backlog of e-mails, junking most of the news group messages without reading them, I'm afraid. It still feels more like sorting mail than cruising the agora. Phone friends in the other, still imagined home on the other side of the globe. We discuss the findings from Tooting.

Fremantle is a place that in its history and its fabric embodies a sense of both *here* and *there*, of *now* and a largely repressed *then*. It is a port city that reinvented itself as a tourist attraction for the America's Cup yacht race in the early nineteen eighties. It shares much of the insouciant and slightly raffish urbanity of Brighton, my last home in England. (One of Brighton's favourite sons, the comedian Max Miller, described it as the sort of town you'd expect to find helping the police with their enquiries. Alan Bond, the West Australian businessman and local hero who wrested the America's Cup away from the United States for the first time, and so brought the race to Fremantle, is now in jail for his business and financial misdeeds.) Fremantle, however, for all its charm, also bears the weight of a traumatic past. It was the first port of call for generations of migrants, willing or unwilling, to Australia. It still retains a certain aura of displaced Europeanness – a point Australian friends often make when commenting on our choice of a place to live. That point of reference, architectural, geographical and historical, tends to overlay another memory of Fremantle. Rottnest Island, a few kilometres out to sea, is today celebrated as a restful spot for camping, sailing or cycling (no cars allowed), and, once a year, as the place where high school kids go to get drunk out of their skulls after the big exams are over. In the past, though, it was Devil's Island, a prison for Aboriginals, and so the location for some of the terrible events that make up this country's troubled racial history.

With children finally in bed, it is my turn for a video. Indulging my train of thought on the plane, I return to a witty cinematic reflection on the revival of *flânerie*, Patrick Keiller's *London*, released in 1994. The film is structured around a number of investigative walks taken by its two fictional and unseen protagonists: Robinson, a ship's photographer recently returned home, and his lover, the narrator (gorgeously spoken by Paul Scofield). The two men set themselves a project. They begin to trace the location of little known episodes concerning artists and authors like Apollinaire, Rimbaud and Alexander Herzen while they were living in the capital. These archaeological rambles through the hidden past of London are interspersed with musings about modernism, and a commentary on events that took place during 1992: the general election, an IRA bombing in the City, the Queen Mum's unveiling of a statue of 'Bomber' Harris, who masterminded the war-time destruction of Dresden, and so forth.

One question the film raises, for me, is again why *flânerie* became so fashionable in the nineteen eighties and nineties, and not just among academics. The film, like the attitude of *flânerie*, mixes a detective's obsession with bringing past events to light with an observant, semiotic relationship to space. Its style of understanding is at once aesthetic and social. Another fan of Keiller's is the novelist Iain Sinclair, who in *White Chapell: Scarlet Tracings* and *Downriver* also excavates the arcane histories of London, especially the more poisonous ones. (One of his anecdotes in *Downriver* concerns the first Australian cricket team, all Aboriginals, to visit England in 1868. A match at Lord's drew a large crowd, 'six thousand of the curious, sportsmen and their ladies'. Two weeks later, the Australian captain, King Cole, was dead, killed by England's cold foul air, and buried in 'a pauper's grave in Victoria Park Cemetery, East London; long accepted as a necropolis of the unregarded. . . . The particular site where they folded King Cole into the earth is now diligently disguised as "Meath Gardens": a light-repelling reservation, amputated from its original host by the twin cuts of Old Ford and Roman Road.'[47]) In his explorations across space as well as time, Sinclair too justifies *flânerie* as epistemology, although in a splenetically Situationist register.

> Walking is the best way to explore and exploit the city; the changes, shifts, breaks in the cloud helmet, movement of light on water. Drifting purposefully is the recommended mode, trampling asphalted earth in alert reverie, allowing the fiction of an underlying pattern to reveal itself. To the no-bullshit materialist this sounds suspiciously like *fin-de-siècle* decadence, a poetic of entropy – but the born-again *flâneur* is a stubborn creature, less interested in texture and fabric, eavesdropping on philosophical conversation pieces, than in noticing *everything*. Alignments of telephone kiosks, maps made from moss on the slopes of Victorian sepulchres, collections of prostitutes' cards, torn and defaced promotional bills for cancelled events at York Hall, visits to the homes of dead writers, bronze casts on war memorials, plaster dogs, beer mats, concentrations of used condoms, the crystalline patterns of glass shards surrounding an imploded BMW quarter-light window, meditations on the relationship between the brain-damage suffered by the super-middleweight boxer Gerald McClellan (lights out in the Royal London Hospital, Whitechapel) and the

simultaneous collapse of Barings, bankers to the Queen. Walking, moving across a retreating townscape, stitches it all together: the illicit cocktail of bodily exhaustion and a raging carbon monoxide high.[48]

This is an aesthetically voracious psychogeography of London. Sinclair's technique is the *dérive*. The leading Situationist Guy Debord defined this as a kind of 'playful-constructive' drift through the city, partly a spontaneous response to places, people and events, partly a premeditated alertness. Like the *flâneur*, the Situationist drifter moves through the crowd, but (supposedly) with a more critical and less compromised eye. As one commentator rather earnestly puts it: 'For the Situationists, . . . the *dérive* was distinguished from *flânerie* primarily by its critical attitude toward the hegemonic scopic regime of modernity.'[49] Whatever Sinclair's attitude to the scopic regime of modernity, his pedestrian speech acts produce some fine insights. Docklands, for example, he gets dead right: Dickens rendered through Céline.

> The whole glass raft is a mistake, glitter forms of anachronistic postmodernism (the swamp where *that* word crawled to die). Instant antiques. Skin grafts peeling before completion. The seductive sky/water cemetery of Thatcherism, cloud-reflecting sepulchre towers: an evil that delights the eye (the eye in the triangle). An astonishingly obvious solicitation of the pyramid, a corrupt thirst for eternity. . . . The planners have dabbled in geomancy, appeased the energy lines (while attempting to subvert them), and have achieved nothing beyond futile decoration. A city state built on self-regard. A colony where news dies (Fleet Street in charge of its own obituary), and where VDU screens play back electronic wavelets, green lines filling the machines with poisoned water, responding to the tides outside the window.[50]

Even so, I find myself resistant to the perspective of the Situationist drifter. I just don't believe that this way of seeing breaks out of the eroticised and colonising gaze of *flânerie*. There is also, in the end, something self-regarding and, however witty, self-important about it. The drifter notices a lot, but not *everything*. Concerned with the cleverness and redemption of the observer – nobody's fool, your Situationist – this *flânerie* doesn't want to risk being tainted by 'eavesdropping on philosophical conversation pieces'. I am less persuaded by the purity of empiricism.

In the end, I am more sympathetic to Keiller's way of seeing London than to Sinclair's. Could it be that that Keiller's cinematic vision embodies a sharper critical edge and a more revealing distance than his *flânerie*? This vision is not Vertov's Kino-eye, the explosive epistemological power of montage championed by Benjamin. On the contrary, Keiller remains stubbornly, even eccentrically, committed to the principle of *photogénie* as an aesthetic strategy. In the avant-garde film theory of the nineteen twenties, *photogénie* offered an alternative to montage as a principle of cinematic composition. For Keiller, it means a belief in the power of the camera to reveal the strangeness of familiar objects. His camera therefore remains resolutely still as it frames places or spaces – which? While the voice over adds layer upon layer of significance to the opaque surface of the city as it describes the protagonists' walks (place), the motionless and unyielding gaze of the camera gradually hollows out the *doxa*, the conventional meanings, from its landscapes (pure space).

The film thus raises questions about the legibility of space, and especially about the opaque layers of past events in space. This makes me think again about Deleuze, and about thinking the past against the present (here through the cinematic image) in order to resist the present in favour of the future.[51] More straightforwardly, it makes me think that there may be something more than nostalgia to my investment in cinema and the city even though I *know* that, sociologically, they are now less important than television and the suburb.

For Roger Silverstone, 'suburbia offers a coincidence of the architectural and the televisual', a coincidence that again reveals Habermas's ideal of the public sphere to be both backward looking and too literally spatial.[52] In the suburban world of television, and the televisual world of the suburb, there emerges 'a new kind of neo-participatory politics based on self-interest and grounded in defensive anxiety.'[53] Margaret Morse agrees. A post-urban ontology of television, mall and freeway has rendered even the idea of publicness pretty hopeless: 'older notions of the public realm and of paramount reality have been largely undermined, and a return to a pre-televisual world of politics, the street, or the marketplace is unlikely.'[54] They are right, of course, although I would again say that this means we should think of publicness as a phantom, as an immaterial yet effective social force, rather than a lost reality or a dead community.

But what would it mean to think about space and community from the perspective of television rather than cinema? Victor Burgin, although resolutely a city dweller rather than a suburbanite, chides Fredric Jameson for structuring his discussion of space allegorically around cinema, not television. He does so on the grounds of a comparison between the temporalities of the two media.

> The urban dweller who turns away from the image on her or his television screen, to look out of the window, may see the same program playing on other screens, behind other windows, or, more likely, will be aware if a simultaneity of different programs. Returning from this casual act of voyeurism they may 'zap' through channels, or 'flip' through magazines. Just as Benjamin refers to architecture as appreciated 'in a state of distraction', so television and photography are received in much the same way. The cinematic experience is temporally linear. For all that narrative codes may shuffle the pack of events, the spatial modulations that occur in the diegesis are nevertheless *successively* ordered and experienced as a *passage* through space and time. The global space-time of television, however, is fractured and kaleidoscopic.[55]

I hesitate for two reasons. First, I think Burgin just gets it wrong here about the temporality of cinema. Yes, the experience of watching a film is temporally linear. But cinema isn't the experience of a single film, any more than the cinema is the only place we watch films. Cinema – the *phantom* cinema – is the layered and worked over memory of all those narratives, all those images, all those occasions of viewing; as Burgin himself shows brilliantly when he creatively remembers Hitchcock's film in his essay 'Diderot, Barthes, *Vertigo*' and then works that memory into his photographic work *The Bridge*.[56] Second, Burgin argues that we should think with television because its temporality is *like* the 'global space-time' on the other side of the urban window. Does that homology really help us much in trying to understand the imaginative space, the analytical space, *between* (to use an important word for Victor Burgin) our private worlds and the public world of the city?[57] Italo Calvino suggests not. He recalls the way that cinema 'satisfied a need for disorientation, for the projection of my attention into a different space, a need which I believe corresponds to a primary function of our assuming our place in the world.' That, I must say, is how I experience it. Television enacts presence and sameness. Imaginatively, the different space, the space of difference, is still cinema.

My possibly eccentric argument is that in order to think about the reality of the suburbs and television (and the globe and the Internet) as part of an anthropology of the present, it is still useful to hang onto the epistemological poetics of the city and cinema. On my side of the argument, Kevin Robins holds out against the 'death of cinema', against the denial of its imaginative and creative possibilities, and in defence of 'the need to continually transform – to de-integrate – structures of vision and visibility'.[58] John Frow cites the enthusiasm for television by the fictional academic Murray in Don DeLillo's novel *White Noise*. Murray's students do not share his postcritical celebration of the medium. For them, television is 'worse than junk mail. Television is the death throes of human consciousness, according to them. They're ashamed of their television past. They want to talk about movies.' 'Murray is a postmodernist,' comments Frow. 'His students, wishing to return to the high modernism of cinema, are postpostmodernists.'[59]

In that preposterous postpostmodernist spirit, I have tried to show how thinking the city through cinema makes it possible to realise Sue Golding's political ethic: 'the whole focus now comes upon the importance – no, the *necessity* – to re-cover 'urban-ness' in all its anomie, and rather chaotic heterogeneity, if we are indeed serious about creating a radically pluralistic and democratic society.'[60] This imaginative recovery of the city is the only way I know to think on behalf of a time to come, of future places and people. John Rajchman again:

> The principle of such other, invisible, future peoples is not some recognition withheld by a state or its majority. Rather, we can invent the other peoples that we already are or may become as singular beings only if our being and being-together are indeterminate – not identifiable, given, recognizable in space and time – in other words, if our future remains unknown and our past indeterminate such that our very narratives can go out of joint, exposing other histories in our histories, releasing the strange powers of an artifice in our very 'nature'. Fiction and cinema have both explored the powers, the times, the spaces of this principle of the future city.[61]

In the end, it turns out to be the enigmatic *principle of the city* that I have been looking for in so many built, planned, governed, unbuildable, fictional and cinematic cities. That search has been driven by a political commitment. I share the affirmation of the future city passionately expressed by Lefebvre. 'The *right to the city* cannot be conceived of as a simple visiting right or as a return to traditional cities. It can only be formulated as a transformed and renewed *right to urban life*.'[62] That's it. The right to more equitably governed cities, even as we question and often oppose the rationalities and techniques of government. At the same time, the right to a different urbanity, an ethic that acknowledges indeterminacy and the inevitability of desire and violence without renouncing hope in the negotiability of our living together. The right, finally, to a living city, the phantom city, unimaginably rebuilt and renewed. Imagine.

Notes

Notes to Preface

1. Manuel Castells, *The Informational City: Information Technology, Economic Restructuring and the Urban-Regional Process*, Oxford: Blackwell, 1989; Anthony D. King, *Urbanism, Colonialism and the World Economy*, London: Routledge, 1989; Saskia Sassen, *The Global City: New York, London, Tokyo*, Princeton: Princeton University Press, 1991.
2. Christopher Prendergast, *Paris in the Nineteenth Century*, Oxford: Blackwell, 1992; Victor Burgin, *Some Cities*, London: Reaktion, 1996; Mike Davis, *City of Quartz: Excavating the Future of Los Angeles*, London: Verso, 1990; Sharon Zukin, *Landscapes of Power*, Berkeley: University of California Press, 1991; Ackbar Abbas, *Hong Kong: Culture and the Politics of Disappearance*, Minneapolis: University of Minnesota Press, 1997.
3. Marshall Berman, *All That Is Solid Melts Into Air*, London: Verso, 1982.
4. See, most influentially, David Harvey, *The Condition of Postmodernity*, Oxford: Blackwell, 1989; Fredric Jameson, *Postmodernism or the Cultural Logic of Late Capitalism*, London: Verso, 1991; Edward Soja, *Postmodern Geographies*, London: Verso, 1989.
5. See also Victor Burgin's video *Venise*, on Marseilles, Algiers and San Francisco, and his book *Some Cities*.
6. Roger Silverstone (ed.), *Visions of Suburbia*, London: Routledge, 1997, p.4.
7. Ernesto Laclau and Chantal Mouffe, *Hegemony and Socialist Strategy*, London: Verso, 1985, p.77.
8. For one possible answer, linking radical democracy to AIDS activism and urban geography, see Michael P. Brown, *Replacing Citizenship*, New York: The Guildford Press, 1997.
9. Gianni Vattimo, 'The End of Modernity, the End of the Project?' in Neil Leach (ed.), *Rethinking Architecture*, London: Routledge, 1997, p.148.

Notes to Chapter 1

1. Kevin Lynch, *Good City Form*, Cambridge, Mass.: MIT Press, 1981, pp.147–50.
2. William Sharpe and Leonard Wallock (eds.), *Visions of the Modern City*, Baltimore: Johns Hopkins Press, 1987, p.17.
3. T. S. Eliot, *The Wasteland*, London: Faber (paperback edn 1972), 1922.
4. Raymond Williams, *The Country and the City*, London: Chatto and Windus, 1973, p.243.
5. Williams, p.243.
6. In Liz Heron (ed.), *Streets of Desire: Women's Fictions of the Twentieth-Century City*, London: Virago, 1993, pp.44–45.
7. W.R. Burnett, *The Asphalt Jungle*, London: Macdonald, 1950.
8. Louis Wirth (1938), 'Urbanism as a Way of Life', in Philip Kasinitz (ed.), *Metropolis: Center and Symbol of Our Times*, New York: New York University Press, 1995, p.75.
9. Quoted in Kasinitz, p.17.
10. Ken Gelder and Sarah Thornton (eds.), *Subcultures Reader*, London: Routledge, 1997, p.27.

11. The argument I am making here echoes Slavoj Zizek, *Mapping Ideology*, London: Verso, 1994, pp.20–21.

12. Ihab Hassan, 'Cities of Mind, Urban Words', in Michael C. Jaye and Ann Chalmers Watts (eds.), *Literature and the Urban Experience*, New Brunswick: Rutgers University Press, 1981, p.94.

13. Benedict Anderson, *Imagined Communities*, London: Verso, 1983.

14. Victor Burgin, *Some Cities*, London: Reaktion Books, p.48.

15. David Frisby, *Fragments of Modernity*, Cambridge: Polity Press, 1985, p.2.

16. Georg Simmel, 'The Metropolis and Mental Life', in David Frisby and Mike Featherstone (eds.), *Simmel on Culture: Selected Writings*, London: Sage, 1997, p.175.

17. Simmel, p.184.

18. Simmel, p.181; translation modified.

19. Williams, p.243. Deena Weinstein and Michael A. Weinstein, *Postmodern(ized) Simmel*, London: Routledge, 1993, pp.66–67.

20. Simmel, p.183; translation modified.

21. Simmel, p.181.

22. Henri Lefebvre, *The Production of Space*, Oxford: Basil Blackwell, 1991, p.18. Both Victor Burgin and Derek Gregory see this as the key to his spatial archtectonics. See Burgin, p.31 and Derek Gregory, 'Lacan and Geography: the Production of Space Revisited', in Georges Benko and Ulf Strohmayer (eds.). *Space and Social Theory: Interpreting Modernity and Postmodernity*, Oxford: Blackwell, 1993, p.207.

23. Lefebvre, pp.38–39.

24. Lefebvre, p.203. Here I am following Gregory's discussion, pp.222–223.

25. Gregory makes a persuasive case that the underlying logic of *The Production of Space* is a sustained, and for the most part intransigent, engagement with Lacan's ideas.

26. Michel de Certeau, *The Practice of Everyday Life*, Berkeley: University of California Press, 1984.

27. De Certeau, p.94.

28. De Certeau, p.95.

29. De Certeau, p.93.

30. Meaghan Morris, 'Great Moments in Social Climbing: King Kong and the Human Fly', in Beatriz Colomina (ed.), *Sexuality and Space*, New York: Princeton University Press, 1992, p.13.

31. De Certeau, p.95; also Morris.

32. See, for example, Tony Bennett, *Culture: A Reformer's Science*, St Leonards, Sydney: Allen & Unwin, 1998, ch. 7.

33. De Certeau, p.110. I say more about this linkage in Chapter Three.

34. De Certeau p.108.

35. Zizek, *Mapping Ideology*, p.21.

36. Zizek, p.21.

37. For an account of the phenomenological tradition of thought on imagination, see Richard Kearney, *Poetics of Imagining: Husserl to Lyotard*, London: Harper Collins, 1991, especially p.6; and Cornelius Castoriadis, *The Castoriadis Reader*, (ed. David Ames Curtis) Oxford: Blackwell, 1997, especially pp.321–322.

38. Kearney, especially p.6. For Richard Kearney, 'imagining does not involve a courier service between body and mind but an original synthesis which precedes the age-old opposition between the sensible and the intelligible.'

39. Cornelius Castoriadis uses the term *radical imagination* (as opposed to the purely representational forms of secondary imagination) in order to 'emphasise the idea that this imagination is *before* the distinction between 'real' and 'fictitious'. To put it bluntly: it is because radical imagination exists that 'reality' exists *for us*—exists *tout court*–and exists *as* it exists.' Castoriadis, p.321.

40. Kearney, p.6.

41. Sue Golding, 'Quantum Philosophy, Impossible Geographies and a Few Small Points about Life, Liberty and the Pursuit of Sex (All in the Name of Democracy)', in Michael Keith and Steve Pile, *Place and the Politics of Identity*, London: Routledge, 1993, p.211; also Burgin, p.36.

42. Golding, p.217.

43. This suggestion is made, after Bruno Latour, by John Frow, *Time and Commodity Culture*, Oxford: Clarendon, 1997.

44. Michel Foucault, 'Kant on Enlightenment and Revolution', *Economy and Society*, 1986, vol. 15, no. 1, p.88.

45. Michel Foucault, 'What is Enlightenment?' in Paul Rabinow (ed.), *The Foucault Reader*, London: Penguin, 1984, pp.38–39.

46. Andrew Barry, Thomas Osborne and Nikolas Rose (eds.), *Foucault and Political Reason: Liberalism, Neo-Liberalism and Rationalities of Government*, London: UCL Press, 1996, p.3.

47. Barry, Osborne and Rose, p.5.

48. Rosalyn Deutsche and Doreen Massey don't *quite* say it either, but they make the point quite forcefully. See Deutsche, 'Men in Space', *Artforum*, February 1990; Massey, 'Flexible Sexism', in *Space, Place and Gender*, Cambridge: Polity, 1994.

49. Foucault, pp.39, 42.

50. Foucault, pp.40, 41.

51. Thomas Osborne, 'Drains, Liberalism and Power in the Nineteenth Century', in Barry, Osborne and Rose, pp.114–115. My emphasis.

52. Quoted in Peter Stallybrass and Allon White, *The Politics and Poetics of Transgression* London: Methuen, 1986, p.141.

53. Stallybrass and White, p.142.

Notes to Chapter 2

1. Anthony Vidler, 'Bodies in Space/Subjects in the City: Psychopathologies of Modern Urbanism', *differences*, vol. 5, no. 3, 1993, p.36.

2. In the context of the Open University course *Understanding Modern Societies*.

3. G. Davison, 'The City as a Natural System: Theories of Urban Society in Early Nineteenth Century Britain', in D. Fraser and A. Sutcliffe (eds.), *The Pursuit of Urban History*, London: Edward Arnold, 1983, pp.349–50.

4. Quoted in Davison, p.354.

5. Davison, p.369.

6. Quoted in Frank Mort, *Dangerous Sexualities: Medico-Moral Problems in England since 1830*, London: Routledge and Kegan Paul, 1987, pp.19–20.

7. Quoted in Mort, p.21.

8. On this aspect, see Mary Poovey, *Making a Social Body: British Cultural Formation 1830–1864*, Chicago: University of Chicago Press, 1995. Poovey draws similar conclusions about the importance of organic and mechanical metaphors.

9. Quoted in Ian Hunter, *Culture and Government: The Emergence of Literary Education*, London: Macmillan, 1988, pp.55–6.

10. Michel Foucault, *Politics, Philosophy, Culture*, (ed. L.D. Kritzman), New York: Routledge, 1988, p.67.

11. Ian Hacking, 'Biopower and the Avalanche of Printed Numbers', *Humanities in Society*, vol. 5, nos. 3/4 (Summer/Fall), 1982, p.292. See also his *Reconstructing Individualism*, Stanford: Stanford University Press, 1986, especially the chapter 'Making Up People'.

12. Foucault, *Politics, Philosophy, Culture*, p.82.

13. Foucault, *Politics, Philosophy, Culture*, p.83.

14. Paul Rabinow, *French Modern: Norms and Forms of Social Environment*, Cambridge, Mass.: MIT Press, 1989, p.39.

15. Rabinow, p.67.

16. Davison, p.368.

17. Steven Marcus, 'Reading the Illegible', in H.J. Dyos and M. Wolff (eds.), *The Victorian City: Images and Realities*, London: Routledge and Kegan Paul, 1973, p.258.

18. The following quotations are taken from Friedrich Engels, *The Condition of the Working Class in England in 1844*, London: Allen and Unwin, 1892, pp.45–54. First published in 1845.

19. Marcus, p.263.

20. John Tagg, 'God's Sanitary Law: Slum Clearance and Photography in Late Nineteenth-Century Leeds', in *The Burden of Representation: Essays on Photographies and Histories*,

London: Macmillan, 1988. My account here is also influenced by the television programme *Imagining the Modern City* which I scripted for the BBC/Open University in 1992, and to which John Tagg contributed.

21. Tagg, p.119.
22. Tagg, p.143.
23. Tagg, p.144.
24. M. Christine Boyer, *The City of Collective Memory: Its Historical Imagery and Architectural Entertainments*, Cambridge, Mass.: MIT Press, 1994, pp.240–1.
25. Boyer, pp.243–4.
26. Walter Benjamin, 'The Work of Art in the Age of Mechanical Reproduction', in *Illuminations*, London: Fontana, 1973, p.228.
27. Benjamin, 'The Work of Art'.
28. Walter Benjamin, 'A Short History of Photography' in Alan Trachtenberg (ed.), *Classic Essays in Photography*, New Haven: Leete's Island Books, 1980, p.209.
29. Benjamin, 'A Short History', pp.209, 210.
30. Walter Benjamin, *Charles Baudelaire: A Lyric Poet in the Era of High Capitalism*, London: New Left Books, 1973; Susan Buck-Morss, *The Dialectics of Seeing: Walter Benjamin and the Arcades Project*, Cambridge, Mass.: MIT Press, 1989; Marshall Berman, *All That Is Solid Melts into Air: The Experience of Modernity*, London: Verso, 1983.
31. Quoted in Buck-Morss, p.83.
32. See Tagg, *Grounds of Dispute: Art History, Cultural Politics and the Discursive Field*, Minneapolis: University of Minnesota Press, 1992, pp.135–6.
33. On Manet, see T.J. Clark, *The Painting of Modern Life: Paris in the Art of Manet and his Followers*, London: Thames and Hudson, 1984.
34. Here following David Frisby, 'The *Flâneur* in Social Theory', in Keith Tester (ed.) *The Flâneur*, London: Routledge, 1994, pp.85–86.
35. Quoted in David Frisby, *Fragments of Modernity*, Cambridge: Polity Press, 1985, pp.18–19.
36. Benjamin, *Baudelaire*, p.69.
37. Frisby, 'The *Flâneur*', pp.82–3.
38. Clark, pp.37–8; Buck-Morss, pp.89–90; Boyer, p.185.
39. Rabinow, p.77.
40. Friedrich Engels, *Marx-Engels Selected Works*, 2 vols, Moscow, 1955, I, pp.559, 606–9. (Cited in. Berman, p. 153.)
41. Buck-Morss, pp.83–86.
42. Buck-Morss, p.50.
43. Benjamin, *Baudelaire*, p.170.
44. Benjamin, *Baudelaire*, p.54.
45. See Anne Friedberg, *Window Shopping: Cinema and the Postmodern*, Berkeley: University of California Press, 1993; Miriam Hansen, *Babel and Babylon: Spectatorship in American Silent Film*, Cambridge, Mass.: Harvard University Press, 1991.
46. The literature on this topic is now extensive. See, for example, Janet Woolf, 'The Invisible *Flâneuse*: Women and the Literature of Modernity', *Theory, Culture and Society*, vol. 2, no. 3, 1985, reprinted in her *Feminine Sentences*, Cambridge: Polity, 1990; Woolf, 'The Artist and the *Flâneur*', in Tester, *Flâneur*; Griselda Pollock, 'Modernity and the Spaces of Femininity', in *Vision and Difference: Femininity, Feminism and Histories of Art*, London: Routledge, 1988; Elizabeth Wilson, *The Sphinx in the City*, London: Virago, 1991; Friedberg, *Window Shopping*; Rachel Bowlby, *Just Looking: Consumer Culture in Dreiser, Gissing and Zola*, London: Methuen, 1985; Mica Nava, 'Modernity's Disavowal', in Mica Nava and Alan O'Shea (eds.), *Modern Times: Reflections on a Century of English Modernity*, London: Routledge, 1996; Anke Gleber, 'Female Flânerie and the *Symphony of the City*', in Katharina von Ankum (ed.), *Women in the Metropolis: Gender and Modernity in Weimar Culture*, Berkeley: University of California Press, 1997, 67–88.
47. William Sharpe and Leonard Wallock (eds.), *Visions of the Modern City*, Baltimore: Johns Hopkins University Press, 1987, p.13; Raymond Williams, *The Country and the City*, London: Chatto and Windus, 1973, p.235.
48. Buck-Morss, pp.253–4.

49. Carl Schorske, *Fin-de-Siécle Vienna: Politics and Culture*, London: Weidenfeld and Nicolson, 1980.

50. Schorske, pp.62–72.

51. Schorske, pp.73–4.

52. Rudolf Wittkower, in Carlo Palazzolo and Riccardo Vio *In the Footsteps of Le Corbusier*, New York: Rizzoli, 1991, p.11. In this account, I draw primarily on James Holston, *The Modernist City: An Anthropological Critique of Brasilia*, Chicago: University of Chicago Press, 1989, Chapter 2, and Françoise Choay, 'Urbanism in Question', in M. Gottdiener and A.Ph. Lagopoulos (eds.), *The City and the Sign*, New York: Columbia University Press, 1986: otherwise unattributed quotations from Le Corbusier appear in these two sources.

53. Henri Lefebvre *Writing in Cities*, Oxford: Basil Blackwell, 1996, p.207.

54. Le Corbusier, *Vers une architecture*, cited in Beatriz Colomina, *Privacy and Publicity: Modern Architecture as Mass Media*, Cambridge, Mass., MIT Press, 1994, p.141

55. See Colomina.

56. Alan Colquhoun, *Modernity and the Classical Tradition : Architectural Essays 1980–1987*, Cambridge, Mass.: MIT Press, 1989, p.104.

57. Le Corbusier, *The City of Tomorrow and its Planning*, London: John Rodker, 1929, p.53.

58. Le Corbusier, *City of Tomorrow*, p.8.

59. Colquhoun, p.104.

60. See Michel Foucault, 'Space, Knowledge and Power (Interview Conducted with Paul Rabinow)', in Neil Leach (ed.), *Rethinking Architecture: A Reader in Cultural Theory*, London: Routledge, p.370.

61. Colquhoun, p.90.

62. Le Corbusier, *City of Tomorrow*, p.xxiii.

63. Le Corbusier, *Radiant City*, p.341; cited in Holston, p.41.

64. Holston, p.44.

65. Le Corbusier, *Radiant City*, p.176; Holston, p.50.

66. Holston, p.55.

67. Le Corbusier, *Radiant City*, p.143; Holston, p.56.

68. Colquhoun, p.108.

69. Colquhoun, pp.108, 115.

70. Rabinow, p.322.

71. Rosemary Mellor, 'Urban Sociology: A Trend Report', *Sociology*, vol. 23, no. 2, 1989, p.246.

Notes to Chapter 3

1. Adrienne Rich, *The Dream of a Common Language*, New York: W.W. Norton, 1978, p.25.

2. Le Corbusier, *The City of Tomorrow and its Planning*, London: John Rodker, 1929, p.94.

3. Peter Fritzsche, *Reading Berlin 1900*, Cambridge, Mass.: Harvard University Press, 1996, p.18.

4. Fritzsche, p.248.

5. See Douglas Gomery, *Shared Pleasures: A History of Movie Presentation in the United States*, London: British Film Institute, 1992, ch. 3.

6. See Raymond Williams, *Television, Technology and Cultural Form*, London: Fontana, 1974, ch. 1; Lynn Spigel, *Make Room for TV: Television and the Family Ideal in Post-war America*, Chicago: Chicago University Press, 1992; Roger Silverstone, *Visions of Suburbia*, London: Routledge, 1997.

7. The Commission on Educational and Cultural Films, *The Film in National Life*, London, 1932, p.10; quoted in James Donald 'Stars', in Pam Cook (ed.), *The Cinema Book*, London: British Film Institute, 1985, p.50.

8. The issues raised in the following paragraphs are also discussed in James Donald and Stephanie Donald, 'The Publicness of Cinema', in Christine Gledhill and Linda Williams (eds.), *Re-inventing Film Studies*, London: Edward Arnold, forthcoming.

9. Jonathan Crary, 'Dr. Mabuse and Mr. Edison', in Kerry Brougher, Russell Ferguson and Jonathan Crary (eds.), *Art and Film Since 1945: Hall of Mirrors*, Los Angeles: Museum of Contemporary Art/Monacelli Press, 1996, p.265. See also Crary, 'Unbinding Vision: Manet and the Attentive Observer', in Leo Charney and Vanessa Schwartz (eds.), *Cinema and Modernity*, Berkeley: University of California Press, 1995.

10. Miriam Hansen, *Babel and Babylon: Spectatorship in American Silent Film*, Harvard University Press, 1991, p.16.

11. Hansen, *Babel*, pp.2–3. See also Anne Friedberg, *Window Shopping: Cinema and the Postmodern*, Berkeley: University of California Press, 1992.

12. Hansen, *Babel*, pp.1–2.

13. This is also the argument (or roughly so) of Anne Friedberg's *Window Shopping*. She emphasises the mobilised virtual gaze.

14. Miriam Hansen, 'America, Paris, the Alps: Kracauer (and Benjamin) on cinema and modernity', in Charney and Schwartz, pp.365–6.

15. Hansen, 'America, Paris', p.374.

16. Siegfried Kracauer, *The Mass Ornament: Weimar Essays*, (ed. and trans. Thomas Y. Levin), New Haven: Harvard University Press, 1995, pp.325–6. The quotes are from 'The Cult of Distraction', first published 1926.

17. See James Donald, Anne Friedberg, and Laura Marcus, *Close Up, 1927–1933: Cinema and Modernism*, London: Cassell, 1998.

18. Donald, Friedberg, and Marcus, p.160. Here I am following Laura Marcus's argument.

19. Donald, Friedberg, and Marcus, pp.204, 174, 171.

20. Margaret Morse, 'An Ontology of Everyday Distraction: The Freeway, the Mall, and Television', in Patricia Mellencamp (ed.), *Logics of Television*, Bloomington: Indiana University Press/London: BFI Publishing, 1990, p.193.

21. Michel de Certeau, *The Practice of Everyday Life*, Berkeley: University of California Press, 1984, p.95.

22. Anthony Vidler, *The Architectural Uncanny: Essays in the Modern Unhomely*, Cambridge, Mass.: MIT Press, 1992, p.3.

23. Jeanne Favret-Saarda, *Deadly Words*, Cambridge: Cambridge University Press, 1980, ch. 1.

24. Marc Eli Blanchard, *In Search of the City: Engels, Baudelaire, Rimbaud*, Stanford, Calif.: Amna Libri, 1985, p.95.

25. Christopher Prendergast, *Paris and the Nineteenth Century*, Oxford: Blackwell, 1992, pp.142–43; Blanchard, p.90.

26. Vidler, pp.ix-x.

27. De Certeau, p.105. My reading of de Certeau here follows Victor Burgin, 'Chance Encounters: *Flâneur* and *Detraquée* in Breton's *Nadja*', *New Formations*, no. 11, Summer 1990, p.80.

28. De Certeau, p.110.

29. Mladen Dolar, ''I Shall Be with You on your Wedding-night': Lacan and the Uncanny', *October*, no. 58, Fall 1991, p.23.

30. See David Frisby, *Fragments of Modernity*, Cambridge: Polity Press, 1985; Prendergast, p.143.

31. Here I follow Susan Buck-Morss's wonderfully imaginative variations on the *Passagen-Werk*: see *The Dialectics of Seeing: Walter Benjamin and the Arcades Project*, Cambridge, Mass.: MIT Press, p.254.

32. Vidler, p.172. The argument in this paragraph is his.

33. Walter Benjamin, 'The Work of Art in the Age of Mechanical Reproduction', in *Illuminations*, London: Fontana, 1973, p.230.

34. Georg Simmel, 'The Metropolis and Mental Life', in David Frisby and Mike Featherstone (eds.), *Simmel on Culture: Selected Writings*, London: Sage, 1997, p.175; Benjamin, 'Work of Art', p.227; Benjamin, *Charles Baudelaire: A Lyric Poet in the Era of High Capitalism*, London: New Left Books, 1973, p.132.

35. Stephen Kern, *The Culture of Time and Space 1880–1918*, Cambridge: Harvard University Press, 1983, pp.142–43, 74.

36. Münsterberg quoted in Kern, p.71; László Moholy-Nagy, *Painting, Photography, Film*, London: Lund Humphries, 1969, p.122. I am grateful to Roger Cardinal for pointing out the particular relevance of Citroën's montage, and to Annette Michelson for telling me about Moholy-Nagy's sketch.

37. Sergei Eisenstein, *The Film Sense*, London: Faber & Faber, 1968, pp.82–83.

38. Eisenstein, pp.83–84

39. Quoted in Friedberg, *Window Shopping*, p.50.

40. Benjamin, 'Work of Art', p.229.

41. See Giuliana Bruno, *Streetwalking on a Ruined Map: Cultural Theory and the City Films of Elvira Notari*, Princeton: Princeton University Press, 1993. Bruno discusses a specifically Neapolitan genre of city films, primarily focused on the lives of women, that lasted roughly from the beginning of the century until the end of the nineteen twenties.

42. Quoted in Vlada Petric, *Constructivism in Film: The Man with the Movie Camera*, Cambridge: Cambridge University Press, 1987, p.82.

43. A point brought out in the geographer Wolfgang Natter's account of the film, 'The City as Cinematic Space: Modernism and Place in *Berlin, Symphony of a City*', in S.C. Aitken and L.E. Zonn (eds.) *Place, Power, Situation and Spectacle: A Geography of Film*, Lanham, Md.: Rowman and Littlefield, 1994, p.218.

44. Natter, p.219.

45. Natter, p.218. I think Natter may have seen a more complete version of the film than I have, or at least a different print. I did not notice all the elements he mentions. I certainly have to take his word on which districts in Berlin are shown.

46. For an alternative reading see Anke Gleber, 'Female Flânerie and the *Symphony of the City*', in Katharina von Ankum (ed.), *Women in the Metropolis: Gender and Modernity in Weimar Culture*, Berkeley: University of California Press, 1997, pp.67–88. For the reasons I stick to my account, see my review of Gleber's book *The Art of Taking a Walk: Flânerie, Literature, and Film in Weimar Culture* (Princeton: Princeton University Press, 1999) – 'Talking the Talk, Walking the Walk', *Screen*, vol. xx, no. xx, 1999.

47. Herbert Marshall (trans. and ed.), *Mayakovsky*, London: Dennis Dobson, 1965, p.352; quoted in Petric, p.29.

48. Quoted in Petric, p.130.

49. Siegfried Kracauer, *FrankfurterZeitung*, 13 November 1927, quoted in Natter, p.220.

50. Siegfried Kracauer, *From Caligari to Hitler: A Psychological History of the German Film*, Princeton: Princeton University Press, 1947, pp.185–87.

51. This is Natter's case for the film. See Natter, pp.221–222.

52. Quoted in Miriam Hansen, 'America, Paris', p.106.

53. Gleber, p.79; my emphasis.

54. Patrice Petro, *Joyless Streets: Women and Melodramatic Representation in Weimar Germany*, Princeton: Princeton University Press, 1989, ch. 2. Petro sees Benjamin and Kracauer as part of this tradition, and not just as commentators on it.

55. Vertov quoted in Petric, pp.12–13, 6.

56. This is Christine Buci-Glucksmann's formulation in *Baroque Reason: The Aesthetics of Modernity*, London: Sage, 1994, p.76.

57. Peter Wollen, 'Delirious Projections', *Sight and Sound*, August 1992, p.25. Benjamin defends 'profane illumination' in 'Surrealism', in *One Way Street*, London: New Left Books, 1979, p.237, where he also discusses *Nadja*.

58. See Giuliana Bruno, 'Ramble City: Postmodernism and *Blade Runner*', *October* no. 41, Summer 1987.

59. These days, the most dangerous technologies that might run out of control are often identified as media or information technologies. David Cronenberg's *Videodrome* and Kathryn Bigelow's *Strange Days* are just two examples.

60. Andreas Huyssen, 'The Vamp and the Machine: Fritz Lang's *Metropolis*', in *After the Great Divide: Modernism, Mass Culture, Postmodernism*, Bloomington: Indiana University Press, 1986. Janet Lungstrum, '*Metropolis* and the Technosexual Woman', in von Ankum, *Women in the Metropolis*.

61. Vidler, pp.12–13.

62. Buci-Glucksmann, p.43.

Notes to Chapter 4

1. See David Rosenberg (ed.), *The Movie that Changed my Life*, New York: Viking, 1991.

2. Specularity and alterity come from Kaja Silverman, *Male Subjectivity at the Margins*, London: Routledge, 1992.

3. Jürgen Habermas, 'Yet Again: German Identity – A Unified Nation of Angry DM-Burghers?', *New German Critique*, 1992.

4. Habermas, p.98.

5. Rogers Brubaker, *Citizenship and Nationhood in France and Germany*, New Haven: Harvard University Press, 1992, p.182.

6. Brubaker, p.1.

7. Brubaker, p.1.

8. Slavoj Zizek, *Looking Awry*, Cambridge Mass.: MIT Press, 1991, p.163.

9. Renata Salecl, *The Spoils of Freedom: Psychoanalysis and Feminism after the Fall of Socialism*, London: Routledge, 1994, p.119.

10. Quoted in Salecl, p.121.

11. Salecl, p.126.

12. Zizek, p.163.

13. Chantal Mouffe, 'Citizenship and Political Community', in Miami Theory Collective (eds.), *Community at Loose Ends*, Minneapolis: University of Minnesota Press, 1991, p.78.

14. René Descartes, *The Philosophical Writngs of Descartes* (trans. John Cottingham, Robert Stoothoff and Dugald Murdoch), Cambridge: Cambridge University Press, 1985, p.2.

15. Marcel Mauss, 'A Category of the Human Mind, the Notion of Person; the Notion of Self', in *Sociology and Psychology: Essays* (trans. Ben Brewster), London: Routledge and Kegan Paul, 1979, p.78.

16. Mauss, p.84.

17. Mauss, pp.85–6. See also Nikolas Rose's discussion in *Governing the Soul: The Shaping of the Private Self*, London: Routledge, 1990, pp.217–219.

18. Mauss, p.89. Emphasis added.

19. Etienne Balibar, 'Citizen Subject', in Eduardo Cadava, Peter Connor and Jean-Luc Nancy (eds.), *Who Comes After the Subject?*, London: Routledge, 1991, p.45.

20. Friedrich Schiller, *On the Aesthetic Education of Man* [1791], Oxford: Clarendon Press, 1967, p.33. See the discussions in Ian Hunter, 'Setting limits to culture', *New Formations*, no. 4, Spring 1988, and Jeffrey Minson, *Questions of Conduct: Sexual Harassment, Citizenship, Government*, London: Macmillan, 1993.

21. Jean-Jacques Rousseau, *Émile* (trans. Barbara Foxley), London: J.M. Dent, 1974, p.254.

22. Richard Sennett, *The Fall of Public Man*, Cambridge: Cambridge University Press, 1974, p.115.

23. Rousseau, *La Nouvelle Héloïse*, quoted in Charles E. Ellison, 'Rousseau and the Modern City: The Politics of Speech and Dress', *Political Theory*, vol. 13, no. 4, 1985, p.507.

24. Rousseau, *Letter to d'Alembert*, quoted in Sennett, p.118.

25. See Ellison, p.526.

26. Rousseau, *Julie*, quoted in Sennett, p.119.

27. *Letter to d'Alembert*, in John Hope Mason, *The Indispensable Rousseau*, London: Quartet, 1979, p.129.

28. Michel Foucault, *Power/Knowledge* (ed. Colin Gordon), Brighton: Harvester, 1980, p.152.

29. *Émile*, quoted in Ellison, p.518.

30. Alfred Loos, 'Ornament and Crime', quoted in Beatriz Colomina, *Privacy and Publicity: Modern Architecture as Mass Media*, Cambridge Mass.: MIT Press, 1994, p.35.

31. Georg Simmel, 'The Metropolis and Mental Life', in David Frisby and Mike Featherstone (eds.), *Simmel on Culture: Selected Writings*, London: Sage, 1997, p.175.

32. See Colomina, p.37.

33. Simmel, 'Fashion' 1904, quoted in Colomina, p.273.

34. Nietzsche, 'On the Uses and Disadvantages of History for Life,' quoted in Colomina, pp.32, 8.

35. Alfred Loos, 'Architecture' [1910], quoted in Colomina, p.274.

36. Georg Simmel, 'The Problem of Style' [1910], quoted and discussed in David Frisby, *Fragments of Modernity*, Cambridge: Polity, 1985, p.101.

37. Quoted in Colomina, p.35.

38. Quoted in Stephen Heath, 'Joan Riviere and the Masquerade', in Victor Burgin, James Donald, and Cora Kaplan (eds.), *Formations of Fantasy*, London: Methuen, 1986, p.56.

39. Quoted in Silverman, pp.6–7.

40. See Riviere and Heath in *Formations of Fantasy*. Also the essays on masquerade by

Mary Ann Doane, *Femmes Fatales: Feminism, Film Theory, Psychoanalysis*, London: Routledge, 1991.

41. See chapter 2, note 46.
42. Quoted in Wolff, p.126.
43. Quoted in Derek Gregory, 'Lacan and Geography: the Production of Space Revisited', in Georges Benko and Ulf Strohmayer (eds.). *Space and Social Theory: Interpreting Modernity and Postmodernity*, Oxford: Blackwell, 1993, p.225.
44. Joan Copjec, 'The Orthopsychic Subject: Film Theory and the Reception of Lacan', in *Read My Desire*, Cambridge, Mass.: MIT Press, 1994, p.34.
45. Quoted in Gleber, p.87, n.24.
46. The danger is always of reducing the argument to a male/female binarism when the issue is the mobility and volatility of identification and performance within a polarised symbolic field.
47. Iris Marion Young, 'City Life and Difference', in Philip Kasinitz (ed.), *Metropolis: Center and Symbol of Our Times*, New York: New York University Press, 1995, p.266.
48. David Marquand, 'Civic republicans and liberal individualists: the case of Britain', *Archive of European Sociology*, XXXII, 1991, p.343.
49. The phrase is Minson's.
50. Salecl, p.116.
51. Salecl, p.133.
52. Claude Lévi-Strauss, *Introduction to the Works of Marcel Mauss* [1950], London: Routledge and Kegan Paul, 1987, p.35.
53. Gianni Vattimo, *The Transparent Society*, Cambridge: Polity, 1992, p.8.
54. I am grateful to Christine Blake for reminding me of this passage and its relevance.
55. Here I follow Stephen Heath's analysis of the story: 'Psychopathia Sexualis: Stevenson's *Strange Case*', *Critical Quarterly*, vol. 28, nos. 1/2, 1986.
56. Quoted in Heath, p.97.
57. Mladen Dolar, ''I Shall Be With You On Your Wedding-Night': Lacan and the Uncanny', *October*, no. 58, 1991, p.7.
58. Slavoj Zizek, *Enjoy Your Symptom!*, London: Routledge, 1992, p.136.
59. Roberto Unger quoted in Minson, p.193; Michael Sandel, *Liberalism and the Limits of Justice*, Cambridge: Cambridge University Press, 1982, p.173. See the discussion in Iris Marion Young, *Justice and the Politics of Difference*, Princeton: Princeton University Press, 1990, p.230

Notes to Chapter 5
1. Cited in Ihab Hassan, 'Cities of Mind, Urban Words', in M.C. Jaye and A. Chalmers Watts (eds.), *Literature and the Urban Experience*, New Brunswick, NJ: Rutgers University Press, 1981, p.97.
2. On this characterisation of the city, see Iris Marion Young, *Justice and the Politics of Difference*, Princeton: Princeton University Press, 1990.
3. Victor Burgin, 'Geometry and Abjection', in James Donald (ed.), *Thresholds: Psychoanalysis and Cultural theory*, London: Macmillan, 1991. See also Anthony Vidler, 'Bodies in Space/Subjects in the City: Psychopathologies of Modern Urbanism', *differences*, vol. 5, no. 3, 1993, pp.32–33.
4. See J Hillis Miller, *Topographies*, Stanford: Stanford University Press, 1995, p.6.
5. Miller, p.7.
6. Henri Lefebvre makes a similar point, through his distinction between the representation of space and representational space. See *The Production of Space*, Oxford: Basil Blackwell, 1991.
7. Lefebvre, p.8
8. Cited in Malcolm Bowie, *Psychoanalysis and the Future of Theory*, Oxford: Blackwell, 1993, p.18.
9. Bowie, pp.34, 26.
10. Bowie, p.35.
11. Bowie, p.45.
12. John Rajchman, *Truth and Eros: Foucault, Lacan and the Question of Ethics*, London: Routledge, 1991, pp.145–6.

13. Richard Kearney, *Poetics of Imagining: Husserl to Lyotard*, London: Harper Collins, 1991, p.226.

14. Virginia Woolf, *Moments of Being: Unpublished Autobiographical Writings* (ed. Jeanne Schulkind), New York: Harcourt Brace Jovanovich, 1976, pp.159–60.

15. Woolf, p.132; cited in Susan M. Squier, *Virginia Woolf and London: The Sexual Politics of the City*, Chapel Hill: University of North Carolina Press, 1988, p.20.

16. Bowie, p.26.

17. Christopher Prendergast, *Paris and the Nineteenth Century*, Oxford: Blackwell, 1992, p.221. See also Raymond Williams, *The Country and the City*, London: Chatto and Windus, 1973; D.A. Miller, *The Novel and the Police*, Berkeley: University of California Press, 1988; and Klaus R. Scherpe, 'The City as Narrator: The Modern Text in Alfred Döblin's *Berlin Alexanderplatz*', in Andreas Huyssen and David Bathrick (eds.), *Modernity and the Text: Revisions of German Modernism*, New York: Columbia University Press, 1989.

18. Virginia Woolf, *Mrs Dalloway* [1925], Oxford: Oxford University Press (The World's Classics), 1992; Alfred Döblin, *Berlin Alexanderplatz* [1929], trans. Eugene Jolas, Harmondsworth: Penguin, 1978. Page references given in the text.

19. Dietrich Scheunemann, *Romankrise: Die Entstehungsgeschichte der modernen Romanpoetik in Deutschland*, Heidelberg: Quelle & Meyer, 1978, p.176; cited in David B. Dollenmayer, *The Berlin Novels of Alfred Döblin*, Berkeley: University of California Press, 1988, p.69.

20. Scheunemann, pp.167–74, 182–83. The case for the influence of Ruttman's film is strengthened by viewing Piel Jutzi's 1931 film of *Berlin Alexanderplatz*, for which Döblin wrote the script. To complete the circle, Joyce apparently expressed the wish that Ruttmann should make a film of Ulysses.

21. In this reading I follow Dollenmayer.

22. Quoted in Maria Dibattista, 'Joyce, Woolf and the Modern Mind', in Patricia Clements and Isobel Grundy (eds.), *Virginia Woolf: New Critical Essays*, London: Vision and Barnes & Noble, 1983, p.96.

23. Virginia Woolf, 'Modern Fiction', in *The Crowded Dance of Modern Life. Selected Essays; Volume Two* (ed. Rachel Bowlby), Harmondsworth: Penguin, 1993, p.8.

24. Woolf, 'Modern Fiction', p.9.

25. Quoted in John Mepham, 'Mourning and Modernism', in Clements and Grundy, p.137.

26. Laura Marcus, 'Women, Modernism, Cinema', in James Donald and Stephanie Donald (eds.), *The City, the Cinema: Modern Spaces*, CulCom Research Papers in Media and Cultural Studies, vol. 3, Falmer: University of Sussex, 1995, p.28.

27. Virginia Woolf, 'The Cinema', in Andrew McNeillie (ed.), *The Essays of Virginia Woolf*, Volume 4: 1925–1928, London: Hogarth Press, 1994, p. 595. See Marcus, 'Women, Modernism, Cinema', pp.31–32.

28. See Rachel Bowlby, 'Walking, Women and Writing: Virginia Woolf as *Flâneuse*', in *Still Crazy After All These Years*, London: Routledge, 1992; and Jeremy Tambling, 'Repression in *Mrs Dalloway*', *Essays in Criticism*, vol. 39, 1989, p.141.

29. Georg Simmel, 'The Metropolis and Mental Life', in David Frisby and Mike Featherstone (eds.), *Simmel on Culture: Selected Writings*, London: Sage, 1997, p.175.

30. See Vidler, p.35.

31. Vidler, pp.43, 45.

32. Quoted in Scherpe, p.173. On the narratibility of the city, see pp.167/68.

33. See Beatriz Colomina, *Privacy and Publicity: Modern Architecture as Mass Media*, Cambridge, Mass.: MIT Press, 1994.

34. Vidler, p.36 ff.

35. Quoted in Vidler., pp. 41–42. I am following Vidler's argument closely here.

36. Le Corbusier cited in Kevin Robins, 'Collective Emotion and Urban Culture', in P. Healey, S. Cameron, S. Davoudi, S. Graham & A. Madani-Pour (eds.), *Managing Cities: The New Urban Context*, Chichester: John Wiley & Sons, 1995, pp.50, 51.

37. Franco Bianchini and Hermann Schwengel, quoted in Robins, p.47.

38. Robins, p.47.

39. Mike Davis, *City of Quartz*, London: Verso, 1990; Manuel Castells, *The Informational City*, Oxford: Blackwell, 1989; Saskia Sassen, *The Global City*, Princeton: Princeton University Press, 1991.

40. Doreen Massey, 'A Place Called Home?', in *Space, Place and Gender*, Cambridge: Polity, 1994, p.163.
41. Robins, p.53.
42. See, for example, Doreen Massey's critique of Laclau's anti-spatialism in 'Politics and Space/Time', in *Space, Place and Gender*, pp.250–269.
43. Ernesto Laclau, *New Reflections on the Revolution of Our Time*, London: Verso, 1990, p.82.
44. Bernard Tschumi, *Architecture and Disjuncture*, Cambridge, Mass.: MIT Press, 1994, p.217.
45. Tschumi, pp.191 ff.
46. Tschumi, pp.181, 185
47. Tschumi, p.193
48. Elizabeth Grosz, 'Women, *Chora*, Dwelling', in *Space, Time and Perversion*, St Leonards: Allen & Unwin, 1995, p.112.
49. Jacques Derrida, 'Where the Desire May Live', in Neil Leach (ed.), *Rethinking Architecture*, London: Routledge, 1997, p.322.
50. Derrida, p.323.
51. Quoted in Andrew Benjamin, 'Eisenman and the Housing of Tradition', in Leach, *Rethinking Architecture*, p.294.
52. Mary McLeod, 'Everyday and 'Other' Spaces', in Debra Coleman, Elizabeth Danze and Carol Henderson (eds.), *Architecture and Feminism*, New York: Princeton Architectural Press, 1996, p.11.
53. Grosz, pp.123–124.
54. Vidler, p.48.
55. This is Iris Marion Young's phrase.
56. Rajchman, p.144.

Notes to Chapter 6
1. John Rajchman, *Truth and Eros: Foucault, Lacan and the Question of Ethics*, London: Routledge, 1991, p.144.
2. Raymond Williams, *The Country and the City*, London: Chatto & Windus, 1973, p.84.
3. Doreen Massey, *Space, Place, Gender*, Cambridge: Polity Press, 1994, p.153.
4. The relevant passages were clinically taken apart by Paul Gilroy in *There Ain't No Black in the Union Jack*, London: Unwin Hyman, 1987.
5. Raymond Williams, *Towards 2000*, Harmondsworth: Penguin, 1985, p.195
6. Williams, *Towards 2000*, p.196, my emphasis.
7. Williams, *Towards 2000*, p.196, my emphasis.
8. Williams, *Towards 2000*, p.195–6
9. Raymond Williams, *The Country and the City*, pp.5–6; my emphasis.
10. Raymond Williams, 'Culture is Ordinary', in Robin Gable (ed.), *Resources of Hope*, London: Verso, 1989, p.9.
11. Salman Rushdie, 'In Good Faith', in *Imaginary Homelands*, London: Granta Books, 1992, p.394.
12. Jean-Francois Lyotard, *The Inhuman*, Stanford: Stanford University Press, 1992.
13. Raymond Williams, *Television: Technology and Cultural Form*, London: Fontana, 1974, ch. 1.
14. Lyotard, pp.201–2.
15. See Norman Denzin's chapter on the film in *Images of Postmodern Society*, London: Sage, 1991.
16. The distinction is drawn by Jonathan Rosenbaum, *Movies as Politics*, Berkeley: University of California Press, 1997.
17. Jean-Luc Nancy, *The Inoperative Community*, Minneapolis: University of Minnesota press, 1991, p.xxxvi.
18. Nancy, p.xxxviii.
19. See Iris Marion Young, *Justice and the Politics of Difference*, Princeton: Princeton University Press, 1990.
20. Georg Simmel, 'The Stranger' (1908), in Charles Lemert (ed.), *Social Theory: The Multicultural and Classic Readings*, Boulder: Westview, 1993, p.200.
21. Simmel, p.203.

22. Homi Bhabha, 'Novel Metropolis', *New Statesman and Society*, 16 February 1990, p.16.
23. Julia Kristeva, *Strangers to Ourselves*, London: Harvester Wheatsheaf, 1991, p.170.
24. Kristeva, p.192.
25. Michael Walzer, *On Toleration*, New Haven: Yale University Press, 1997, p.89.
26. Nancy, p.12.
27. Charles Taylor, *Multiculturalism and 'The Politics of Recognition'*, Princeton: Princeton Univrsity Press, 1992; Will Kymlicka (ed.), *The Rights of Minority Cultures*, New York: Oxford University Press, 1995; Young, *Justice*.
28. David Harvey, 'Social Justice, Postmodernism and the City', in Susan Fainstein and Scott Campbell (eds.), *Readings in Urban Theory*, Oxford: Blackwell, 1996, p.416.
29. Harvey, 'Social Justice', pp.417–418. Quotes are Iain Chambers 'Maps for the Metropolis: A Possible Guide to the Present', *Cultural Studies*, 1, 1985, pp.1–22; Young, *Justice*, p.227; Jane Jacobs, *The Death and Life of Great American Cities*, New York: Vintage, 1961.
30. Harvey, pp.419–420.
31. David Harvey, 'Contested Cities: Social Process and Spatial Form', in Nick Jewson and Susanne MacGregor (eds.) *Transforming Cities: Contested Governance and New Spatial Divisions*, London: Routledge, 1997, p.24.
32. Harvey, 'Contested Cities', p.24.
33. Massey, p.243.
34. David Harvey, *The Condition of Postmodernity*, Oxford: Blackwell, 1990, p.355
35. David Harvey, *Justice, Nature and the Geography of Difference*, Oxford: Blackwell, 1996, p.108.
36. Harvey, *Justice, Nature*, p.431.
37. Nancy, p.40.
38. Dick Hebdidge, 'The Impossible Object: Towards a Sociology of the Sublime', *New Formations*, no. 1, spring 1987, p.66.
39. Nancy, pp.xil–xl.
40. Nancy, pp.xxxvii–xxxviii.
41. In Liz Heron (ed.), *Streets of Desire: Women's Fictions of the Twentieth-Century City*, London: Virago, 1993, pp.247–8.
42 Nancy, p.xxxviii.
43. Walzer, *Toleration*, p.9.
44. Walzer, *Toleration*, pp.10–11.
45. Walzer, *Toleration*, p.11.
46. Quoted in Richard Kearney, *Poetics of Imagining: Husserl to Lyotard*, London: Harper Collins, 1991, p.225.
47. Kearney, p.210.
48. Quoted in Jacques Derrida, *Politics of Friendship*, London: Verso, 1997, p.60.
49. Derrida, p.60.
50. Derrida, p.252.
51. Michael Walzer, 'Pleasures and Costs of Urbanity', in Philip Kasinitz (ed.), *Metropolis: Center and Symbol of Our Times*, New York: New York University Press, 1995, p.323.
52. Richard Rogers and Mark Fisher, *A New London*, Harmondsworth: Penguin, p.xv.
53. See Christopher Fynsk, 'Foreword' to Nancy, *Inoperative Community*.
54. Ernesto Laclau, *New Reflections on the Revolution of Our Time*, London: Verso, 1990, p.34.
55. Laclau, p.35.
56. See Jeremy Gilbert, 'Soundtrack to an Uncivil Society: Rave Culture, the Criminal Justice Act and the Politics of Modernity', *New Formations*, no. 31, 1997.
57. Iris Marion Young, 'Communication and the Other: Beyond Deliberative Democracy', in Seyla Benhabib (ed.), *Democracy and Difference: Contesting the Boundaries of the Political*, Princeton: Princeton University Press, 1996, p.120.
58. Young, 'Communication', p.120.
59. Seyla Benhabib, 'Toward a Deliberative Model of Democratic Legitimacy', in Benhabib, *Democracy and Difference*, p.83.
60. Young, 'Communication', p.129.
61. Nancy, pp.xil-xl.
62. Laclau, p.xv.

63. I take this phrase from Stephanie Donald. See her *Public Secrets, Public Spaces: Cinema and Civility in China*, Boulder: Rowman and Littlefield, 1999.
64. Nancy, p.19.

Notes to Chapter 7

1. Jacques Derrida, *The Post Card: From Socrates to Freud and Beyond*, Chicago: Chicago University Press, 1987, pp.100–1.
2. Gilles Deleuze, *Foucault*, Minneapolis: University of Minnesota Press, 1988, p. 119; quoted in Nigel Thrift, *Spatial Formations*, London: Sage, 1996, p.295.
3. See John Frow, *Time and Commodity Culture: Essays in Cultural Theory and Postmodernity*, Oxford: Clarendon Press, 1997, esp. 'Introduction'; Homi K. Bhabha, *The Location of Culture*, London: Routledge, 1994, 'Conclusion'.
4. Anthony King, *Global Cities: Post-Imperialism and the Internationalization of London*, London: Routledge, 1990, p.143.
5. Quoted in David Harvey, *Justice, Nature and the Geography of Difference*, Oxford: Blackwell, 1996, p.421.
6. Richard Sennett in Nan Ellin (ed.), *Architecture of Fear*, New York: Princeton Architectural Press, 1997, p.62.
7. Manuel Castells, *The Informational City*, Oxford: Blackwell, 1989, p.348.
8. David Turnbull, 'Soc. Culture; Singapore:', in Ellin, *Architecture*, p.227.
9. Turnbull, p.227.
10. Turnbull, p.228.
11. Turnbull, p.228.
12. Stephen Graham and Simon Marvin, *Telecommunications and the City: Electronic Spaces, Urban Places*, London: Routledge, 1996, p.143.
13. Bill Schwarz, 'Where Horses Shit a Hundred Sparrows Feed: Docklands and East London during the Thatcher Years', in John Corner and Sylvia Harvey (eds.), *Enterprise and Heritage: Crosscurrents of National Culture*, London: Routledge, 1991, p.86.
14. Peter Ambrose, *Urban Process and Power*, London: Routledge, 1994, pp.180–181.
15. All quotes from Widgery taken from Ambrose, pp.180–182.
16. Docklands Community Poster Project, in Brian Wallis, (1991) *If You Lived here: The City in Art, Theory, and Social Activism. A Project by Martha Rosler*, Seattle: Bay Press, 1991, pp.300–303.
17. Schwarz, 'Horses', pp.79–80.
18. Quoted in Jane M. Jacobs, *Edge of Empire: Postcolonialism and the City*, London: Routledge, 1996, p.70.
19. Stuart Hall, Chas Critcher, Tony Jefferson, John Clarke and Brian Roberts, *Policing the Crisis: Mugging, the State, and Law and Order*, London: Macmillan, 1978.
20. Rosemary Mellor, 'Urban Sociology: A Trend Report', *Sociology*, vol. 23, no. 2, 1989, p.246.
21. Nikolas Rose, 'The Death of the Social', unpublished paper, 1994.
22. Rose, 'Death', pp. 5–6.
23. Turnbull, 'Singapore', p.227.
24. See for example Sophie Watson and Katherine Gibson (eds.), *Postmodern Cities and Spaces*, Oxford,: Blackwell, 1995; Leonie Sandecock, *Towards Cosmopolis*, London: John Wiley, 1998.
25. Michael Walzer, 'Pleasures and Costs of Urbanity', in Philip Kasinitz (ed.), *Metropolis: Center and Symbol of Our Times*, New York: New York University Press, 1995, p.321.
26. This continued a collaboration begun in work on the *London As It Could Be* exhibition at the Royal Academy in London in 1986. In 1992, Rogers and Fisher also published the book *A New London*, Harmondsworth: Penguin.
27. Rem Koolhaas, *Conversations with Students*, New York: Princeton Architectural Press, 1996, p.45.
28. John Rajchman, *Constructions*, Cambridge, Mass.: MIT Press, 1998, pp.111–112.
29. John Eade (ed.), *Living the Global City: Globalization as Local Process*, London: Routledge, 1997.
30. Jörg Dürrschmidt, 'The Delinking of Locale and Milieu', in Eade, p.70.
31. Martin Albrow, 'Travelling Beyond Local Cultures', in Eade, p.51.

32. Albrow in Eade, p.52.
33. Castells, p.349; Marc Augé, *Non-Places: Introduction to an Anthropology of Supermodernity*, London: Verso, 1995, p.107.
34. William J. Mitchell, *City of Bits*, Cambridge, Mass.: MIT Press, 1995.
35. Mitchell, p.8.
36. Mitchell, pp.118–119.
37. Mitchell, p.24.
38. Mitchell, p.121.
39. Mitchell, p.119.
40. Mitchell, p.7.
41. Paul Virilio, cited in Kevin Robins, *Into the Image: Culture and Politics in the Field of Vision*, London: Routledge, 1996, p.103.
42. Mitchell, *City*, p.172.
43. Mitchell, p.8.
44. Mitchell, p.160.
45. See Bruce Robbins (ed.). *The Phantom Public Sphere*, Minnesota: University of Minneapolis Press, 1993, especially Thomas Keenan, 'Windows: Of Vulnerability'.
46. Rosalyn Deutsche, 'Agoraphobia', in *Evictions: Art and Spatial Politics*, Cambridge, Mass.: MIT, 1996, pp.325–6.
47. Iain Sinclair, *Downriver*, London: Paladin, 1991, pp.82–83.
48. Iain Sinclair, *Lights Out for the Territory*, London: Granta, 1997, p.4.
49. Thomas F. McDonagh, 'Situationist Space', *October*, no. 67, Winter 1994, p.73. See also Simon Sadler, *The Situationist City*, Cambridge, Mass.: MIT Press, 1998, esp. 79–80.
50. Sinclair, *Lights Out*, pp.40–41.
51. I have yet to get to grips with Deleuze's work on cinema. Nevertheless, one comment on the image as, in D.N. Rodowick's account, 'a grouping of temporal relations', suggests another possible way of thinking through the epistemological power of cinema and virtuality. 'The image itself is the system of the relationships between its elements, that is, a set of relationships of time from which the variable present only flows. . . . What is specific to the image . . . is to make perceptible, to make visible, relationships of time which cannot be seen in the represented object and do not allow themselves to be reduced to the present.' Quoted in D. N. Rodowick, *Gilles Deleuze's Time Machine*, Durham: Duke University Press, 1997, p.8.
52. Roger Silverstone, *Visions of Suburbia*, London: Routledge, 1997, p.11.
53. Silverstone, p.12.
54. Margaret Morse, 'An Ontology of Everyday Distraction', in Patricia Mellencamp (ed.), *Logics of Television*, London: BFI, 1990, p.213.
55. Victor Burgin, *In/Different Spaces*, Berkeley: University of California Press, 1996, p.34.
56. Victor Burgin, 'Diderot, Barthes,*Vertigo*', in Victor Burgin, James Donald and Cora Kaplan (eds.), *Formations of Fantasy*, London: Methuen, 1986.
57. Robins, *Image*, p.143. Victor Burgin, *Between*, Oxford: Blackwell/London: Institute of Contemporary Arts, 1986.
58. Robins, p.145.
59. Frow, *Time*, p.26
60. Sue Golding, 'Quantum Philosophy, Impossible Geographies and a Few Small Points about Life, Liberty and the Pursuit of Sex (All in the Name of Democracy)', in Michael Keith and Steve Pile, *Place and the Politics of Identity*, London: Routledge, 1993, p.216.
61. Rajchman, *Constructions*, p.113.
62. Henri Lefebvre, *Writings on Cities*, Oxford: Blackwell, 1996, p.158.

Bibliography

Abbas, Ackbar, *Hong Kong: Culture and the Politics of Disappearance*, Minneapolis: University of Minnesota Press, 1997.

Aitken, S.C. and L.E. Zonn (eds.), *Place, Power, Situation and Spectacle: A Geography of Film*, Lanham, Md.: Rowman and Littlefield, 1994.

Albrow, Martin, 'Travelling Beyond Local Cultures', in John Eade (ed.), *Living the Global City: Globalization as Local Process*, London: Routledge, 1997.

Ambrose, Peter, *Urban Process and Power*, London: Routledge, 1994.

Anderson, Benedict, *Imagined Communities*, London: Verso, 1983.

Augé, Marc, *Non-Places: Introduction to an Anthropology of Supermodernity*, London: Verso, 1995.

Balibar, Etienne, 'Citizen Subject', in Eduardo Cadava, Peter Connor and Jean-Luc Nancy (eds.), *Who Comes After the Subject?*, London: Routledge, 1991.

Barry, Andrew, Thomas Osborne and Nikolas Rose (eds.), *Foucault and Political Reason: Liberalism, Neo-Liberalism and Rationalities of Government*, London: UCL Press, 1996.

Benhabib, Seyla (ed.), *Democracy and Difference: Contesting the Boundaries of the Political*, Princeton: Princeton University Press, 1996.

Benhabib, Seyla, 'Toward a Deliberative Model of Democratic Legitimacy', in Seyla Benhabib (ed.), *Democracy and Difference: Contesting the Boundaries of the Political*, Princeton: Princeton University Press, 1996.

Benjamin, Andrew, 'Eisenman and the Housing of Tradition', in Neil Leach (ed.), *Rethinking Architecture*, London: Routledge, 1997.

Benjamin, Walter, 'A Short History of Photography' in Alan Trachtenberg (ed.), *Classic Essays in Photography*, New Haven: Leete's Island Books, 1980.

Benjamin, Walter, 'The Work of Art in the Age of Mechanical Reproduction', in *Illuminations*, London: Fontana, 1973.

Benjamin, Walter, *Charles Baudelaire: A Lyric Poet in the Era of High Capitalism*, London: New Left Books, 1973.

Benjamin, Walter, *One Way Street*, London: New Left Books, 1979.

Benko, Georges, and Ulf Strohmayer (eds.), *Space and Social Theory: Interpreting Modernity and Postmodernity*, Oxford: Blackwell, 1993.

Bennett, Tony, *Culture: A Reformer's Science*, St Leonards, Sydney: Allen & Unwin, 1998.

Berman, Marshall, *All That Is Solid Melts into Air: The Experience of Modernity*, London: Verso, 1983.

Bhabha, Homi K., 'Novel Metropolis', *New Statesman and Society*, 16 February 1990.

Bhabha, Homi K., *The Location of Culture*, London: Routledge, 1994.

Blanchard, Marc Eli, *In Search of the City: Engels, Baudelaire, Rimbaud*, Stanford, Calif.: Amna Libri, 1985.

Bowie, Malcolm, *Psychoanalysis and the Future of Theory*, Oxford: Blackwell, 1993.

Bowlby, Rachel, *Just Looking: Consumer Culture in Dreiser, Gissing and Zola*, London: Methuen, 1985.

Bowlby, Rachel, 'Walking, Women and Writing: Virginia Woolf as *Flaneuse*', in *Still Crazy After All These Years*, London: Routledge, 1992.

Boyer, M. Christine, *The City of Collective Memory: Its Historical Imagery and Architectural Entertainments*, Cambridge, Mass.: MIT Press, 1994.

Brougher, Kerry, Russell Ferguson and Jonathan Crary (eds.), *Art and Film Since 1945: Hall of Mirrors*, Los Angeles: Museum of Contemporary Art/Monacelli Press, 1996.

Brown, Michael P., *Replacing Citizenship*, New York: The Guildford Press, 1997.

Brubaker, Roger, *Citizenship and Nationhood in France and Germany*, New Haven: Harvard University Press, 1992.

Bruno, Giuliana, 'Ramble City: Postmodernism and *Blade Runner*', *October*, no. 41, Summer 1987.

Bruno, Giuliana, *Streetwalking on a Ruined Map: Cultural Theory and the City Films of Elvira Notari*, Princeton: Princeton University Press, 1993.

Buci-Glucksmann, Christine, *Baroque Reason: The Aesthetics of Modernity*, London: Sage, 1994.

Buck-Morss, Susan, *The Dialectics of Seeing: Walter Benjamin and the Arcades Project*, Cambridge, Mass.: MIT Press, 1989.

Burgin, Victor, *Between*, Oxford: Blackwell/London: Institute of Contemporary Arts, 1986.

Burgin, Victor, 'Diderot, Barthes,*Vertigo*', in Victor Burgin, James Donald and Cora Kaplan (eds.), *Formations of Fantasy*, London: Methuen, 1986.

Burgin, Victor, James Donald, and Cora Kaplan (eds.), *Formations of Fantasy*, London: Methuen, 1986.

Burgin, Victor, 'Chance Encounters: *Flâneur* and *Detraquée* in Breton's *Nadja*', *New Formations*, no. 11, Summer 1990.

Burgin, Victor, 'Geometry and Abjection', in James Donald (ed.), *Thresholds: Psychoanalysis and Cultural Theory*, London: Macmillan, 1991.

Burgin, Victor, *Some Cities*, London: Reaktion Books, 1996.

Burgin, Victor, *In/Different Spaces*, Berkeley: University of California Press, 1996.

Burnett, W.R., *The Asphalt Jungle*, London: Macdonald, 1950.

Cadava, Eduardo, Peter Connor and Jean-Luc Nancy (eds.), *Who Comes After the Subject?*, London: Routledge, 1991.

Castells, Manuel, *The Informational City: Information Technology, Economic Restructuring and the Urban-Regional Process*, Oxford: Blackwell, 1989.

Castoriadis, Cornelius, *The Castoriadis Reader*, (ed. David Ames Curtis), Oxford: Blackwell, 1997.

Chambers, Iain, 'Maps for the Metropolis: A Possible Guide to the Present', *Cultural Studies*, 1, 1985.

Charney, Leo, and Vanessa Schwartz (eds.), *Cinema and Modernity*, Berkeley: University of California Press, 1995.

Choay, Françoise, 'Urbanism in Question', in M. Gottdiener and A.Ph. Lagopoulos (eds.), *The City and the Sign*, New York: Columbia University Press, 1986.

Clark, T.J., *The Painting of Modern Life: Paris in the Art of Manet and his Followers*, London: Thames and Hudson, 1984.

Clements, Patricia and Isobel Grundy (eds.), *Virginia Woolf: New Critical Essays*, London: Vision and Barnes & Noble, 1983.

Coleman, Debra, Elizabeth Danze and Carol Henderson (eds.), *Architecture and Feminism*, New York: Princeton Architectural Press, 1996.

Colomina, Beatriz (ed.), *Sexuality and Space*, New York: Princeton University Press, 1992.

Colomina, Beatriz, *Privacy and Publicity: Modern Architecture as Mass Media*, Cambridge, Mass., MIT Press, 1994.

Colquhoun, Alan, *Modernity and the Classical Tradition : Architectural Essays 1980–1987*, Cambridge, Mass.: MIT Press, 1989.

Commission on Educational and Cultural Films, *The Film in National Life*, London, 1932.

Cook, Pam (ed.), *The Cinema Book*, London: British Film Institute, 1985.

Copjec, Joan, *Read My Desire*, Cambridge, Mass.: MIT Press, 1994.

Corner, John and Sylvia Harvey (eds.), *Enterprise and Heritage: Crosscurrents of National Culture*, London: Routledge, 1991.

Crary, Jonathan, 'Unbinding Vision: Manet and the Attentive Observer', in Leo Charney and Vanessa Schwartz (eds.), *Cinema and Modernity*, Berkeley: University of California Press, 1995.

Crary, Jonathan, 'Dr. Mabuse and Mr. Edison', in Kerry Brougher, Russell Ferguson and Jonathan Crary (eds.), *Art and Film Since 1945: Hall of Mirrors*, Los Angeles: Museum of Contemporary Art/Monacelli Press, 1996.

Davis, Mike, *City of Quartz: Excavating the Future of Los Angeles*, London: Verso, 1990.

Davison, Graham, 'The City as a Natural System: Theories of Urban Society in Early Nineteenth Century Britain', in D. Fraser and A. Sutcliffe (eds.), *The Pursuit of Urban History*, London: Edward Arnold, 1983.

De Certeau, Michel, *The Practice of Everyday Life*, Berkeley: University of California Press, 1984.

Deleuze, Gilles, *Foucault*, Minneapolis: University of Minnesota Press, 1988.

Denzin, Norman, *Images of Postmodern Society*, London: Sage, 1991.

Derrida, Jacques, *The Post Card: From Socrates to Freud and Beyond*, Chicago: Chicago University Press, 1987.

Derrida, Jacques, *Politics of Friendship*, London: Verso, 1997.

Derrida, Jacques, 'Where the Desire May Live', in Neil Leach (ed.), *Rethinking Architecture*, London: Routledge, 1997.

Descartes, René, *The Philosophical Writngs of Descartes*, Cambridge: Cambridge University Press, 1985.

Deutsche, Rosalyn, 'Men in Space', *Artforum*, February 1990.

Deutsche, Rosalyn, *Evictions: Art and Spatial Politics*, Cambridge, Mass.: MIT, 1996.

Dibattista, Maria, 'Joyce, Woolf and the Modern Mind', in Patricia Clements and Isobel Grundy, (eds.), *Virginia Woolf: New Critical Essays*, London: Vision and Barnes & Noble, 1983.

Doane, Mary Ann, *Femmes Fatales: Feminism, Film Theory, Psychoanalysis*, London: Routledge, 1991.

Döblin, Alfred, *Berlin Alexanderplatz* [1929], Harmondsworth: Penguin, 1978.

Dolar, Mladen, ' "I Shall Be With You On Your Wedding-Night": Lacan and the Uncanny', *October*, no. 58, 1991.

Dollenmayer, David B., *The Berlin Novels of Alfred Döblin*, Berkeley: University of California Press, 1988.

Donald, James, 'Stars', in Pam Cook (ed.), *The Cinema Book*, London: British Film Institute, 1985.

Donald, James (ed.), *Thresholds: Psychoanalysis and Cultural Theory*, London: Macmillan, 1991.

Donald, James and Stephanie Donald (eds.), *The City, the Cinema: Modern Spaces*, CulCom Research Papers in Media and Cultural Studies, vol. 3, Falmer: University of Sussex, 1995.

Donald, James, Anne Friedberg, and Laura Marcus, *Close Up, 1927–1933: Cinema and Modernism*, London: Cassell, 1998.

Dyos, H.J. and M. Wolff (eds.), *The Victorian City: Images and Realities*, London: Routledge and Kegan Paul, 1973.

Dürrschmidt, Jörg, 'The Delinking of Locale and Milieu', in John Eade (ed.), *Living the Global City: Globalization as Local Process*, London: Routledge, 1997.

Eade, John (ed.), *Living the Global City: Globalization as Local Process*, London: Routledge, 1997.
Eisenstein, Sergei, *The Film Sense*, London: Faber & Faber, 1968.
Eliot, T. S., *The Wasteland* [1922], London: Faber, 1972.
Ellin, Nan (ed.), *Architecture of Fear*, New York: Princeton Architectural Press, 1997.
Ellison, Charles E., 'Rousseau and the Modern City: The Politics of Speech and Dress', *Political Theory*, vol. 13, no. 4, 1985.
Engels, Friedrich, *The Condition of the Working Class in England in 1844*, London: Allen and Unwin, 1892.

Favret-Saarda, Jeanne, *Deadly Words*, Cambridge: Cambridge University Press, 1980.
Foucault, Michel, *The Foucault Reader*, (ed. Paul Rabinow), Harmondsworth: Penguin, 1984.
Foucault, Michel, 'Kant on Enlightenment and Revolution', *Economy and Society*, 1986, vol. 15, no. 1.
Foucault, Michel, *Politics, Philosophy, Culture*, (ed. L.D. Kritzman), New York: Routledge, 1988.
Foucault, Michel, *Power/Knowledge* (ed. Colin Gordon), Brighton: Harvester, 1980.
Foucault, Michel, 'Space, Knowledge and Power (Interview Conducted with Paul Rabinow)', in Neil Leach (ed.), *Rethinking Architecture: A Reader in Cultural Theory*, London: Routledge, 1997.
Fraser, D. and A. Sutcliffe (eds.), *The Pursuit of Urban History*, London: Edward Arnold, 1983.
Friedberg, Anne, *Window Shopping: Cinema and the Postmodern*, Berkeley: University of California Press, 1993.
Frisby, David, *Fragments of Modernity*, Cambridge: Polity Press, 1985.
Frisby, David, 'The *Flâneur* in Social Theory', in Keith Tester (ed.), *The Flâneur*, London: Routledge, 1994.
Fritzsche, Peter, *Reading Berlin 1900*, Cambridge, Mass.: Harvard University Press, 1996.
Frow, John, *Time and Commodity Culture: Essays in Cultural Theory and Postmodernity*, Oxford: Clarendon Press, 1997.

Gelder, Ken and Sarah Thornton (eds.), *Subcultures Reader*, London: Routledge, 1997.
Gilbert, Jeremy, 'Soundtrack to an Uncivil Society: Rave Culture, the Criminal Justice Act and the Politics of Modernity', *New Formations*, no. 31, 1997.
Gilroy, Paul, *There Ain't No Black in the Union Jack*, London: Unwin Hyman, 1987.
Gleber, Anke, 'Female Flânerie and the *Symphony of the City*', in Katharina von Ankum (ed.), *Women in the Metropolis: Gender and Modernity in Weimar Culture*, Berkeley: University of California Press, 1997.
Golding, Sue, 'Quantum Philosophy, Impossible Geographies and a Few Small Points about Life, Liberty and the Pursuit of Sex (All in the Name of Democracy)', in Michael Keith and Steve Pile, *Place and the Politics of Identity*, London: Routledge, 1993.
Gomery, Douglas, *Shared Pleasures: A History of Movie Presentation in the United States*, London: British Film Institute, 1992.
Graham, Stephen and Simon Marvin, *Telecommunications and the City: Electronic Spaces, Urban Places*, London: Routledge, 1996.
Gregory, Derek, 'Lacan and Geography: the Production of Space Revisited', in Georges Benko and Ulf Strohmayer (eds.), *Space and Social Theory: Interpreting Modernity and Post-modernity*, Oxford: Blackwell, 1993.
Grosz, Elizabeth, 'Women, *Chora*, Dwelling', in *Space, Time and Perversion*, St Leonards: Allen & Unwin, 1995.

Habermas, Jürgen, 'Yet Again: German Identity — A Unified Nation of Angry DM-Burghers?', *New German Critique*, 1992.

Hacking, Ian, 'Biopower and the Avalanche of Printed Numbers', *Humanities in Society*, vol. 5, nos. 3/4, Summer/Fall 1982.

Hacking, Ian, *Reconstructing Individualism*, Stanford: Stanford University Press, 1986.

Hall, Stuart, Chas Critcher, Tony Jefferson, John Clarke and Brian Roberts, *Policing the Crisis: Mugging, the State, and Law and Order*, London: Macmillan, 1978.

Hansen, Miriam, *Babel and Babylon: Spectatorship in American Silent Film*, Cambridge, Mass.: Harvard University Press, 1991.

Hansen, Miriam, 'America, Paris, the Alps: Kracauer (and Benjamin) on cinema and modernity', in Leo Charney and Vanessa Schwartz (eds.), *Cinema and Modernity*, Berkeley: University of California Press, 1995.

Harvey, David, *The Condition of Postmodernity*, Oxford: Blackwell, 1989.

Harvey, David, 'Social Justice, Postmodernism and the City', in Susan Fainstein and Scott Campbell (eds.), *Readings in Urban Theory*, Oxford: Blackwell, 1996.

Harvey, David, *Justice, Nature and the Geography of Difference*, Oxford: Blackwell, 1996.

Harvey, David, 'Contested Cities: Social Process and Spatial Form', in Nick Jewson and Susanne MacGregor (eds.), *Transforming Cities: Contested Governance and New Spatial Divisions*, London: Routledge, 1997.

Hassan, Ihab, 'Cities of Mind, Urban Words', in M.C. Jaye and A. Chalmers Watts (eds.), *Literature and the Urban Experience*, New Brunswick, NJ: Rutgers University Press, 1981.

Healey, P., S. Cameron, S. Davoudi, S. Graham and A. Madani-Pour (eds.), *Managing Cities: The New Urban Context*, Chichester: John Wiley & Sons, 1995.

Heath, Stephen, 'Joan Riviere and the Masquerade', in Victor Burgin, James Donald, and Cora Kaplan (eds.), *Formations of Fantasy*, London: Methuen, 1986.

Heath, Stephen, 'Psychopathia Sexualis: Stevenson's *Strange Case*', *Critical Quarterly*, vol. 28, nos. 1/2, 1986.

Hebdidge, Dick, 'The Impossible Object: Towards a Sociology of the Sublime', *New Formations*, no. 1, Spring 1987.

Heron, Liz (ed.), *Streets of Desire: Women's Fictions of the Twentieth-Century City*, London: Virago, 1993.

Holston, James, *The Modernist City: An Anthropological Critique of Brasilia*, Chicago: University of Chicago Press, 1989.

Hunter, Ian, *Culture and Government: The Emergence of Literary Education*, London: Macmillan, 1988.

Hunter, Ian, 'Setting Limits to Culture', *New Formations*, no. 4, Spring 1988.

Huyssen, Andreas, *After the Great Divide: Modernism, Mass Culture, Postmodernism*, Bloomington: Indiana University Press, 1986.

Huyssen, Andreas and David Bathrick (eds.), *Modernity and the Text: Revisions of German Modernism*, New York: Columbia University Press, 1989.

Jacobs, Jane, *The Death and Life of Great American Cities*, New York: Vintage, 1961.

Jacobs, Jane M., *Edge of Empire: Postcolonialism and the City*, London: Routledge, 1996.

Jameson, Fredric, *Postmodernism or the Cultural Logic of Late Capitalism*, London: Verso, 1991.

Jaye, Michael C., and Ann Chalmers Watts (eds.), *Literature and the Urban Experience*, New Brunswick: Rutgers University Press, 1981.

Kasinitz, Philip (ed.), *Metropolis: Center and Symbol of Our Times*, New York: New York University Press, 1995.

Kearney, Richard, *Poetics of Imagining: Husserl to Lyotard*, London: Harper Collins, 1991.

Keith, Michael and Steve Pile, *Place and the Politics of Identity*, London: Routledge, 1993.

Kern, Stephen, *The Culture of Time and Space 1880–1918*, Cambridge: Harvard University Press, 1983.

King, Anthony D., *Urbanism, Colonialism and the World Economy*, London: Routledge, 1989.

King, Anthony, *Global Cities: Post-Imperialism and the Internationalization of London*, London: Routledge, 1990.

Koolhaas, Rem, *Conversations with Students*, New York: Princeton Architectural Press, 1996.

Kracauer, Siegfried, *From Caligari to Hitler: A Psychological History of the German Film*, Princeton: Princeton University Press, 1947.

Kracauer, Siegfried, *The Mass Ornament: Weimar Essays*, New Haven: Harvard University Press, 1995.

Kristeva, Julia, *Strangers to Ourselves*, London: Harvester Wheatsheaf, 1991.

Kymlicka, Will (ed.), *The Rights of Minority Cultures*, New York: Oxford University Press, 1995.

Laclau, Ernesto and Chantal Mouffe, *Hegemony and Socialist Strategy*, London: Verso, 1985.

Laclau, Ernesto, *New Reflections on the Revolution of Our Time*, London: Verso, 1990.

Leach, Neil (ed.), *Rethinking Architecture*, London: Routledge, 1997.

Le Corbusier, *The City of Tomorrow and its Planning*, London: John Rodker, 1929.

Lefebvre, Henri, *The Production of Space*, Oxford: Basil Blackwell, 1991.

Lefebvre, Henri, *Writings on Cities*, Oxford: Basil Blackwell, 1996.

Lévi-Strauss, Claude, *Introduction to the Works of Marcel Mauss* [1950], London: Routledge and Kegan Paul, 1987.

Lungstrum, Janet, '*Metropolis* and the Technosexual Woman', in Katharina von Ankum (ed.), *Women in the Metropolis: Gender and Modernity in Weimar Culture*, Berkeley: University of California Press, 1997.

Lynch, Kevin, *Good City Form*, Cambridge, Mass.: MIT Press, 1981.

Lyotard, Jean-Francois, *The Inhuman*, Stanford: Stanford University Press, 1992.

Marcus, Laura, 'Women, Modernism, Cinema', in James Donald and Stephanie Donald (eds.), *The City, the Cinema: Modern Spaces*, CulCom Research Papers in Media and Cultural Studies, vol. 3, Falmer: University of Sussex, 1995.

Marcus, Steven, 'Reading the Illegible', in H.J. Dyos and M. Wolff (eds.), *The Victorian City: Images and Realities*, London: Routledge and Kegan Paul, 1973.

Marquand, David, 'Civic Republicans and Liberal Individualists: The Case of Britain', *Archive of European Sociology*, vol. 32, 1991.

Marshall, Herbert (trans. and ed.), *Mayakovsky*, London: Dennis Dobson, 1965.

Mason, John Hope, *The Indispensable Rousseau*, London: Quartet, 1979.

Massey, Doreen, *Space, Place and Gender*, Cambridge: Polity Press, 1994.

Mauss, Marcel, *Sociology and Psychology: Essays*, London: Routledge and Kegan Paul, 1979.

McDonagh, Thomas F. 'Situationist Space', *October*, no. 67, Winter 1994.

McLeod, Mary, 'Everyday and 'Other' Spaces', in Debra Coleman, Elizabeth Danze and Carol Henderson (eds.), *Architecture and Feminism*, New York: Princeton Architectural Press, 1996.

Mellencamp, Patricia (ed.), *Logics of Television*, Bloomington: Indiana University Press/London: BFI Publishing, 1990.

Mellor, Rosemary, 'Urban sociology: a trend report', *Sociology*, vol. 23, no.2, 1989.

Mepham, John, 'Mourning and Modernism', in Patricia Clements and Isobel Grundy (eds.), *Virginia Woolf: New Critical Essays*, London: Vision and Barnes & Noble, 1983.

Miami Theory Collective (eds.), *Community at Loose Ends*, Minneapolis: University of Minnesota Press, 1991.

Miller, D.A., *The Novel and the Police*, Berkeley: University of California Press, 1988.

Miller, J Hillis, *Topographies*, Stanford: Stanford University Press, 1995.

Minson, Jeffrey, *Questions of Conduct: Sexual Harassment, Citizenship, Government*, London: Macmillan, 1993.

Mitchell, William J. *City of Bits*, Cambridge, Mass.: MIT Press, 1995.

Moholy-Nagy, László, *Painting, Photography, Film*, London: Lund Humphries, 1969.

Morris, Meaghan, 'Great Moments in Social Climbing: King Kong and the Human Fly', in Beatriz Colomina (ed.), *Sexuality and Space*, New York: Princeton University Press, 1992.

Morse, Margaret, 'An Ontology of Everyday Distraction: The Freeway, the Mall, and Television', in Patricia Mellencamp (ed.), *Logics of Television*, Bloomington: Indiana University Press/London: BFI Publishing, 1990.

Mort, Frank, *Dangerous Sexualities: Medico-Moral Problems in England since 1830*, London: Routledge and Kegan Paul, 1987.

Mouffe, Chantal, 'Citizenship and Political Community', in Miami Theory Collective (eds.), *Community at Loose Ends*, Minneapolis: University of Minnesota Press, 1991.

Nancy, Jean-Luc, *The Inoperative Community*, Minneapolis: University of Minnesota Press, 1991.

Natter, Wolfgang, 'The City as Cinematic Space: Modernism and Place in *Berlin, Symphony of a City*', in S.C. Aitken and L.E. Zonn (eds.), *Place, Power, Situation and Spectacle: A Geography of Film*, Lanham, Md.: Rowman and Littlefield, 1994.

Nava, Mica, 'Modernity's Disavowal', in Mica Nava and Alan O'Shea (eds.), *Modern Times: Reflections on a Century of English Modernity*, London: Routledge, 1996.

Nava, Mica and Alan O'shea (eds.), *Modern Times: Reflections on a Century of English Modernity*, London: Routledge, 1996.

Palazzolo, Carlo, and Riccardo Vio (eds.), *In the Footsteps of Le Corbusier*, New York: Rizzoli, 1991.

Petric, Vlada, *Constructivism in Film: The Man with the Movie Camera*, Cambridge: Cambridge University Press, 1987.

Petro, Patrice, *Joyless Streets: Women and Melodramatic Representation in Weimar Germany*, Princeton: Princeton University Press, 1989.

Pollock, Griselda, *Vision and Difference: Femininity, Feminism and Histories of Art*, London: Routledge, 1988.

Poovey, Mary, *Making a Social Body: British Cultural Formation 1830–1864*, Chicago: University of Chicago Press, 1995.

Prendergast, Christopher, *Paris and the Nineteenth Century*, Oxford: Blackwell, 1992.

Rabinow, Paul, *French Modern: Norms and Forms of Social Environment*, Cambridge, Mass.: MIT Press, 1989.

Rajchman, John, *Truth and Eros: Foucault, Lacan and the Question of Ethics*, London: Routledge, 1991.

Rajchman, John, *Constructions*, Cambridge, Mass.: MIT Press, 1998.

Rich, Adrienne, *The Dream of a Common Language*, New York: W. W. Norton, 1978.

Robbins, Bruce (ed.), *The Phantom Public Sphere*, Minnesota: University of Minneapolis Press, 1993.

Robins, Kevin, *Into the Image: Culture and Politics in the Field of Vision*, London: Routledge, 1996.

Robins, Kevin, 'Collective Emotion and Urban Culture', in P. Healey, S. Cameron, S. Davoudi, S. Graham and A. Madani-Pour (eds.), *Managing Cities: The New Urban Context*, Chichester: John Wiley & Sons, 1995.

Rodowick, D.N., *Gilles Deleuze's Time Machine*, Durham: Duke University Press, 1997.

Rogers, Richard and Mark Fisher, *A New London*, Harmondsworth: Penguin, 1992.

Rose, Nikolas, *Governing the Soul: The Shaping of the Private Self*, London: Routledge, 1990.

Rose, Nikolas, 'The Death of the Social', unpublished paper, 1994.

Rosenbaum, Jonathan, *Movies as Politics*, Berkeley: University of California Press, 1997.

Rosenberg David, (ed.), *The Movie that Changed my Life*, New York: Viking, 1991.

Rousseau, Jean-Jacques, *Émile*, London: J.M. Dent, 1974.

Rushdie, Salman, *Imaginary Homelands*, London: Granta Books, 1992.

Sadler, Simon,*The Situationist City*, Cambridge, Mass.: MIT Press, 1998.

Salecl, Renata, *The Spoils of Freedom: Psychoanalysis and Feminism after the Fall of Socialism*, London: Routledge, 1994.

Sandecock, Leonie, *Towards Cosmopolis*, London: John Wiley, 1998.

Sandel, Michael, *Liberalism and the Limits of Justice*, Cambridge: Cambridge University Press, 1982.

Sassen, Saskia, *The Global City: New York, London, Tokyo*, Princeton: Princeton University Press, 1991.

Scherpe, Klaus R., 'The City as Narrator: The Modern Text in Alfred Döblin's *Berlin Alexanderplatz*', in Andreas Huyssen and David Bathrick (eds.), *Modernity and the Text: Revisions of German Modernism*, New York: Columbia University Press, 1989.

Scheunemann, Dietrich, *Romankrise: Die Entstehungsgeschichte der modernen Romanpoetik in Deutschland*, Heidelberg: Quelle & Meyer, 1978.

Schiller, Friedrich, *On the Aesthetic Education of Man* [1791], Oxford: Clarendon Press, 1967.

Schorske, Carl, *Fin-de-Siécle Vienna: Politics and Culture*, London: Weidenfeld and Nicolson, 1980.

Schwarz, Bill, 'Where Horses Shit a Hundred Sparrows Feed: Docklands and East London during the Thatcher Years', in John Corner and Sylvia Harvey (eds.), *Enterprise and Heritage: Crosscurrents of National Culture*, London: Routledge, 1991.

Sennett, Richard, *The Fall of Public Man*, Cambridge: Cambridge University Press, 1974.

Sharpe, William and Leonard Wallock (eds.), *Visions of the Modern City*, Baltimore: Johns Hopkins Press, 1987.

Silverman, Kaja, *Male Subjectivity at the Margins*, London: Routledge, 1992.

Silverstone, Roger, *Visions of Suburbia*, London: Routledge, 1997.

Simmel, Georg, 'The Metropolis and Mental Life', in David Frisby and Mike Featherstone (eds.), *Simmel on Culture: Selected Writings*, London: Sage, 1997.

Simmel, Georg, 'The Stranger' (1908), in Charles Lemert (ed.), *Social Theory: The Multicultural and Classic Readings*, Boulder: Westview, 1993.

Sinclair, Iain, *Downriver*, London: Paladin, 1991.

Sinclair, Iain, *Lights Out for the Territory*, London: Granta, 1997.

Soja, Edward, *Postmodern Geographies*, London: Verso, 1989.

Spigel, Lynn, *Make Room for TV: Television and the Family Ideal in Post-war America*, Chicago: Chicago University Press, 1992.

Squier, Susan M., *Virginia Woolf and London: The Sexual Politics of the City*, Chapel Hill: University of North Carolina Press, 1988.

Stallybrass, Peter and Allon White, *The Politics and Poetics of Transgression*, London: Methuen, 1986.

Tagg, John, *The Burden of Representation: Essays on Photographies and Histories*, London: Macmillan, 1988.

Tagg, John, *Grounds of Dispute: Art History, Cultural Politics and the Discursive Field*, Minneapolis: University of Minnesota Press, 1992.

Tambling, Jeremy, 'Repression in *Mrs Dalloway*', *Essays in Criticism*, vol. 39, 1989.

Taylor, Charles, *Multiculturalism and 'The Politics of Recognition'*, Princeton: Princeton University Press, 1992.

Tester, Keith (ed.), *The Flâneur*, London: Routledge, 1994.

Thrift, Nigel, *Spatial Formations*, London: Sage, 1996.

Trachtenberg, Alan (ed.), *Classic Essays in Photography*, New Haven: Leete's Island Books, 1980.

Tschumi, Bernard, *Architecture and Disjuncture*, Cambridge, Mass.: MIT Press, 1994.

Turnbull, David, 'Soc. Culture; Singapore:', in Nan Ellin (ed.), *Architecture of Fear*, New York: Princeton Architectural Press, 1997.

Vattimo, Gianni, *The Transparent Society*, Cambridge: Polity Press, 1992.

Vattimo, Gianni, 'The End of Modernity, the End of the Project?' in Neil Leach (ed.), *Rethinking Architecture*, London: Routledge, 1997.

Vidler, Anthony, *The Architectural Uncanny: Essays in the Modern Unhomely*, Cambridge, Mass.: MIT Press, 1992.

Vidler, Anthony, 'Bodies in Space/Subjects in the City: Psychopathologies of Modern Urbanism', *differences*, vol. 5, no. 3, 1993.

von Ankum, Katharina (ed.), *Women in the Metropolis: Gender and Modernity in Weimar Culture*, Berkeley: University of California Press, 1997.

Wallis, Brian, *If You Lived Here: The City in Art, Theory, and Social Activism. A Project by Martha Rosler*, Seattle: Bay Press, 1991.

Walzer, Michael, 'Pleasures and Costs of Urbanity', in Philip Kasinitz (ed.), *Metropolis: Center and Symbol of Our Times*, New York: New York University Press, 1995.

Walzer, Michael, *On Toleration*, New Haven: Yale University Press, 1997.

Watson, Sophie and Katherine Gibson (eds.), *Postmodern Cities and Spaces*, Oxford: Blackwell, 1995.

Weinstein, Deena and Michael A. Weinstein, *Postmodern(ized) Simmel*, London: Routledge, 1993.

Williams, Raymond, *The Country and the City*, London: Chatto and Windus, 1973.

Williams, Raymond, *Television, Technology and Cultural Form*, London: Fontana, 1974.

Williams, Raymond, *Towards 2000*, Harmondsworth: Penguin, 1985.

Williams, Raymond, *Resources of Hope*, (Robin Gable, ed.), London: Verso, 1989.

Wilson, Elizabeth *The Sphinx in the City*, London: Virago, 1991.

Wittkower, Rudolf, in Carlo Palazzolo and Riccardo Vio (eds.), *In the Footsteps of Le Corbusier*, New York: 1991.

Wolff, Janet, 'The Invisible *Flâneuse*: Women and the Literature of Modernity', *Theory, Culture and Society*, vol. 2, no. 3, 1985.

Wolff, Janet, *Feminine Sentences*, Cambridge: Polity, 1990.

Wolff, Janet, 'The Artist and the *Flâneur*', in Keith Tester (ed.), *The Flâneur*, London: Routledge, 1994.

Wollen, Peter, 'Delirious Projections', *Sight and Sound*, August 1992.

Woolf, Virginia, *Moments of Being: Unpublished Autobiographical Writings*, ed. Jeanne Schulkind, New York: Harcourt Brace Jovanovich, 1976.

Woolf, Virginia, *Mrs Dalloway* [1925], Oxford: Oxford University Press (The World's Classics), 1992.

Woolf, Virginia, *The Crowded Dance of Modern Life. Selected Essays; Volume Two* (ed. Rachel Bowlby), Harmondsworth: Penguin, 1993.

Woolf, Virginia, 'The cinema', in Andrew McNeillie (ed.), *The Essays of Virginia Woolf*, Volume 4: 1925–1928, London: Hogarth Press, 1994.

Young, Iris Marion, *Justice and the Politics of Difference*, Princeton: Princeton University Press, 1990.

Young, Iris Marion, 'City Life and Difference' in Philip Kasinitz (ed.), *Metropolis: Center and Symbol of Our Times*, New York: New York University Press, 1995.

Young, Iris Marion, 'Communication and the other: Beyond Deliberative Democracy', in Seyla Benhabib (ed.), *Democracy and Difference: Contesting the Boundaries of the Political*, Princeton: Princeton University Press, 1996.

Zizek, Slavoj, *Enjoy Your Symptom!*, London: Routledge, 1992.

Zizek, Slavoj, *Looking Awry*, Cambridge MA: MIT Press, 1991.

Zizek, Slavoj, *Mapping Ideology*, London: Verso, 1994.

Zukin, Sharon, *Landscapes of Power*, Berkeley: University of California Press, 1991.

Index

Page numbers in italics refer to illustrations.

Á Propos de Nice (1930), 77
Abbas, Ackbar, x
advertising, 5, 47
Akira (1989), 86, 173
Albrow, Martin, 181
Apollinaire, Guillaume, 184
arcades, 11, 42, 44, 45, 49, 65
architecture, 8, 27, 37, 41, 44, 51, 52,
   54–5, 71, 76, 77, 86, 89, 107, 124, 127,
   132, 140, 142, 143–4, 167, 178, 179–80,
   181, 182
Arendt, Hannah, 167
Aristotle, 96, 155, 167, 182
Arnott, Neil, 29
Atget, Eugene, 41–2, *43*, 44, 82, *83*
Augé, Marc, 3, 180, 181
Australia, 183

Balibar, Etienne, 102, 103, 180
Balzac, Honoré de, 70, 127
Barry, Andrew, 20–4
Bashkirtoff, Marie, 112
Batman (1989), 86, 89
Baudelaire, Charles, 3, 19, 21–2, 42, 44,
   45–6, 47, 49, 52, 59, 70, 71, 72, 74, 89,
   136, 182
Benhabib, Seyla, 169
Benjamin, Walter, 11, 41–5, 47–9, 51,
   52, 65, 66, 68, 70, 72, 73–4, 76–7, 79,
   82, 86, 92, 112, 128, 136, 185
Bennett, Tony, 17

Bentham, Jeremy, 73
Berlin, 18, 63, 64, 66, 69, 77–9, 82, 127,
   128–9, 135, 162
Berlin: Symphony of a Great City (1927),
   77–9, 128
Berman, Marshall, x
Bhabha, Homi, 156
Bianchini, Franco, 138
Blade Runner (1982/1992), 86, 89, *91*, 173
boulevards, 41, 44, 46–7, 49, 71
Boyer, Christine, 41
Braques, Georges, 74
Brazil (1986), 86
Brecht, Bertolt, 128
Breton, André, 86
Brubaker, Rogers, 98, 167
Buci-Glucksmann, Christine, 92
Buckham, Alfred G., *134*
Burgin, Victor, x, 8–10, 122, 186
Burnett, W.R., 7; *The Asphalt Jungle*, 5–7

Caché, Bernard, 179
Calvino, Italo, 186–7; *Invisible Cities*, x
Cameron, Dr James Spottiswoode,
   39–42
Candyman (1992), 69–70, 86, 92
Castells, Manuel, 138, 175, 176
Castoriadis, Cornelius, 18
Cavalcanti, Alberto, 77
Chadwick, Edwin, 29, 32, 33, 36, 47, 136,
   176

Chambers, Iain, 159
Chicago, 5–7, 64, 69
Chicago School, 6–7
Churchill, Winston, 125
Cinema, xii, 5, 11, 49, 63–8, 73–4, 77, 137, 142
Citizens, 97–9, 102, 104, 105, 106, 109, 114, 117–19, 143, 145, 155, 162, 167, 179
Citizenship, xii, 96–101, 102, 116, 123, 148, 151, 155, 167, 169, 170
Citroën, Paul, 74, 75, 173
City, and economic relations, 35–6; and nature, 2; and social engineering, 33, 51, 52, 59; as a frame of mind, 73; as a place of politics, 96; as a problem, 30, 70, 179; as a representation, 8; as a state of mind, 8–19; as abstraction, 8; as archive, 7, 39; as category of thought & experience, 121; as disease, 27, 29–31, 57; as dream space, 86; as human laboratory, 52; as imagined, 5, 7, 8–19, 27, 59, 60, 68, 96, 127, 147, 174; as informed by society, 32; as machine, 6, 27, 57, 84; as object of government, 73, 127; as object of knowledge, 127; as psychic space, 73, 130, 136, 145; as self-correcting, 61; as spectacle, 42; as text, 71, 182; as unsolvable enigma, 71; as work of art, 52; Concept City, 14–17, 42, 46, 51, 59, 73, 92, 161; Ideal City, xi; in novels, 127–37, 145; Modernist city, 6, 173; photographic evidence of, 39–42, 127; republican city, 96, 98; theatre of the, xii
City Symphony (1930), 77
Community, 147–9, 151–62, 166, 168, 169, 170, 171, 177, 178, 179, 182–3, 186
Constructivism, 79, 86
Copjec, Jean, 114
Corbett, Harvey Wiley, 86
Cornelius, Henry, 152
Crary, Jonathan, 65
Cubism, 76, 77, 79, 122
Cultural Studies, 147, 151, 159, 160
Cyborg, 89

Davis, Mike, 138; *City of Quartz*, x

De Certeau, Michel, 14–17, 18, 46, 55, 69, 71–2, 82, 89, 92, 144, 173
de Oliveira, Manoel, 77
Debord, Guy, 92, 185
Deconstruction, 159–60
Delaunay, Robert, 74
Deleuze, Gilles, 174, 181, 185
DeLillo, Don, 187
Democracy, 97–8, 100, 116, 139, 151, 157, 167, 169, 170, 182
Department stores, 44, 49, 64, 65, 112
Derrida, Jacques, 17, 140, 143, 166–7, 173
Descartes, René, 101, 102
Desire, 84, 100, 103, 104, 112, 116, 123, 127, 145, 187
Detective, 69–70, 96, 184
Deutsche, Rosalyn, 183
Dickens, Charles, 10, 24, 28, 69, 77, 130, 176, 185; *Bleak House*, 1, 5
Difference, 164–5, 169, 170, 179
Disney, Walt, 183
Distraction, 65, 68, 69
Do The Right Thing (1989), 152–5, 159
Döblin, Alfred, 132, 135; *Berlin Alexanderplatz*, 127, 128–30, 135–8, 142
Docklands, 176, 185
Dolar, Mladen, 72
Douro, Faina, Fluvial (1931), 77
Dreams, 72, 73, 76, 86, 89, 123–4

East Enders, 177
Eisenman, Peter, 143–4
Eisenstein, Sergei, 76, 77, 81, 142
Eliot, T.S., 6; *The Wasteland*, 3
Engels, Friedrich, 33–7, 44, 47, 60, 70–1, 176
Epstein, Jacob, 125
Evans, Walker, *111*

Fantasy, 116, 124, 140
Favret-Saarda, Jeanne, 70
Ferris, Hugh, 86
Fichte, Johan G., 102
Flânerie, 45, 49, 73, 79, 82, 96, 114, 117, 133, 139, 184–5
Flâneur, 44–51, 71, 82, 112, 114, 116, 127, 136, 182, 185

Flâneuse, 49, 112, 116
Foucault, Michel, 20–2, 31–2, 73, 105, 124, 174
Freeways, 69, 186
Fremantle, 183
Freud, Sigmund, 71, 82, 116, 118, 122, 123, 152
Friedberg, Anne, 65, 79
Frisby, David, 45
Fritzsche, Peter, 63–4
Frow, John, 187
Futurism, 79, 86

Geneva, 104, 105, 106
Gibson, William, 138
Gleber, Anke, 82
Globalisation, 174, 175, 180
Golding, Sue, 19, 187
Government, 28, 30, 31, 32, 33, 37, 44, 61, 65, 105, 178, 180, 187
Great Exhibitions, 44
Grosz, Elizabeth, 74, 144

Habermas, Jürgen, 97–9, 102, 104, 105, 106, 109, 114, 117–19, 138, 151, 162, 169, 186
Hacking, Ian, 31–2
Hall, Stuart, 177
Hansen, Miriam, 65–6
Harvey, David, x, 19, 157–61, 167, 169
Hassan, Ihab, 8
Haussman, Georges, Baron, 41, 42, 44, 46–9, 51, 54, 57, 74
Hebdige, Dick, 161–6, 167, 168
Hegel, G.F.W., 64
Heidegger, Martin, xi
Henry, O., 95–6, 109
Herzen, Alexander, 184
Hillis Miller, J., 122–3, 125, 127, 139, 143, 183
Hitchcock, Alfred, 186
Hoffman, E.T.A., 82
Hoggart, Richard, 147
Hölderlin, Friedrich, xi
Home, 150–1, 168, 180, 183
Hong Kong, 175
Howard, Ebenezer, 60
Hugo, Victor, *Les Misérables*, 22–4

Identity, 89, 97, 98, 100, 102, 103, 109, 112, 116, 118, 122, 125, 138, 147, 148, 151, 152, 155, 156, 161, 162, 167, 168, 170, 171
Imagination, 10, 17–18, 19, 47, 140, 144, 174, 182 politics of, 124
India, 180
Internet, 181, 182–3, 187

Jacobs, Jane, 121, 123, 127, 137, 138, 159, 178–9
Jameson, Fredric, x, 186
Joyce, James, 6, 17, 181, 182; *Ulysses*, 3–5, 128, 132; *Dubliners*, 4–5

Kant, Immanuel, 20, 21, 102
Kay-Shuttleworth, Sir James, 29–36, 37, 39, 47, 60, 136, 176
Kearney, Richard, 122, 124, 165
Keiller, Patrick, 184, 185
King Kong (1933), 86, 89, *90*
King, Martin Luther, 152
Koolhaas Rem, 92, 179–80, 182–3
Kracauer, Siegfried, 11, 66, 68, 69, 81, 86, 112
Kristeva, Julia, 157
Kundera, Milan, 165
Kymlicka, Will, 157

Lacan, Jacques, 109, 122, 125
Laclau, Ernesto, xi, 139, 168, 169, 170
Lang, Fritz, 86
Law, 99–100, 101, 104
Le Corbusier, 19–20, 27, 28, 52–60, *58*, 73, 84, 86, 89, 92, 105, 122, 123, 137, 139, 143, 145, 175, 176, 178, 179
Lee, Spike, 152
Leeds, 37–9
LEF Group, 74
Lefebvre, Henri, 13–14, 17, 18, 52, 68, 123, 144, 187
Lefort, Charles, 100
Lemoine-Luccioni, Eugénie, 109
Lessing, Doris, *The Four-Gated City*, 122
Levi-Strauss, Claude, 117
Liberalism, 178
Logos, 167

London, 1, 24, 28, 55, 66–8, 122, 124, 125, 127, 130, 132, 133, 135, 136, 138, 152, 156, 174, 175, 176, 177, 178, 179, 180, 183, 184, 185
London (1994), 184
Loos, Alfred, 106, 107, *108*, 109, 118, 170
Lumière Brothers, 73
Lynch, Kevin, 2
Lyotard, Jean-François, 149–51

Malcolm X, 152
Malls, 69, 186
Malthus, Thomas, 29
Manchester, 27, 28–37, 44, 47, 70, 71, 176
Manet, Edouard, 44
Manhatta (1921), 77
Marcus, Laura, 132
Marcus, Steven, 33
Marquand, David, 116, 118
Marville, Charles, 41
Marxism, 161
Masks, 101–2, 109
Mass media, 54, 63, 137
Massey, Doreen, 138, 160, 180
Mauss, Marcel, 101–2, 117
Mayakovsky, Vladimir, 79
Mayhew, Henry, 176
McLeod, Mary, 144
Memory, 125, 151, 181
Men's clothing, 106–9
Mental life, 8–10, 13, 14, 17, 49, 52, 59, 65, 71, 128, 156, 181
Metaphors of the city, xii, 27, 139; organic metaphor, 27, 28, 29–31, 52, 57, 59, 147; mechanical metaphor, 27, 51, 52, 59, 148; medical metaphor, 51, 136
Metropolis (1926), 86, *88*
Mitchell, William J., 181–3
Modernisation, 44, 46
Modernity (theorisation of), 19–24
Moholy-Nagy, László, 74
Montage, 74, 76, 77, 81, 82, 122, 128, 129, 142, 181, 185
Morris, Meaghan, 14–17
Morse, Margaret, 68, 186
Moscow, 79

Mouffe, Chantal, xi
Münsterberg, Hugo, 74
Myth, 69, 70, 73, 84, 104, 117, 181

Nancy, Jean-Luc, 154–5, 157, 161, 162, 164, 166, 167, 170, 171
Napoleon III, 46
Natter, Wolfgang, 77
Necropolis, 145
Neighbours, 166, 167, 169
New York, 64, 84, 89, 95, 96, 152, 157, 170, 173, 175, 177
Newspapers, 63–4
Nietzsche, Friedrich, 21, 107, 117, 174

Osborne, Thomas, 20–4

Paley, William, 28
Paris, 27, 32, 41, 42–51, 71, 72, 73, 74, 77, 84, 104, 106, 140, 175, 182
Park, Robert, 6–8, 10; and imagination, 18
Passport to Pimlico (1949), 152–6
Performance, 162, 166, 167
Phobia, 136, 138
Picasso, Pablo, 74
Planning, 27, 37, 51, 52, 54, 57, 59, 60, 122, 123, 137, 140, 177, 178–9, 180
Plato, 143
Police, 31–2, 36–7, 127
Polis, 155, 167, 171, 182
Political (the), 168–9, 171, 180
Pound, Ezra, 74
Prendergast, Christopher, x
Prince Charles, 123, 138, 177
Publicness, 65, 100, 179, 181, 182, 183, 186
Pynchon, Thomas, *The Crying of Lot 49*, 138

Quarry Hill, Leeds, 37, 41

Rabinow, Paul, 32, 33, 60
Rajchman, John, 147, 151, 155, 168, 187
Representation, 10, 27
Respect, 166, 167
Responsibility, 162, 164, 166, 167, 171
Richardson, Dorothy, 4, 6, 17, 66–8, 181
Rien que les heures (1926), 77

Rimbaud, Arthur, 184
Riviere, Joan, 109
Robins, Kevin, 138, 139, 187
Rogers, Richard, 55, 138, 170, 176, 179
Romero, George, 118
Rose, Bernard, 69
Rose, Gillian, 114
Rose, Nikolas, 20–4, 178
Rossi, Aldo, 176
Rousseau, Jean-Jacques, 103, 104, 105, 106, 116, 118, 167
Rushdie, Salman, 150, 151; *Satanic Verses*, 138, 149, 152, 156
Ruttman, Walter, 77–9, *78*, 81–4, 128

Saint-Simon, Claude de Rouvroy, Comte de, 33, 46
Salecl, Renata, 116–17
Sandel, Michael, 119
Sander, August, *67*, *110*
Sant'Elia, Antonio, 86, *87*
Sassen, Saskia, 138
Schiller, Friedrich, 103, 116
Scholvin, Ulrike, 114
Schwarz, Bill, 177
Second World War, xii, 60, 70
Seine, 46
Self, 101–2, 103, 104, 105, 106, 116, 117, 118, 123, 136, 167, 170
Sennett, Richard, 104, 175
Sewers, 22–4
Sexual differentiation, 109, 116
Sexuality, 89, 118
Sheeler, Charles, 77
Silverstone, Roger, 186
Simmel, Georg, 7, 10–13, 14, 17, 18, 52, 54, 63, 64, 70, 71, 73–4, 77, 106, 107–9, 118, 132, 135, 136, 137, 155–6, 167, 181, 183
Sinclair, Ian, 184–5; *Downriver*, 138, 184; *White Chapel: Scarlet Tracings*, 184
Singapore, 173–6, 178, 180
Sitte, Camillo, 51–2, 60
Situationists, 13, 140, 185
Slums, 30, 37, 39, 44, 46, 57, 68
Smith, Adam, 29
Social (the), 178–9, 183
Social welfare, 31, 33, 178

Society, 29, 30, 32–3, 96, 104, 106, 116, 139, 140, 187
Soja, Edward, x
Southwood Smith, Thomas, 29, 33
Space, x, 13–14, 27, 121–2, 123, 128, 132, 139–40, 142, 143, 144, 155, 168, 170, 171, 179, 185, 187
Spice Girls, 179
Stallybrass, Peter, 22
Statistics, 14, 31–2, 37, 127
Stefan, Verena, *Shedding*, 162–4, 165, 166, 167
Stevenson, Robert Louis, 117–19; *Strange Case of Dr Jekyll and Mr Hyde*, 117–19
Strand, Paul, 77
Stranger (the), 137–8, 147, 149, 151, 155–6, 161, 169
Subjectivity, 96, 100, 104, 109, 116, 119
Suburbia, xi, 64, 186, 187
Surrealists, 13, 41–2
Surveillance, 14, 31, 32, 36, 73, 84, 105
Sweden, 180

Tagg, John, 37–9
Tay Keng Soon, 178
Taylor, Charles, 157
Technologies, 5, 6, 11, 74, 89, 139, 142, 181
Telephone, 180, 181
Television, 68, 69, 150, 186, 187
Temporality, 74, 76, 152, 186
Terror, 71, 73, 89, 137
Teshigahara, Hiroshi, ix
Thatcher, Margaret, 176
The Communist Manifesto, 174
The Man With the Movie Camera (1929), 77, 79–81, *80*, *85*
Tokyo, 175
Tolerance, 162, 164, 166, 167, 171
Traffic, 69, 77, 175, 179, 183
Transparency, 73, 105, 106, 114, 123, 137, 162, 183
Tschumi, Bernard, 140–3, *141*, 179
Turnbull, David, 175

Uncanny (the), 71, 81, 82, 84, 86, 89, 92, 137, 156

Unger, Roberto, 119
Urbanisation, 29, 30, 36

Valentino, Rudolph, 65
Vattimo, Gianni, xi–xii, 17, 117
Vertov, Dziga, 77, 79–81, 84, 86, 92, 142, 185
Vidler, Anthony, 27, 69, 73, 136, 145
Vienna, 28, 51–2, 69
Vigo, Jean, 77
Violence, 138, 152, 161, 165, 187

Wagner, Otto, 51–2, *53*, 54
Walzer, Michael, 156–7, 164–5, 167, 170, 179
Weber, Max, 72
Weinberg, Herman, 77
Welfare, 21, 30, 31, 32, 47, 51
welfare state, 60, 177
Wells, H.G., 149
Wenders, Wim, *Wings of Desire*, 18
Western Australia, 180
Whately, Richard, 28
White, Allon, 22
Who Framed Roger Rabbit? (1988), 123

Widgery, David, 176–7
Williams, Raymond, 3–4, 19, 147–51, 154, 156; *The Country and the City*, 148–9; *Towards 2000*, 148–9
Wirth, Louis, 6
Wolfe, Tom, 177
Wollen, Peter, 86
women, 84, 104; and cinema, 65, 66–9; and citizenship, 112–17; and masquerade, 109–12, 166; and space, 144
Woolf, Virginia, 19, 123, 124, 125, 132; *Mrs Dalloway*, 7, 127–8, 130, 133–8, 142
work, 77, 81
Worpole, Ken, 138

Young, Iris Marion, 114, 155, 157, 159, 164, 169–70

Zizek, Slavoj, 103, 118–19; Derrida and spectre, 17–18; substancelessness of citizenship, 99
Zola, Emile, 127
Zukin, Sharon, x